MAGICAL ALPHABETS

NIGEL PENNICK

MAGICAL ALPHABETS

SAMUEL WEISER, INC.

York Beach, Mai

First American edition published in 1992 by
Samuel Weiser, Inc.
Box 612
York Beach, Maine 03910

Second printing, 1993

Library of Congress Cataloging-in-Publication Data

Pennick, Nigel.
   Magical alphabets / Nigel Pennick.
      p.   cm.
   Includes bibliographical references.
    1. Magic   2. Alphabets--Miscellanea.   I. Title
BF1623.A45P46 1992
133.4'3--dc20   92-7859
                                          CIP

ISBN 0-87728-747-3
BJ

All illustrations in this book were made by the author, except for
numbers 6, 7, 10, 15, 24, 25, 36, 43, 55, 56, 57, 61-63, which are
historic illustrations from the author's picture collection.

Printed in the United States of America

The paper used in this publication meets the minimum requirements
of the American National Standard for Permanence of Paper for
Printed Library Materials Z39.48-1984.

Contents

I call strong Pan, the substance of the whole,
Etherial, marine, earthly, general soul,
Undying fire; for all the world is thine,
And all are parts of thee, O pow'r divine . . .
All parts of matter, various form'd, obey,
All Nature's change thro' thy protecting care,
And all mankind thy lib'ral bounties share,
For these where'er dispersed thro' boundless space,
Still find thy providence support their race.

The Orphic Hymn to Pan

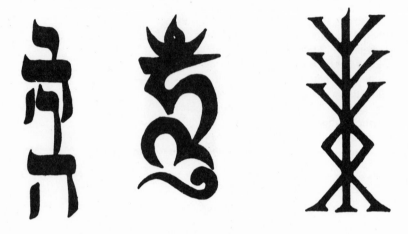

Fig. 1. Letter-trees: the Hebrew name of God, the Buddhist mantra Hum, and the Northern Tradition tree bind-rune.

Introduction

A symbol is ever, to him who has eyes for it, some dimmer or clearer revelation of the God-like.

HELENA BLAVATSKY

At a first, cursory glance, the subject of alphabets, secret or otherwise, may not appear to tell us much about the world and ourselves. But another, longer, look will show anyone of this opinion that he or she is wrong. Alphabets are one of the most highly sophisticated means by which we humans can try to gain some understanding of the world, and our place within it. When constructed properly, as all ancient ones are, each alphabet is metaphorical in nature. Language itself is a metaphor, for it represents objects and concepts whilst it is not those objects and concepts themselves.

The very basis of language is metaphorical. We usually distinguish things by comparison; our basic description of the world around us is full of examples. When we ask, 'What is it?', we tend to reply by making a comparison: we say it is *like* another thing which resembles it in some way, real or imagined. Within the described thing, object or quality, we seek some character by which it can be fitted into some human conceptual framework. We can see this process in action with reference to the human body. We speak of a body of water, a body of work, even a body of men. We speak of the head of a bed, a table, a page, a nail, a stream of water, a household or an organization. A clock has a face, just as does a playing card, a rock and a piece of planed wood. A hill has a brow, a cup possesses a lip, as does a crater; combs and gear-wheels have teeth, and a page has a foot. Weapons are called arms. A race or a contest may be divided into a number of legs. A shoe may have a tongue, as does a certain type of carpentry joint, and the pointwork of railways and tramways. Needles, potatoes and storms all have eyes. There are many more examples. Much of language, then, perceives the world in terms of metaphors of known objects, especially the human body and its parts. This is a continuous process: new language is generated as and when it is needed.

Philosophically, this metaphorical nature of language is manifested in the concept of 'man the microcosm', which lies at the foundation of western esoteric thought. This is encapsulated in the Hermetic maxim ascribed to the mythological Egyptian founder of science, Hermes Trismegistus, 'as above, so below'. This insightful understanding of reality states that that which is below is actually a reflection of that which is above. The 'little world', or microcosm, represented by the human being's physical and psychic constitution, reflects and is a part of the 'greater world', the macrocosm or universe. This reflection exists at all levels: the basic forms or structures that occur on a galactic scale are reproduced in the whirlpools of a river or the subatomic structure of matter itself. Similarly patterns of 'the way things happen', the phenomenon I call 'transvolution', occur on time-scales that range from millions of years to milliseconds. It is by the recognition of these patterns, and their meaning, that we can gain an insight into the nature of our own reality, and thereby attain enlightenment.

Like language, the alphabet is a metaphysical description of reality. The most important function of magical alphabets is to enable the seeker to experience transformative processes. They provide a series of accessible images of a reality that sometimes cannot be comprehended by any other means. They can be used to go beyond the outward appearance of things, to access deeper meanings within reality. Dynamically operative *now*, constantly they recombine the new ways that express concepts, describe structures, feelings, and the otherwise inexplicable nature of transvolution. In their esoteric aspects, they can convey meaning that cannot be expressed adequately by any other means. They are symbols that can express non-verbal experiences that can alter one's consciousness drastically. Suddenly, they can change the direction of flow of one's mind, diverting it into new and unexpected channels. Users of magical alphabets may experience a flood of new understanding, accompanied by an immediate recognition of completely new viewpoints of life. After such experiences, the whole aspect of life is transformed. This inner transformation is one of the main objectives of the study of magical alphabets of all traditions, and it can be accomplished by any of the alphabet systems described in this book.

On a more general level, magical alphabets represent the presence of the infinite within the finite. According to the philosophical system to which they belong, this may be seen as the presence of God within the world, or the many as yet unrealized possibilities of existence that may come into being if the right conditions manifest themselves. Letters in an alphabet are metaphors of reality: in themselves, most of the individual characters or shape-forms have no transcendent external meaning – their meaning is in the minds of those who use or have learnt them. The transcendent forms are those which relate to certain geometrical forms which underlie natural structures, such as the hexagonal lattice. But generally, the letters of magical alphabets are complex symbolic structures that work within the context of the individual alphabet's system. But many different alphabets use the same shape-form to represent different phonetic sounds, or different concepts.

To suggest, as some people have done, that certain specific uses are correct, and that others are wrong, is a form of cultural arrogance. For example, the character that takes the form 'X' means different things in different alphabets. As the letter Chi in Greek, it has the phonetic value of 'Ch'; in the Roman alphabet, it is 'X'; in the runes, and one version of the Westphalian alphabet, it has the value of 'G'. The first Coelbren of the Welsh bard Meurig Dafydd makes this character denote 'A', whilst the German Femgenossen scripts and the Inquisitorial one give it the value of 'H'. The secret bardic alphabet known as Bobileth gives it the value 'O', as does the supposedly ancient Greek Apollonian, whilst one Renaissance alchemical alphabet uses it for 'T'. The Tifinag script of North Africa also gives it the value 'T'. A supposed 'Templar' script has 'N' as its equivalent. Thus the character with the form 'X' has the value of A, Ch, G, H, N, O and T as well as X. And this is only in the major magical alphabets. This is ample proof that it is rarely through the outward forms of the letters that we can gain insights. It is by means of their inner meanings that we must come to understand each individual letter of any given alphabet. Overall, these alphabets can be viewed in the same way as languages, in which quite different words and syntax may be used to describe the same objective phenomena. None is any better than the other, but one or other may be more appropriate under different circumstances.

The known human use of artificial signs is of great antiquity. In Europe, archaic ideomorphs are known from many Magdalenian cave sites (12,000–17,000 years before the present). Although nothing concrete is known about their meaning, some of these ideomorphs resemble the characters of later alphabets. A fine example of this is the series of linear symbols that were found painted with tiver (red ochre) on a mammoth skull discovered at Mezhirich in the Ukraine. It dates from around 14,000 years ago. These signs are of such enormous antiquity that it is well nigh impossible to interpret them. They do show, however, that our human ancestors were very like us. Much later, in the fifth millennium BCE, in what is now Hungary, Czechoslovakia, Romania and Yugoslavia, was a

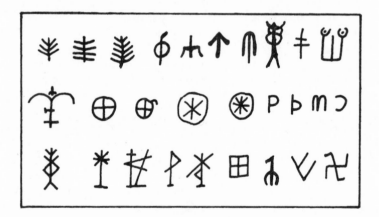

Fig. 2. Ancient rock-carved ideomorphs from many places distant from one another show related forms, the predecessors of alphabet characters: (*left to right, top line*) (i) Dowth, Ireland; (ii, iii) Sleive na Cailleach, Ireland; (iv, v) Vishera, Perm, USSR; (vi) Taja Amarillo, Spain; (vii) Cueva de las Paomas, Spain; (viii, ix) Val Camonica, Italy; (x) Bohuslän, Sweden; (*middle line*) (xi) Bohuslän; (xii) Knockmary, Ireland; (xii) Ostergötland, Sweden; (xiv) Dowth; (xv) Sleive na Cailleach; (xvi–xix) Locmariquer, Brittany; (*bottom line*) (xx) Tomsk, USSR; (xxi–xxiii) Athlone, Ireland; (xxiv) Seine, France; (xxv) Tras os Monte, Portugal; (xxvi) Puerto de los Ruedas, Portugal; (xxvi–xxviii) Val Camonica.

high culture that produced many artefacts with symbols that are recognizable in modern terms. These identifiable symbols are the most archaic of Europe. They include many that survived into later days as alphabetic letters, such as runes, and also as magical and religious symbols, such as the cross and the swastika. The pottery dishes and figures from Bylany, Czechoslovakia, dated as coming from around the end of the sixth millennium BCE, and miniature vessels from the Vinca site in Romania bear many such inscriptions. Other examples can be seen in the National Museum in Belgrade. These artefacts from 5000 BCE are recognizably part of the tradition that continues today, seven millennia later.

It is generally recognized that all archaic symbols had a magical and religious significance. In legend, they were given by the gods to human beings. According to Greek tradition, it was Hermes, the god of travel, commerce and writing who invented letters when he saw a flock of cranes flying through the sky. Their various different forms gave him the idea that characters could be arranged to represent sounds. Another version of the origin of letters tells that they were made by Cadmus the Phoenician. Historically, it was from the Phoenician script that Greek originated. But modern research on human perception may provide us with another possibility, one embedded deeply within our own human consciousness. Modern neurophysiology has identified phosphenes, geometrical shapes and images that are present subconsciously in the visual cortex and neural system. These are present in all humans: they are described as *entopic*, being visible when the eyes are shut. They can also be seen when the consciousness is altered by some means: during meditation, in trance, or in hallucinations induced by fatigue, illness or drugs. Geometric shapes related to letters are often perceived in the early stages of trance.

These states of consciousness are the domain of the shaman, the human who treads the thin line between life and death in his or her quest for enlightenment. The Norse legend of the origin of the runes is founded in the fatigue and agony of the shaman-god Odin's self-torture on the 'windswept tree'. Such shamanic practices of self-torture still exist in the indigenous religions of North America and Central Asia, and also in certain sects of Japanese Buddhism. By means of their esoteric techniques, altered and novel states of consciousness can be achieved, through which new insights can be obtained. As a matter of necessity, to be transmitted to other human beings at all, these insights must appear within a format which coincides with the inherent patterns of human consciousness. The legend of Odin's inner rune quest is a textbook example of the conscious realization and formalization of these inherent phosphene patterns. Thus the concept that letters, whether they be from the Hebrew, Greek, Etruscan, Latin, Runic, Coelbren, Gothic, Westphalian or even those of our familiar Roman alphabet, are inherent aspects of the neural 'circuitry' of each human being. At the same time, they are also metaphors for the various aspects of the nature of reality. It is through the study of these entopic patterns in the light of the universal that we may find the key to the many magical alphabets detailed in this book, and most importantly, the key to the door of personal enlightenment.

1
The Hebrew Alphabet

In the beginning was the Word, and the Word was with God, and the Word was God. The same was in the beginning with God.

THE GOSPEL ACCORDING TO ST JOHN, 1:1–2

An alphabet is a system of writing that expresses a language's sounds, both consonants and vowels, by means of single characters. Historically, the Phoenician (West Semitic) alphabet was the first to do this, in and around what is now the Lebanon. This alphabet was the starting-point of all of the later European alphabets, as well as Hebrew and Arabic. The Phoenician alphabet differs from the later European alphabets only in that it does not use vowels. The definitive version of the Phoenician alphabet is the inscription on the sarcophagus of King Ahiram of Byblos, 1000 BCE. This systematized alphabet of 22 characters had come into use around 1200 BCE, one version of the various character sets used around the eastern end of the Mediterranean at that time.

It is thought that although they used the cumbersome hieroglyphic system of writing, the ancient Egyptians originated the 'one sound, one sign' principle of writing. By themselves, Egyptian heieroglyphs were ambiguous. A hieroglyph could represent the object that it depicted, a corresponding sound, or a magical correspondence. But, as written, it was unclear whether object, sound or analogy was meant, and so additional characters were needed to indicate the way that the hieroglyphs were intended to be read. Usually, it was necessary to indicate sound and, eventually, a system of 24 consonantal signs was formalized. These extra characters were used in combination with hieroglyphs, but gradually, as more and more foreign words and names, for which there were no hieroglyphs, crept into the Egyptian language, this system was used to write these alien words. The Egyptians themselves did not use the 24-character consonantal system as an alphabet however, but it is clear that these characters had some influence on the two writing systems that preceded Phoenician: the 'proto-Canaanite' writing, known from the Canaanite town of Gebal, and the 'Sinaitic' script, known from the Egyptian mines at Serabit el-Khedem in Sinai.

The standardized script of King Ahiram of Byblos was disseminated widely by traders and colonists. It reached along the coast of North Africa, where it became the Punic script, and further west where it influenced the Tartessian script of Spain. A Phoenician inscription is known from a Cretan Geometric tomb at Knossos. In Italy, it may have been the starting-point for the Etruscan alphabet, and it was certainly the influence from which the Greek alphabet was developed during the middle of the eighth century BCE. The Hebrew script, which is a consonantal system with 22 characters, is part of this family of alphabets, based ultimately upon the Phoenician script.

QABALISTIC SPECULATIONS

The Hebrew script was formalized around the same time as the early Greek, but the characters took a different form. Hebrew was, and still is, written from right to left, and the 'handing' of the letters is in this direction. For example, Resh, with the phonetic value 'R', resembles the lower case Roman 'r', written the opposite way round. The magical connotations of the Phoenician alphabet are uncertain, but many of the exoteric and esoteric meanings of the Hebrew letters are paralleled by those in Greek, and some in runic. But, more than Greek, runic and other comparable spiritually based symbolic alphabets, the mysteries of the Hebrew alphabet are grounded in a coherent philosophical system, developed over a long period – the Qabalah. The book known as the *Sepher Yetzirah* is considered by many qabalists to be the cornerstone of the Qabalah. Dating from somewhere between the third and sixth centuries CE, it details a doctrine which is said to have been received first by Abraham. This is an inner-initiated teaching. The rabbinical tradition held that these teachings were to be kept secret, away from the knowledge of profane people. In

Fig. 3. The Hebrew alphabet, with its numerical values.

the minds and hands of the profane, they could only destroy a simple faith in God, and give them access to the techniques of black magic. So the knowledge was passed orally from master to pupil.

The esoteric Jewish conception of the nature of existence is not the same as that asserted exoterically by rabbinical Judaism. Esoteric belief states that the God of the Bible who created material things is not transcendent. This god is a limited being, subordinate to a higher form of existence, the 'Ain-Soph', which is translated as 'without end'. In the qabalistic tradition, it is the name of the ineffable. Its transcendence means that it cannot be localized in time or space. The Ain-Soph exists beyond the realms of cause and effect, beyond desire, even beyond the realms of being and non-being. Its nature is thus beyond human understanding. As the God of creation is only an agent of the Ain-Soph, the creation of the universe itself has come directly from the Ain-Soph through a complex process, achieved by the operation of certain emanations of the Ain-Soph, the 'Sephiroth'. Appearing in the Qabalah, the Sephiroth are the link between the material universe and the Ain-Soph.

Like many other culturally bound esoteric traditions, the Jewish Qabalah is based not on the outer experiences of the five senses, but on an inner, visionary experience, expressing that direct access to knowledge that underlies the most

9

powerful of the known magical alphabets. The *Sepher Yetzirah* deals with Jewish cosmogony and cosmology. It is divided into two parts, the first of which deals with the esoteric mysteries of the ten numbers, whilst the second covers the 22 letters of the Hebrew alphabet. According to the first chapter of the *Sepher Yetzirah*:

> *JHVH, through the 32 paths, inscribed his name using the three forms of expression called letters, numbers and sound. There are ten sacred Sephiroth. The foundation of things are the 22 letters. Of these, three are mothers; seven double and twelve simple are the remainder. The sacred Sephiroth are ten in number. They are the ten fingers of the hands, five corresponding with five . . .*

Later on, the *Sepher Yetzirah* tells us:

> *The Sephiroth reveal the ten numbers. In the first, the spirit of the god of life, more resplendent than the Living God. The sound of the voice, of the spirit and of the word are of this spirit. The second: God produces air from this spirit and converts it into 22 sounds, the letters of the alphabet . . . But even above these does the spirit stand in value . . .*

From the letters of the alphabet, which were manifestations of the Divine Breath (known in various traditions as Ki, Pneuma, önd, Nwyvre, etc.), God chose three as his Magnificent Name. These were IHV:

> *By him, with this name, was the universe sealed in the six directions. The fifth: height was sealed with IHV, this he did while looking upwards. Sixth: depth was sealed with IVH. This he did while looking downwards. Seventh: the east was sealed with IVH. This he did while looking forward. Eighth: the west was sealed with IVH. This he did while looking behind him. Ninth: the south was sealed with IVH. This he did while looking rightwards. Tenth: the north was sealed with IVH. This he did while looking leftwards. Look! The spirit of the air, water, fire, height, depth, east, west, north and south emanate out of the ten divine Sephiroth!*

Fig. 4. The Hebrew 'rose' showing the 3–7–12 arrangement of characters. With the addition of a cross at the centre, this is the badge of some Rosicrucian groups.

The creative power that gave rise to the cosmos is thus seen as giving rise simultaneously to the numbers and letters. According to the *Sepher Yetzirah*, the foundation of all things is comprised of the 22 letters of the Hebrew alphabet. Of these 22 characters, three are considered to be the 'mothers', seven are 'doubles' and twelve are 'simples'. The three mothers comprise the letters Aleph (A), Mem (M), and Shin (Sh), which represent the three elements of air, water and fire respectively. All of creation was believed to emanate from these three elements. The earth is composed of water, and the heavens of fire. Between these poles, air symbolizes the spirit which mediates between them. As microcosmic reflections of the macrocosm, the parts of the human body were connected with these three letters. Aleph rules the chest (the breath), Mem the stomach, and Shin, the head (fire, the intellect). These three primal element letters are also connected with time: Aleph represents the seasons of spring and autumn, the time of the equinoxes; Shin symbolizes the summer, whilst Mem is wintertime. There are three classes of letters in the Hebrew alphabet: aspirates, mutes and sibilants. The three 'mother' letters are supposed to be the key characters of each of these three classes. The first, Aleph, is pronounced with silent breathing as an aspirate, so it symbolizes the element of air. Mem is a mute character, made by putting the lips together, and Shin is a sibilant, connected with the Hebrew word 'Esh', fire.

The concept that the universe emanates from the three 'mother' letters is also present in the bardic tradition of Wales. In the Hebrew alphabet, after these three 'mothers', the seven 'doubles' are most important. They are thus named as they symbolize the pairs of opposites which compose existence, and as they signify two phonetic values, a hard and a soft sound. These letters are Beth (B), Gimel (G), Daleth (D), Kaph (K), Pe (P), Resh (R) and Tau (T). Beth signifies life-death; Gimel, harmony-conflict; Daleth, knowledge-ignorance; Kaph, abundance-scarcity; Pe, grace-sin; Resh, fertility-barrenness; Tau, power-powerlessness. In addition to specific dualities of qualities, they signify the seven directions: the four directions of north, east, west and south, above and below and the centre. Pe marks the north, Daleth the east, Resh is at the south, Kaph is to the west, Beth lies above, Gimel below, and Tau is at the centre. According to the *Sefer Yetzirah*, the seven planets and the days of the week were also formed from these letters by God. Microcosmically, the seven 'gates of the soul', corresponding with the planets, were derived from these letters. These are the mouth, the two ears, two eyes and two nostrils.

The remaining 12 Hebrew characters are the 'simple letters'. These have correspondences to the signs of the zodiac, and to certain faculites inherent in the human body. He (H), Aries, is associated with the sight; Vau (U and V), Taurus, the faculty of hearing; Zain (Z), Gemini, the sense of smell; Cheth (CH), Cancer, the power of speech; Teth (TH), Leo, the taste; Yod (Y), Virgo, sexuality; Lamed (L), Libra, the ability to work; Nun (N), Scorpio, the power of movement; Samekh (S), Sagittarius, and Ain (O), Capricorn, the qualities of anger and humour respectively; Tzaddi (TZ), Aquarius, the power of imagination; and Qoph (Q), Pisces, the ability to sleep. These characters are also assigned to the directions of the compass rose; however, unlike the seven 'doubles', they are laid out only on one plane. The direction correspondences of the

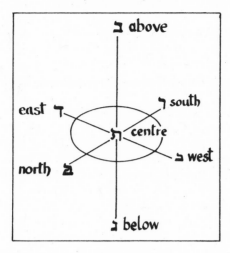

Fig. 5. The seven 'double' Hebrew letters in their relationship to the seven directions of space, which they are believed to have formed.

'simple letters' are composed of two divisions, an inner and an outer. The inner division of four characters represents the cardinal directions, Yod, Cheth, Qoph and Ain. The outer division with eight characters represents the cardinal and intercardinal directions, the letters Teth, He, Zain, Vau, Tzaddi, Lamed, Samekh and Nun. In the inner zone, north is connected with Yod; the east, Cheth; the south, Qoph, and the west Ain. On the outer zone, north is Teth; north-east is He; east is Zain; south-east, Vau; south, Tzaddi; south-west, Lamed; west, Samekh, and north-west, Nun.

THE MEANING OF HEBREW LETTERS

Several esoterically based alphabets share a common feature, in which each individual character has a name and represents a specific object or quality. This concept is developed to a very sophisticated level in Greek, the Celtic oghams, and, most notably, in the Nordic runes. At the most basic human level, they are all linked to the fundamental neurophysiological patterns within our human constitution – our basic biological abilities that interpret our perception of the universe. On a cultural level, this concept may derive from the supposed ancient Egyptian origin of the phonetic alphabet. Equally, it may be an assimilation of earlier pictographs into the particular alphabetic system. It is particularly unfortunate that for the starting-point of all western alphabets, the Phoenician one of 3000 years ago, we have no knowledge of the letters' meanings. Each of the characters of the Hebrew alphabet is named after a corresponding object. In Hebrew, the alphabet has almost the same order as the familiar Roman alphabet in which this book is set. The first letter is A, the second B, and so on. As with the Greek, Ogham and Gaelic alphabets, each Hebrew character also has a numerical equivalent.

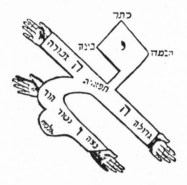

Fig. 6. Qabalistic interpretation of the character Aleph, from *Oedipus Aegyptiacus* by Athanasius Kircher, 1652.

The first letter of the Hebrew alphabet is Aleph, the equivalent of the Roman letter 'A'. This has the exoteric meaning of 'cattle' or 'ox', and the esoteric meaning of 'wealth'. Probably, the letter's shape is derived from the pictogram for a cow's or bull's horned head. As the first character, it reflects the concerns of a pastoral society with the main source of wealth – cattle. In traditional society, the cow was the animal upon which all humans depended, as from her comes milk, horn, hides and meat. The esoteric meaning of Aleph is thus absolute independence from others, self-sufficiency, but recognizing that this condition can exist only in equilibrium with surrounding existence, both on the material and also on the spiritual planes. Thus Aleph may be taken as representing the Hermetic maxim, 'As above, so below'. Esoterically, as the first letter, it is a manifestation of the Father, the ruler of the family in patriarchal societies like ancient Israel. Aleph has the numerical equivalent of 1, which is Achad, meaning unity. Astrologically, it is linked with Taurus, and the constellation Orion.

Beth is the second Hebrew letter, with the equivalent value of 'B'. Its meaning is 'house', and its shape is clearly derived from a pictogram of a house. The house is that human artefact which expresses the will of having arrived and meaning to stay. It represents stability, ownership and continuity of the family in one place. Beth is the possession of one's own ancestral property. In its position as the zenith, Beth signifies the enclosure of space, the roof that is the defining nature of the house. It can also mean the family, reproduction and progeny, continuity of the bloodline in the family homestead. In this aspect, it represents the Mother. On a higher level, this letter is Beth-El, the 'house of God'. Here, it is the letter of creation, the first letter of Genesis. The numerical value of Beth is 2, Sheni, that which repeats, the essence of creation. Astronomically, Beth is allied with the constellation of Cassiopeia.

Gimel is the third. Its value is 'G', and it has the meaning of 'camel'. The camel is the means of travelling through the desert with safety. It can carry humans and goods for vast distances unaffected by the hot, dry conditions. Thus the camel signifies the ability to get through bad places or bad times successfully. It represents self-reliance and inner strength through being in harmony with the prevailing conditions. An esoteric interpretation of Gimel is thus 'nature', which, without human interference, is always a self-regulating system. The numerical value of Gimel is 3, Shalosh, the triad. Astrologically, it is connected with Virgo.

Daleth, the door, is the fourth letter, with a value of 'D'. Unlike the walls of a house or town, which cannot be penetrated, the door allows access. But this access is selective. The door excludes those who should not enter, and admits those who should. The outcome differs, depending on whether the door is shut or open. In this aspect, Daleth therefore represents opening and shutting, access and denial of access. Esoterically, Daleth is thus 'authority'. It is interesting to note that in both the ogham and runic alphabets the letters with the value of 'D' (Duir and Dag) have an identical meaning. As a double letter, Daleth represents knowledge and ignorance, well symbolized by the open or closed door. Daleth's numerical equivalent is 4, Arba, foursquare.

He, 'H', the fifth character, signifies a window, that which admits light into a building. Unlike the door, the previous character, Daleth, which admits humans, the window admits only light and air. It is the place which links the inner world of the house with the outer would surrounding it. Similarly, in human terms, according to the *Sefer Yetzirah*, He is the 'foundation of sight'. Sight links the inner world of the individual with the outer world of his or her surrounding environment, enabling control to be exerted. He is thus a letter of linking the inner with the outer, and one of illumination. Esoterically. He is 'religion', that which 'links' people together with each other, and with the divine outside them. He has the number equivalent of 5, which is Chamesh, 'armed'. Astologically, He is linked with Aries.

Vau, the sixth, with the phonetic value of 'V', represents a nail, doorknob or small hook. The bright head of the nail reflects the light of day. Traditionally, nails have been used in a form of divination in which the patterns of sunlight reflected from the nail-head is interpreted as a letter or letters, providing the answer to any question posed. The nail is also the pivot around which the heavens circle, and Vau is thus connected with the 24-hour day and time. In the human being, the character Vau is connected with the hearing and, esoterically, it has the meaning of 'liberty'. In this respect, the attribution of 'doorknob', that which opens the door, is appropriate, Vau has the numerical value of 6, Shesh, meaning white or bright.

Zain, the seventh letter, means 'sword' or more generally 'weapon' or 'decorated staff'. As the sword, it is usually interpreted as the sword in its scabbard, at rest. Thus Zain has the meaning of repose and forgiveness under the guidance of authority. Esoterically, it has the meaning of 'ownership', that which needs to be defended. This links it with the whole complex mythos of the sword, the militarism of the ancient world, and later European chivalry. It has a value of 'Z'. Zain's numerical equivalent is 7, Shebay, 'at rest'.

The eighth character is Cheth or Heth. Its equivalent is 'CH', and it means 'fence' or 'hurdle'. The fence is that which divides the inner from the outer. It is a barrier which serves an owner of something. It keeps those things in which the owner wants kept in, and keeps out those things which must be excluded. It is thus a letter of discrimination, the separation of things of worth from the worthless. Another related interpretation of Cheth is abundance and energy, the basic characteristics that separate the living from the dead. Esoterically, Cheth means 'distribution', the primary function of energy. It has the number-equivalent of 8, Shemonah, fertility, and is connected astrologically with Libra.

The ninth is Teth, the letter T, the serpent. Teth represents organic unity. It is the brazen serpent of the Old Testament, Aaron's Rod, a Jewish parallel with the magic staff of Hermes, the Caduceus and the Christian cross of Christ. Organic unity can only exist when the universal flow of energy maintains it, and this is represented in all cultures by the serpent, dragon, Nwyvre or Orm. Esoterically, Teth signifies the quality of 'prudence', with the numerical value of 9, Thshay, 'the gate'.

Yod or Jod is the tenth character, with the phonetic value of 'I'. It means the hand, and signifies completion and fullness. The hand is the organ by means of which all human intellectual ingenuity is translated into physical reality. Human control of anything is through the power and agility of the hands, and thus Yod's esoteric meaning is 'order', destiny as directed by God. This meaning parallels that of the Greek letter Iota, which also means 'destiny'. Yod's numerical equivalent is 10, Ayser, all.

Kaph, the 11th, means 'the palm of the hand'. It has the phonetic value of 'K'. The palm is an important part of the body, for it is from there that radiates the bodily energy known variously as 'Pneuma', 'önd', 'Odyle' and 'Nwyvre'. It is best

17

known from the oriental martial arts as 'Ki'. This is the subtle energy that is involved in healing from the 'laying on of the hands', and in the spectacular feats associated with the martial arts. In Christian symbolism, the palms of Jesus are pierced with the crucifying nails, destroying his ability to radiate beneficial healing energy. The radiation of energy from the palms is depicted sometimes in images of the Virgin. Esoterically, Kaph has the meaning of 'force', and the number-equivalent of 20. Astrologically, Kaph is allied with Leo.

Lamed, the 12th letter, with the value of 'L', represents the tool known as an ox-goad or cattle-prod. This is the character that encapsulates the quality of 'getting things going'. This parallels its companion letters in Greek and Runic, where the letters which stand for 'L', Lambda and Lagu, are also to do with flow and progress. Lamed is the directed energy that one requires to initiate any action, and the sacrifices that one must inevitably incur in the process. The esoteric significance of Lamed is thus 'sacrifice'. Lamed's numerical equivalent is 30.

Mem, the 13th, has a value of 'M'. Exoterically, Mem signifies water. This represents flow, flux, more esoterically, the changes brought about by death. As the thirteenth character, it bears the same esoteric significance as the thirteenth letter in the other main alphabets. It is related by its common Phoenician origin to the Greek letter Mu, also originally the thirteenth letter of the Greek alphabet. It can signify the fixed stars, and hence represents the fatalistic astrological interpretation of human destiny. Its astrological correspondence is the constellation of Draco. Mem has the numerical value of 40, a number of completion in Jewish tradition.

Nun, the 14th, represents 'a fish'. It has the value of 'N'. This is another letter which bears some relationship to the preceding one (such as Daleth/He and Yod/Kaph). The fish is an animal that lives in an environment hostile to humans. It has symbolized both the principle of evil, and also, through the Hellenistic interpretations of Poseidon and Jesus, salvation. In this respect, it signifies the astrological sign of Aquarius. Esoterically, Nun signifies reversibility. This parallels the meaning of the runic letter Nyd, which means 'necessity', the quality of turning round a problem and finding the solution that lies, unseen, within it. Nun has similar connotations. It has the number equivalent of 50.

The 15th character is Samekh, 'S'. This signifies a prop or support. Without a support, many things cannot stand up, and so this letter represents the complementary qualities that some people or some things need in order to exist. The prop and the object supported have a mutual need for one another. Without the prop, the person or thing falls. Without the thing to be supported, the prop has no function. Samekh thus signifies mutual independence that exists between people, things or God and humanity. Esoterically, it signifies universal being. It has the numerical value of 60.

The 16th is Ayin or Ayn, with the value of 'O'. This signifies the eye. In human terms, Ayin is the physical equivalent of He. It is through the eye that we see, and Ayin therefore represents the ability to perceive all things. It is a character of vision, esoterically representing 'foresight', the power to see the processes at work within events. Ayin parallels the Greek letter Omicron, which represents the sun and its light, creating the necessary conditions for us to see. Astrologically, Ayin is related to the constellation Ophiucus, and the sign of Scorpio. It has the numerical value of 70.

Seventeenth comes Pe, the letter 'P', meaning 'mouth', the seat of speech, so this letter is one of eloquence and command. Just as a person's words may outlive his or her physical body, the esoteric significance of this character is 'immortality'. It is the origin of the 'word', the primal vibration from which emanated material existence. In this respect, Pe is equivalent to the runic letter Peorth. This character has the esoteric meaning of the womb of the Cosmic Mother, from which emanates existence itself. Astrologically, Pe corresponds with the constellation of Andromeda and the zodical sign of Pisces, Pe's numerical equivalent is 80.

Tzaddi, Tsade or Sadhe is the 18th letter, with the value of 'TZ', representing a fish hook or a javelin. The hook is the means by which the terrestrial human can catch the aquatic fish. This character therefore represents the instrument for which things in one element may be taken into another element, linking two separate worlds – the penetration of one by another in order that something may be removed from it. Symbolically, Tzaddi represents the shadow or reflection of any given thing, the necessary opposite that any state of being must bring with it. It has the number equivalent of 90.

Qoph, the 19th, signifies the back of the head, the part of the body which it is not possible for the individual to see directly. Esoterically, Qoph signifies the light, that inner illumination that cannot be experienced directly through the five senses. It is the result of God's command, 'Yehre aur!' – 'Let there be light!'. Qoph represents the sound 'Q', and its astrological correspondence is Gemini. It has the numerical value of 100.

Resh is the 20th Hebrew character which has the phonetic value of 'R'. It is another of those letters whose meaning is related to the previous one. In this case, it is the middle of three. Technically, it can be considered to incorporate both the preceding and subsequent letters, for Resh represents the head and, esoterically, 'recognition', which in any human is primarily based upon the appearance of someone's face. This letter has the numerical value of 200.

Twenty-first comes Shin, 'SH', which represents the teeth, the means by which we can make food edible. When the body decays, and even the bones are reduced to dust, it is the teeth that remain as the last material traces of physical being. Yet they can be lost whilst the body yet lives. In both their aspects of eating, loss and long existence, Shin as the tenth is connected with comsumption and transformation. Esoterically, it is the divine fire that transforms one state into another. In Christian qabalistic terms it is the illuminating fire of the Holy Spirit, transforming the material into the spiritual. Added to the four-letter name of God, it brings into being the Messiah. Shin's numerical equivalent is 300.

The final, 22nd, Hebrew character is Tau, with the value of 'TH'. This represents both the phallus and the sign of the cross, the mark of the 'chosen ones'. As a symbol, it is cognate with the ancient Egyptian sign of life, the Ankh or Crux Ansata. According to some Christian qabalistic thought, all those who do not bear the mark of the Tau are doomed to perish. Tau has the numerical value of 400, the highest single-figure number in the Hebrew counting system. Esoterically, this represents the 400 Sephiroth of the four worlds, which is 'synthesis'. It is the completion of the utterance of God, and thus encompasses creation.

QABALISTIC LETTER MANIPULATIONS

According to Jewish tradition, when Moses acquired the written Law (known as Torah she-bi-khetav) on the holy mountain of Sinai, he received also the oral Law, the Torah she-be-al-peh. Later rabbinical lore asserts that these two Torahs are parts of the same whole, complementary to one another. The written Torah is the basis for the oral Torah in that this latter Law is composed of commentaries and interpretations of the written one. This has been built up over the years by the insights and interpretations of learned scholars and rabbis. Jewish mystical thought asserts that within both the written and oral Torahs is a magical structure, the basis for qabalistic speculation and research. As with all 'religions of the book', qabalistic doctrine states that the Jewish scriptures are literally the Word of God, containing within themselves something of the divine essence. The Spanish commentator Moses ben Nahman (1194–1270, also known as Nahmanides) stated that the whole Torah was composed of the names of God. Furthermore, the very words in the Torah can be interpreted as manifestations of occult names. Fortunately, or by God's providence, this hidden meaning is not embedded so deeply that it cannot be deciphered. Within the sacred scriptural words is an encrypted meaning which, by the use of certain esoteric techniques, it is possible to reveal. In Jewish tradition there are three techniques by which these hidden meanings may be discovered. They are known as 'Gematria', 'Notarikon' and 'Temurah'.

Gematria is a technique in which each letter of the alphabet denotes a numerical equivalent. Each word therefore can be represented as the numbers of each letter added together. Then, this number is linked magically with any other word which has the same number. Any number thus may link a series of words, each with the same value, all magically interpretative of one another. In gematria there is also the convention of 'colel' which allows a discrepancy of one between any two word totals, allowing a little leeway in interpretation. The Hebrew alphabet has a numerical correspondence for every character. Of course, in former times, these were used in everyday arithmetical workings before the more functional Roman and then Arabic numerals came into use. The numbers are arranged in groups. The first nine characters represent 1 to 9; then the next nine stand for 10 to 90; whilst the remaining four have the values of 100 to 400. A similar system was developed in parallel for the Greek alphabet. In Hebrew, Aleph has a value of 1; Beth, 2; Gimel, 3; Daleth, 4; He, 5; Vau, 6; Zain, 7; Cheth, 8, and Teth, 9. The next group has equivalents in the tens: Yod, 10, Kaph, 20; Lamed, 30; Mem, 40; Nun, 50; Samech, 60; Ain, 70; Pe, 80, and Tzaddi, 90. The final characters are numbered in the hundreds: Qoph is 100; Resh is 200; Shin is 300, and Tau is 400. By combining these letters, any number can be generated. A similar system exists in the Greek alphabet, though the numbers rise to a higher level. Because of this numerological basis of the alphabet, Jewish scriptures can be interpreted in terms of number. Passages, words or names with the same number are held to be representative of one another, mystically linked and mutually interpretative. For example, through gematria, Genesis 49:10 was taken by qabalists as a prophecy of the Messiah: 'The sceptre shall not depart from Judah, nor a lawgiver from between his feet, until Shiloh come; and unto him shall the gathering of the people be'. In gematria, 'until Shiloh come' (IBA ShILH) has the number 358. Similarly, the number 358 is the Gematria value of 'Messiah', spelt MShIch. Also the number 358 occurs in the book of Numbers 21:9. This reads: 'And Moses made a serpent of brass, and put it upon a pole; and it shall come to pass, that if a serpent had bitten any man, when he beheld the serpent of brass, he lived.' This Mosaic serpent, in Hebrew, Nachash (NChSh) also has the 'Messiah' number of 358. Christian Hebrew gematrialists saw this connection as evidence that the brazen serpent of Moses was the 'antitype' that prefigured their Messiah, Christ, on the Tau-shaped cross.

Fig. 7. Hebrew tetragrammaton and other inscriptions on the round tower of Copenhagen Cathedral, Denmark, 1642.

Another important example of Hebrew gematria was pointed out by the qabalistic commentator Menesseh ben Israel. He noted that the first word of the Mosaic Pentateuch, 'BRASHITH', has the numerical value of 913. By gematria, this is equivalent to the words in Hebrew, 'He created the Law'. This is a perfect example of the workings of gematria, though more usually it is restricted to the cross-referencing of individual words and names. According to tradition, the Law of the Jews was written down in its entirety by Moses, from the first letter to the last. This first letter is Beth (B) of the word 'Brashith', the first word in Genesis, and the last letter is Lamed (L), the last letter of 'Israel', the final word of Deuteronomy. Esoterically, the whole fabric of the Mosaic law is included between these two letters. 'Brashith' has the gematrial value of 913, whilst 'Israel' computes at 541. Added together, these numbers make 1454, one less (colel) than the gematrial equivalent of 'Adam Kadmon', the microcosmic man whose body encompasses all things. This alphabet from fundamental Jewish tradition appears to have had an influence as far away as ancient Ireland, where the ogham and other esoteric alphabets begin with the letters B, L. It is probable that this was brought to Ireland from Egypt by Coptic monks, among whom many Near Eastern esoteric traditions flourished.

The idea that all of creation can be interpreted in words which have numerical correspondences may seem a strange one. A serious problem is that the logical conclusion of this appears to be that all things are predetermined in advance, that is, there is no free will. This fatalistic idea was rejected both by Jewish and Christian mystics as making a mockery of the whole idea of God's creation and the human being's place within it. The founder of the Hasidic sect of Judaism, Baal-Shem Tov, overcame this objection by means of an ingenious explanation. He suggested that the Torah had existed originally as a disordered collection of letters. There was a finite number of these, a certain number of each character. Thus the numerical content of the Torah, the divine energy, was fixed in advance, reflecting the nature and secret life of God himself. But only when an event took place were these letters formed into words, phrases and sentences that make up the written Torah. Thus the letter content and, hence, the spiritual content represented by the letters, was fixed, but the descriptive content could only be written with these letters when it took place. Thus Baal-Shem Tov reconciled these two seemingly opposite concepts, of a content fixed in advance by God that allowed for free will and the natural unfolding of events.

As with everything on the material plane, any system which continues in use for a long period of time must develop, and it was in Europe that Jewish qabalists continued their never-ending search for further esoteric facts. An important step in this process was the appearance in Spain around 1285 of the *Zohar*, which united the speculative and operative aspects of qabalism. The expulsion of the Jews from Spain in 1492 led to the establishment of a qabalistic school at Safed in Palestine. Its most famous members were Moses Cordovero (1522–1570) and Isaac Luria (1533–1572). Cordovero was primarily a theorist, whilst Luria's work was on the practical applications of the mystic knowledge of the Qabalah. Luria's qabalistic methods included many techniques involving numerical and talismanic magic. His authority was felt outside the Jewish community, influencing the Rosicrucian tradition, which came to prominence in Germay during the seventeenth century. This magical belief system incorporated Jewish qabalistic techniques and speculations into a Christian context. The Christian Qabalah writers like Jakob Böhme and Knorr von Rosenroth continued and expanded the use of gematria and other occult letter systems into the area of Christian mythical exegesis.

Some intriguing examples of this tradition still survive to this day. For example, the great qabalistic painting kept in the Trinity church at Bad Teinach in Baden-Württemberg, Germany, is a rare seventeenth-century example of the Christian Qabalah in pictorial form. It was painted in 1673 for Princess Antonia of Württemberg (1613–79). Designed by the mystical princess in association with Christian qabalists, it is a remarkable work, in both artistic and symbolic terms (which, unfortunately, cannot be described here) in which the connections between the 'anti-type' of the Old Testament and the 'type' of the New Testament are made explicit. Among other things, the brazen serpent of Moses is compared with Christ on the cross, the gematrial link of 358 described above. Also within the painting are a number of Hebrew words that describe symbolically the various aspects of the system of Christian Qabalah. In terms of Hebrew gematria, it is one of the few explicit examples. Surrounding the painting is an architectural frame that bears inscriptions in Hebrew letters. These are quotations from the psalms. One from Psalm 31:20: 'Thou shalt hide them in the secret of thy presence from the pride of man: thou shalt keep them secretly in a pavilion from the strife of tongues'. Next to this quotation is the number 2590, the gematria equivalent of the Hebrew words of this text.

The other text is from Psalm 37:4: 'Delight thyself also in the Lord; and he shall give thee the desires of thine heart'. The number of this quotation is 2005.

The second system of cryptic interpretation of scripture is notarikon, of which there are two versions. The first creates a new 'word' from the first and last letters of any word, whilst the second technique employs the letters of one word as being the first or last letters of each word in a sentence. These techniques are related to the modern obsession, beloved of trade unions and government agencies, for acronyms composed of the first letters of other words, such as Aslef for the 'Association of Locomotive Engineers and Firemen'. In Hebrew notarikon, the subject matter is far more lofty. For example, the ending of prayers, 'Amen', is derived by notarikon from the Hebrew phase meaning 'The Lord and Faithful King'. As with gematria, links between two separate words, names, phrases or texts could be discerned by means of the techniques of notarikon. As well as in Jewish esotericism, both gematria and notarikon were used extensively in the Greek tradition, especially with regard to the names of God the Father and Christ.

The third variety of interpretation, known as temurah, is a form of crytography which substitutes one letter, or several, for another. As with other magical alphabets, cryptography was one means of encoding information meant only for initiates. In the runic and Celtic systems, it was used widely in northern Europe. Many simple systems were used by Hebrew cryptographers, such as writing the alphabet in two halves, one in the reverse order, and pairing the letters. A common form is:

k	i	th	ch	z	v	h	d	g	b	a
l	m	n	s	o	p	th	q	r	sh	t

Certain obscure biblical names were derived from other, better-known ones, by temurah, such as Sheshak for Babel. Some of the names of God used in medieval qabalistic magic were derived by means of temurah. But the sacred name or names of God are shrouded in mystery and conflicting claims made by various occultists over the centuries. One important belief, however, is that the 'true' name of God is in some mysterious way directly encoded within scripture, or actually *is* the sacred writings themselves. For example, the Spanish qabalist Moses de Leon expanded the idea put forward by Moses ben Nahman that the entire Torah was made from the names of God. De Leon stated that the whole Torah was the name of God. But, of course, it was scarcely possible to use the entire Torah when calling upon God in prayers or magical workings. In any case, the true name of God was believed to be so sacred and to contain such awesome inherent power, that even to pronounce it out loud was considered to be a blasphemous act that might produce disastrous consequences. According to legend, it was this word that Moses had used to cause the Red Sea to part, so using it for any lesser needs was considered unwise. The only exception to this was the annual event when the High Priest pronounced it in the Holy of Holies of the Temple at Jerusalem.

The divine name was ascribed four letters of the Hebrew alphabet, known by its Greek name of the 'tetragrammaton'. Technically, any four-letter word is a tetragrammaton, but it is restricted usually to the specific four-letter name of God. The Hebrew tetragrammaton has its origin in Exodus 3.14: 'I am that I am'. This has been written in four different ways, of which the first is by far the most common. The first way is the four Hebrew characters JHVH, the letters Yod, He, Vau and He. This is believed to be the first and true name of God. Although its true pronunciation is unknown now, the name derived from this is Yahweh. This has been Europeanized as Jehovah, and contracted into the Jah worshipped in the Rastafarian religion. There are many mysteries that centre upon this tetragrammaton. In gematria, the letter Yod, He, Vau and He add up to the number 26. This number is important in the esoteric mysteries, and has been used sporadically in Jewish and Christian sacred buildings. For example, it is the guiding number of King's College Chapel at Cambridge, built between 1446 and 1515. This is made explicit by the 1615 wood-carving over the west door, which has the Hebrew tetragrammation inside a 16-rayed solar disc.

The Hebrew letters JHVH also correspond to some of the Sephiroth in the tree of life. Yod corresponds with Chokmah, the supernal wisdom. He is ascribed to Binah, ineffable understanding, comprehending all aspects of life. Vau is said

Fig. 8. Tetragrammaton on the west end of King's College Chapel, Cambridge. Wood carving, 1616.

to correspond with the six Sephiroth from Chesed to Yesod, whilst the final He represents Malkuth, the Kingdom, comprehending the unity of God. Written vertically from top to bottom, the JHVH tetragrammaton stands for the human body, the image of God. The other three tetragrammatons are secondary, being 'by-names' of God, three of the 72 'explicatory names' known as 'Shem ha-mephorash' or 'Shemahamphorash'. These are said to be derived from a 72-syllabled name of God, composed of 216 characters. Esoterically, this 'name' was derived by writing down the letters of verse 19 in the correct order; then those of verse 20 were written in reverse order; finally, the characters of verse 21 were written in the correct order. From these, 72 three-letter names were derived, all of which can be combined to make a single name. Furthermore, to each three-letter name were added the letters IH or AL. These then formed the names of the 72 angels guarding Jacob's ladder. The tradition of God having many symbolic names exists in Islam, whose mystics state that God has 99 names. Similar traditions also exist in other religions, for example with the customary 42 by-names of Odin in Asatrú.

But, of course, the correct magical pronunciation of this 72-syllable ineffable name of God was complex, and was lost. According to qabalistic lore, it was rediscovered by certain rabbis around the year 300 CE, who systematized it into the tetragrammaton used today, JHVH. The reduction to four letters was achieved by a variant form of gematria. By gematria, the total value of the tetragrammaton is 26. Yod equals 10; He, 5 and Vau, 6. The values of the letters are added as follows: Yod (10), plus Yod and He (15), plus Yod, He and Vau (21), plus Yod, He, Vau and He (26). 10 + 15 + 21 + 26

28

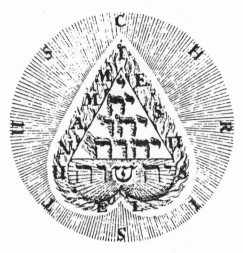

Fig. 9. Christian qabalistic heart-triangle of the name of God, incorporating Jewish and Christian names. From *Libri Apologetici* by Jacob Böhme.

= 72, the number of syllables of Shem ha-mephorash. These numbers occur also in Greek magical tradition, where the numerical values of Zeus and Apollo (612 and 1061 respectively), have the proportion of 15:26. The two variant spellings of Dionysos have the same ratio to one another. The tetragrammaton JHVH was used extensively in medieval and Renaissance ceremonial magic. The inverted heart-shaped mystical tetracyts illustrated in Fig 9 from Jacob Böhme's *Libri Apologetici*, published in London in 1764, has the flaming characters of JHVH arranged in a triangle. Beneath, the addition of the middle letter, Shin, transforms Jehovah into Jehoshua. The Roman letters for 'Immanuel' and 'Iesus', surrounded by 'Christus', show that Böhme was working in the tradition of Christian Qabalah.

The second tetragrammaton is ADNI, with the meaning of 'Lord'. This is generally pronounced in European tradition as Adonai. Knorr von Rosenroth, in his *Kabbala Denudata*, stated that the ADNI tetragrammaton is the divine name that is closest to the material world of created things. The third tetragrammaton is AHIH. This represents the pure being of God, pronounced by western qabalists as 'Eieie'. It represents, by notarikon, the words related to Moses (Exodus 3.14): 'And God said unto Moses, I am that I am: and he said, Thus shalt thou say unto the children of Israel, I Am hath send me unto you'. The final tetragrammaton is AGLA. This is an important word in Christian qabalism and western magic in general. In his *De Arcanis Catholicae Veritatis*, Petrus Galatinus stated that Agla represents the infinite power of the Holy Trinity. According to Eliphas Lévi, Agla contains hieroglyphically all of the mysteries of the Qabalah. Agla represents unity, symbolized by the first Aleph, leading back to unity, represented by the final Aleph. It is a tetragrammaton of the primal nature of God, the fountain of truth. It also signifies the generative principle inherent in Nature. Lévi saw Agla as the perfect word, which, if pronounced in the correct qabalistic manner, would demonstrate the magician's ability to pass all tests of initiation and accomplish the Great Work.

Athough these three tetragrammatons and the Shem hamephorash are the best-known 'names of God' in qabalistic lore, there are others. These are composed of a symbolic number of letters, most commonly 14, 22 and 42 characters. The name of 14 characters is derived by temurah from the 'Shema'. This is the declaration in the book of Deuteronomy (6.4): 'Hear, O Israel, the Lord is our God, the Lord is one'. This special name of God was used almost exclusively in door-protection magic. It was written on the back of the Mezuzah, attached to the right doorpost in order to exclude harmful influences from the household. Further details of this practice can be found in the author's *Earth Harmony* (Rider, 1987). The number fourteen letter became associated, in Christian usage, with the Stations of the Cross, each of which can be considered some sort of gateway in the Passion of Christ.

The name with 22 letters, the same number as the characters in the Hebrew alphabet, was published first in the *Sepher Raziel*. This book, ascribed to Eleazar of Worms, who lived in the thirteenth century, is the book of the Angel Raziel. The 22-letter name of God is believed to be derived by some technique from the letters of the Blessing of the Priests in the Jewish *Authorized Daily Prayer Book*: 'The Lord bless and keep thee: The Lord make his face to shine upon thee and be gracious unto thee: The Lord turn his face unto thee and give thee peace'. The name is 'Anaktam Pastam Papasin Dionsim', which in Hebrew letters would be ANQTM PSTM PSPSYM DYNVNSYM. These words have no meaning in Hebrew. But, during the seventeenth century, this name was very popular among the Jews of central Europe. At one time, it was introduced into the Blessing of the Priest's prayer when it was said in synagogue.

Finally, the name with 42 letters was a little more unwieldy. This name was said to be composed of the first 42 letters in the Bible: ABG YTS QRA STV NGD YCS BTR STG CQB TNA YGL PZQ SQV SYT. Each triplet of letters was believed to be a potent formula in its own right. There are 14 triplets, repeating the mystic double seven of the Mezuzah formula. In Christian mysticism, each of these triplets applies to one of the 14 Stations of the Cross. Its whole number, 42, is a traditionally significant one. There were 42 judges of the dead in the Egyptian *Book of the Dead*, and, later, Christian qabalists pointed out the 42 generations between that of Adam and that of Christ. In the twentieth century, the German geomant Joseph Heinsch found that the number 42 was an important measure in many of the more important ancient and medieval sacred buildings of Europe. And, in his *The Hitchhiker's Guide to the Galaxy*, Douglas Adams ascribed the number 42 as the answer to 'life, the Universe and everything'.

HEBREW MAGIC SQUARES AND GRIDS

All magical traditions have used sacred grids, either physically on the ground, or as a conceptual framework upon which to hang and sort certain aspects of their systems. An esoteric arrangement of the Hebrew Alphabet known as 'Aiq Beker', or the 'Qabalah of Nine Chambers' is the Jewish counterpart of the sacred grid used by the shamans and wise women of the Northern Tradition of Europe. The Hebrew grid arranges the letters of the Hebrew alphabet into the nine-square grid which is also the basic form of indigenous European magic. In this grid, are arranged the 22 characters of the standard Hebrew alphabet, with additional final characters which have specific characteristics. This Qabalah of Nine Chambers arranges three letters in each of the squares. The three letters in each square are related numerically, being the unit, ten and hundred. The arrangement is as follows:

Shin	Lamed	Gimel	Resh	Kaph	Beth	Qoph	Yod	Aleph
300	30	3	200	20	2	100	10	1

Mem (final)	Samekh	Vau	Kaph	Nun	Heh	Tau	Mem	Daleth
600	60	6	500	50	5	400	40	4

Tzaddi (final)	Tzaddi	Teth	Pe (final)	Pe	Cheth	Nun (final)	Ayin	Zain
900	90	9	800	80	8	700	70	7

This arrangement gives nine numerical values: 111, 222, 333, 444, 555, 666, 777, 888 and 999, a total of 4995. Several of these numbers are prominent magically. In making talismans, the Aiq Beker is a means of reducing each letter's numerical value to a unit. Thus, for the purposes of this type of computation, each character in the first square, Aleph, Yod and Qoph, usually equivalent to 1, 10 and 100 are counted as 1. Similarly with the other squares of the grid. By this means, all of the Hebrew letters are given a value between one and nine. This esoteric arrangement of characters is important in the creation of sigils from the names of planetary spirits. It is a form of letter magic closely related to numerical magic squares and in the qabalistic tradition of making talismans, planetary magic squares are used in conjunction with the Aiq Beker grid. The construction of Hebrew magic squares represents the emanation of the Ain-Soph, the qualities of evolution from the monad into the macrocosm, and of its mirror-image, the involution of the macrocosm to the monad. Ultimately, the construction of these squares is an attempt to facilitate the final reunion between the microcosm and the macrocosm. Traditionally, there are seven numerical 'magic squares', each ascribed to one of the seven astrological 'planets'. In the Hebrew and Greek alphabets, where letters stand for numbers, the magic squares are composed of words, intelligble or unintelligble. Each magic square or 'Kamea' is directly related to the sacred grid. Each contains a specific numerical mystery which underlies the physical form that it represents. Like gematria, notaikon and temurah, the creation of a magic letter square is a transformative operation in which thoughts and concepts are transmuted into literal forms of substance, and thence into names and words. These names and words are a direct parallel with the 'mantras' of Indian mysticism, which are chanted in order to create altered states of consciousness with the ultimate aim of the reunification of the individual with the cosmos, or with God.

The seven standard magic squares are assigned to various planetary powers, grading upwards in size from the outermost to the innermost. The square of three is assigned to the outermost of the traditional astrological planets, Saturn, Next, the square of four is that of Jupiter; five is of Mars, six of the Sun, and seven of Venus. The eight by eight square is assigned to Mercury and the nine by nine to the Moon. In a magic square, the numbers of the smaller squares which compose the

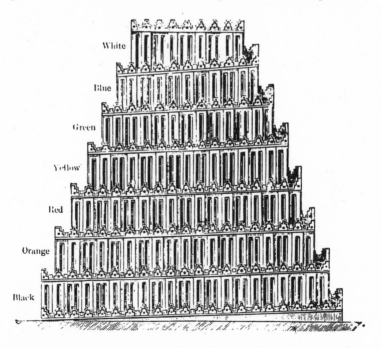

Fig. 10. The arrangement of the planetary colours in the ziggurat at Khorsabad.

larger are arranged in such a manner that, taking any row, the sum of the numbers will be the same. In Hebrew magic, each planet can be seen as a symbol of one of the Sephirah on the tree of life. Saturn signifies Binah, the third Sephirah, whilst Jupiter, corresponds with the fourth Sephirah, Chesed. Mars parallels the fifth Sephirah, Geburah, whilst Mercury is the eighth Sephirah, Hod. This planetary scheme was the basis of Assyrian and Babylonian ziggurats, of which the ill-fated Tower of Babel was an example. In their purest cosmologically defined form, each of the ziggurats' seven stages or platforms represented one of the seven planets. The magic squares are arranged in a sequence that starts with the smallest grid at the outermost. For structural reasons, the outermost square on a ziggurat was the largest. However, it was ruled by the corresponding magic square, and painted in the corresponding colour. The engraving of the Khorsabad ziggurat, reproduced in Fig. 10, gives a good idea of the principle.

The simplest magic square is the square of three by three, ascribed to Saturn, in which each line adds up to 15 and the total of all the numbers added together is 45. This is the square most commonly used by European magicians. Its traditionally associated colour is black, signifying the outermost planet and the bottom tier of the ziggurat.

4	9	2
3	5	7
8	1	6

A four-by-four kamea is assigned to the planet Jupiter. Each rank or file of numbers adds up to 34, and the sum of all the numbers is 136. The traditional colour of this square is tawny or orange.

4	14	15	1
9	7	6	12
5	11	10	8
16	2	3	13

But from the four-by-four grid upwards, there are many alternative magic squares for each number. But only one of these is related to a corresponding planet, the others having different ascriptions. For example, the following four-by-four magic square, which is not the magic square of Jupiter, was used by Albrecht Dürer in his engraving *Melancholia*.

1	14	15	4
8	11	10	5
12	7	6	9
13	2	3	6

But, of course, the total for each line is still 34, and the sum total of all of the numbers 136. This rule of equal line and sum totals applies to all magic squares. Another four-by-four grid, again not the magic square of Jupiter, but a Hindu magical formula, is carved on a stone in the fort at Gwalior in India:

15	10	3	6
4	5	16	9
14	11	2	7
1	8	13	12

From these examples, it is clear that there are many possible arrangements of alphabet letters as numbers to make magic squares, each of which will have their own esoteric reading. The following grid of 25 squares (5 by 5) belongs to Mars, whose colour is red. Each line adding up to 65, making a total of 325.

11	24	7	20	3
4	12	25	8	16
17	5	13	21	9
10	18	1	14	22
23	6	19	2	15

The six-by-six grid of 36 squares is that of the Sun. Its colour is gold or yellow. Each line adds up to 111, and the total is 666. This number is the contentious 'Number of the Beast' described in the Book of Revelation of St John the Divine, and also the total of one of the nine chambers of the Aiq Beker. (The significance and meaning of the number 666 is discussed in Chapter 2.)

35

6	32	3	34	35	1
7	11	27	28	8	30
19	14	16	15	23	24
18	20	22	21	17	13
25	29	10	9	26	12
36	5	33	4	2	31

The fifth grid is that of Venus, which measures seven by seven. Its colour is green-blue. Each rank or file adds up to 175, making a total of 1225 for the entire square.

22	47	16	41	19	35	4
5	23	48	17	42	11	29
30	6	24	49	18	36	12
13	31	7	25	43	19	37
38	14	32	1	26	44	20
21	39	8	33	2	27	45
46	15	40	9	34	3	28

An alternative seven-by-seven grid sometimes encountered is:

30	39	48	1	10	19	28
38	47	7	9	18	27	29
46	6	8	17	26	35	37
5	14	16	25	34	36	45
13	15	24	33	42	44	4
21	23	32	41	43	3	12
22	31	40	49	2	11	20

This square is not ascribed to Venus. The following, sixth, grid is allocated to Mercury, whose colour is light blue. This is the familiar checkerboard grid, upon which such games as chess and English draughts are played, measuring eight by eight. The lines add up to 260 each, making a total of 2080 for the whole grid.

8	58	59	5	4	62	63	1
49	15	14	52	33	11	10	56
41	23	22	44	48	19	18	45
32	34	35	29	25	38	39	28
40	26	27	37	36	30	31	33

17	47	46	20	21	43	42	24
9	55	54	12	13	51	50	16
64	2	3	61	60	6	7	57

The final magic square normally computed is that of the Moon, the innermost of the astrological planets and the top platform of the ziggurat. This magic square measures nine by nine. The traditional colour associated with the Moon is silver or pure white. The added numbers of each line of this grid are 369, making a grand total of 3321. This square is especially important, because it is the first square which is a square of a square (3^4: $3 \times 3 \times 3 \times 3$).

37	78	29	70	21	62	13	54	5
6	38	79	30	71	22	63	14	46
47	7	39	80	31	72	23	55	15
16	48	8	40	81	32	64	24	56
57	17	49	9	41	73	33	65	25
26	58	18	50	1	42	74	34	66
67	27	59	10	51	2	43	75	35
36	68	19	60	11	52	3	44	76
77	28	69	20	61	12	53	4	45

In the nineteenth century, the French magus Éliphas Lévi assigned each of the seven planetary magic squares to one of the ancient Seven Wonders of the World. The magic square of Saturn, which has 9 figures was related to Solomon's Temple in Jerusalem, with the mystic number of 45. The square of Jupiter, comprising 16 numbers, corresponded with the image of Zeus at Olympia, whose mystic number was thus 136. The next square, with 25 numbers, is that of Mars, which represented the Hanging Gardens of Babylon, with the mystic number of 325. The 36-figure magic square of the Sun, whose number is the ominous 666, corresponded with the giant effigy of Apollo, known as the Colossus of Rhodes. For the magic square of Venus, with 49 numbers and a total of 1225, the Tomb of Mausolus was the corresponding 'wonder'. The Pyramids were related to the next magic square, the 64-figure square assigned to the planet Mercury. Their number was 2080. Finally, the magic square of the Moon, with a total of 3321 and 81 numbers, signified the Temple of Diana at Ephesus.

HEBREW LETTER SQUARES AND OTHER AMULETS

Related to these numerically based magic squares are the letter arrays used mainly in talismanic magic. Many of these had a numerical basis through gematria, and almost all of them, generally used in protective magic, referred in some way to the unity of God. For example, Samaritan amulets carried the name of God, such as 'Elohim', read from the centre of what appears to be a magic square. The Samaritan amulet pattern reproduced in Fig. 11 reads 'Lord, great God', 'Elohim'. These amuletic inscriptions are taken from the book of Deuteronomy 6.4: 'Hear, O Israel; The Lord our God is one Lord' (*Shema Israel. Adonai Elohim Adonai Ahat*). The formula Abracadabra, now reduced to use in the repertoire of performing conjurors, was originally used against fever. This formula has a double derivation. It is said to refer to the divinity Abraxas,

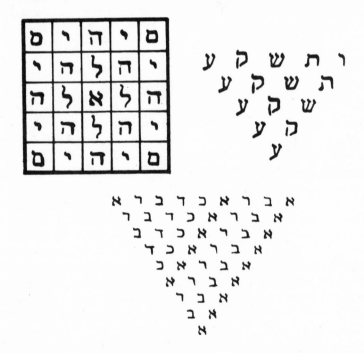

Fig. 11. Medieval Hebrew letter-labryinths: (*top left*) square based upon 'Elohim', read from the middle; (*top right*) Wattish'ka triangle, a talisman against fire; (*below*) Abracadabra formula.

38

whose number in gematria, 365, makes this entity the lord of the year. But the word 'Abracadabra' is probably derived from the Chaldean words, *abbâda ke dåabrå*, which means 'perish like the word', although traditionally it is ascribed to Serenus Sammonicus, physician of the Emperor Caracalla (reigned 211–17 CE). This formula was written as a downward-pointing triangle, with the medical function of magically suppressing fevers. Its relation to Abraxas is that, as god of the whole year, his name will help to restore wholeness. A similar, though smaller, downward-pointing triangle formula was used against fire. This used the Hebrew word 'Wattishk'a' (and the fire dwindled), referring to a passage from the book of Numbers:

And when the people complained, it displeased the Lord: and the Lord heard it; and his anger was kindled; and the fire of the Lord burnt among them, and consumed them that were in the uttermost parts of the camp. And the people cried unto Moses; and when Moses prayed unto the Lord, the fire was quenched.

MEDIEVAL HEBREW-DERIVED ALPHABETS

There are a number of magical alphabets used from the medieval period onwards that are derived from earlier Hebrew characters. These were most prevalent in those European countries whose esoteric culture was most influenced by the Jewish qabalistic tradition in central and eastern Europe, though, of course, they were transmitted readily to students of the arcane sciences in other lands. The main versions of these have names which refer to some aspect of Jewish tradition: Celestial Hebrew, Canaanean, Moabite, Samaritan, Malachim, Solomonian, etc. Some of these are just alternative, cursive, variants of standard 'square' Hebrew. These have letters which resemble, more or less, those cursive Hebrew scripts used to write Yiddish in Germany and Poland in the days before Hitler's inferno. As these scripts developed, variations and alterations took place, and new varieties evolved from earlier ones. In general, these Renaissance scripts are complicated because their creators and users were conversant with not only Hebrew, but also with the Greek and Roman alphabets. Thus we find magical alphabets that have either Hebrew, Greek,

Latin or vernacular equivalents. The Jewish Qabalah concurs in many ways with the philosophy of the Pythagorean, Gnostic, neo-Platonic and Hermetic schools, and so it was natural, as it developed, that it should have influenced and merged with these medieval and Renaissance philosophical tendencies. The embellished and altered forms of Hebrew letters on Renaissance paintings in central Europe display forms that have close parallels with some secret scripts. There are several interesting inscriptions in variant Hebrew on the magnificent four-panelled altarpiece of the Herrenberger Altar, painted in 1519 by the ill-fated mystic artist Jerg Ratgeb, now in the Staatsgalerie in Stuttgart. These forms resemble closely the style of letters in such letter-rows as the Alphabet of the Magiq.

There are two basic forms of Hebrew derivations. One takes the characters and alters them slightly or drastically, but remains basically a pen-written script. This style can be seen in Ratgeb's painting. The other type makes the letters into ornamental sigils by drawing a small circle at the end of each line, and at the junctions of lines. H.C. Agrippa's Celestial script of 1531 is a good example of this. The scripts recorded in 1675 by J. Bartolozzi and C.J. Imbonati are also typical. In his book *The Magus* (1801), Francis Barratt listed several of these ornamental magical alphabets, including versions of Celestial, Malachim and Crossing the River (*Transitus Fluvii*). In modern times, many variants of the bewildering plethora of such 'Hebraic' scripts have been recorded by Fred Gettings in his excellent compilation *Dictionary of Occult, Hermetic and Alchemical Sigils* (1981).

Conventionally, these scripts are classified under certain names, all of which recall their origins with Hebrew connotations. Although it has a Latin name, *Transitus Fluvii* (Crossing the River) is one of the most celebrated occult alphabets. It has been used by several notable magi, and published in several closely related forms. It is a Hebraic script in the 'ornamental sigil' tradition, where basic Hebrew letters were taken, modified and ornamented. In *The Magus*, Francis Barratt listed this with a letter order that is different from that used in standard Hebrew, being related to a species of Temurah. Using his spelling of the letters, his order reads: Lamed, Caph, Jod, Theth, Cheth, Zain, Vau, He, Daleth, Gimel, Beth, Aleph, Tau, Schin, Resh, Kuss, Zade, Pe, Ain, Samech, Nun, Mem.

So-called Chaldean script is another Hebrew-derived variant. The ancient Chaldeans used the Cuneiform script, which has no relationship to scripts based on the Phoenician alphabet. In the medieval period, the word 'Chaldean' was taken to refer to the magi and astrologers of antiquity, as in such texts as *The Chaldean Oracles of Zoroaster*. This alphabet is related to Hebrew by its order, and by many of its characters being embellished versions of standard 'square' Hebrew characters. Several of these letters are altered Hebrew characters turned round by 90 degrees.

The script known as Samaritan is thought to be a parallel version of Hebrew, derived from the ancient Samaritan book script, one of the old semetic alphabets derived directly from Phoenician. In medieval and Renaissance magic, this term applies to a group of related alphabets. Some resemble closely the historic Samaritan script, whilst others are modifications that depart more strongly from the original forms. One form, given in the 1675 book *Biblioteca Magna Rabbinica* by J. Bartolozzi and C.J. Imbonati, follows the historic letters closely. Another Samaritan script was recorded by G. Postel in 1538. Some of the characters of this alphabet are almost the same as the historic Samaritan, while others depart markedly from it, being from the typical repertoire of Renaissance magical alphabet characters. A more distantly related Samaritan script is recorded by B. de Vignere in his 1586 compilation *Traicté des Chiffres, ou Secrètes Manières d'Escrire*. This is an embellished 'ornamental sigil' alphabet that has small circles or dots at the ends and junctions of many of the characters' strokes.

As with all of these mixed and rather personal alphabets, there are a number of scripts which have been given the name Canaanean. One variant of Canaanean is derived directly from Chaldaean, or parallels it. Others are related to the secret scripts attributed to the Spanish Inquisition and the secret German Vehmgericht societies. These scripts were developed as secret codes used only by members of these pernicious organizations. It is ironic that secret organizations that numbered Jewish people among the 'heretics' whom they hunted should use secret alphabets based originally on Hebrew.

The alphabet known as Celestial, used by H.C. Agrippa and his contemporaries, is another variant of Hebrew/Samaritan.

Fig. 12. Three medieval Hebrew-derived magical alphabets: (*top to bottom*) Celestial, Malachim and Transitus Fluvii.

Again, Agrippa's version of this alphabet is of the 'ornamental sigil' type. As with some other magical alphabets he described, Francis Barratt's Celestial was written in his special order. It is the same as that in his Transitus Fluvii, detailed above. His Malachim alphabet, however, has another letter-order, again different from the standard. Some writers call versions of the Celestial script, its parallels and derivatives, by other names, most commonly 'Angelic' or 'Supercelestial'. The interpretation of these scripts has also undergone periodic updating and adaptation to make them more accessible under the changed conditions of modern times. In his *Amulettes, Talismans et Pentacles dans les Traditions Orientales et Occidentales* (1938), J. Marquès-Rivière gave a version of this alphabet, modified with Roman rather than Hebrew equivalents. Fred Gettings has pointed out that many of the letters in Marquès-Rivière's Celestial alphabet are the same as those in his Angelic. Seemingly, there is no end to the permutations of Hebraic magical alphabets, and it is inevitable that yet more versions will come into being as individuals follow their personal paths.

2
The Greek Alphabet

Pythagoras thought that he, who gave things their names, ought to be regarded not only the most intelligent, but the oldest of the wise men. We then search the Scriptures accurately, since they are admitted to be expressed in parables, and from the names hunt out the thoughts which the Holy Spirit, propounded respecting things, reached by imprinting His mind, so to speak, on the expressions. That the names used with various meanings, being made the subject of accurate investigation, may be explained, and that which is hidden under many integuments may, being handled and learned, come to light and gleam forth.
SELECTIONS FROM PROPHETIC SCRIPTURES XXXII, ANTI-NICENE
LIBRARY, VOL. XXIV

Jewish mystics asserted that the Hebrew alphabet was an emanation of the Ain-Soph, but for the ancient Greeks there were several myths concerning the origin of their alphabet. One version of the legend comes down to us from the Roman writer Caius Julius Hyginus, who was the curator of the Paletine Library and a friend of the poet Ovid. In his *Fables*, he wrote that the Fates invented the first seven of the Greek letters. These were Alpha, Beta, Eta, Ypsilon, Iota, Omicron and Tau. After this, Palamedes, son of Nauplius, invented eleven more. Then Epicharmus of Sicily added Theta and Chi (alternatively Pi and Psi). Finally, Simonides contributed the letters Omega, Epsilon, Zeta and Psi (or Phi) to the alphabet. An alternative legend ascribed the letters to Hermes, who, seeing a flight of cranes, was struck with the idea that similar shapes could be used to represent written sounds. Yet another origin myth, historically the most accurate, ascribes the Greek alphabet to Cadmus the Phoenician. As with the Hebrew alphabet, the Phoenician was the model from which the Greek alphabet was developed during the middle of the eighth century BCE. Many of the early Greek characters are very close to archaic Phoenician forms. It is possible that the Greeks learnt the script from Phoenician traders who had settled in such strategically important places as Cos, Crete and Rhodes.

At first, the Greek alphabet had several variant forms, but eventually the Ionic form became standardized, and when adopted formally at Athens in the year 403 BCE, it was the form which survives to this day. In that formalization, the older Greek alphabet was augmented by several new characters. Like modern Greek and all other European scripts except Etruscan, this form of Greek was written from left to right. At the same time, some older compound letters were discarded. But some of these older characters were retained as numerals. By the fifth century BCE, it was taken for granted in Greece that male citizens were literate. From the outset, writing was used for the activities we associate with literacy today: everything from shopping lists to legal documents, from literature to invocations of the Gods. Like Hebrew, but in a subtly different way, the Greek Alphabet attained a high level of development around the third century BCE, when the systems of gematria are believed to have emerged. The alphabet has 24 characters, each of which has a complete system of attributions, symbolic and numerical. Unlike the Roman alphabet, but like the Phoenician and Hebrew, the Greek characters also represent

Fig. 13. The Greek alphabet.

numbers. This has given the alphabet a considerable potential for magical use. Both the numerical system of the followers of the Pagan sage Pythagoras and the number-magic of Christian mysticism are implicit in the Greek alphabet. In addition, the Greek alphabet is a magical system with a complete series of esoteric correspondences which give it a powerful divinitory potential. In this there is a direct parallel with the runes, which are better known in this respect. Like the runes, each Greek letter has a specific name, a meaning and a numerical value which can be used in divination. But whilst the famous ancient Greek oracles of Delphi and Dodona are well known, the divinatory magic of the Greek alphabet has still to receive the attention which is its due.

A major area of Greek sacred alphabet symbolism is in the art of gematria. As in the Hebrew tradition, this is an esoteric system in which each word in Greek letters is converted into a corresponding number. This number is produced by adding the numerical equivalents of the letters together. In the Greek tradition, these numbers are the hidden side of scripture, in both the Pagan and the Christian observances. Different words with the same numerical equivalent can and are used to encode meanings which are then only apparent to practitioners of the art of gematria. Linear dimensions and other associated numbers in sacred buildings can also have a specific meaning when decoded by gematria. In this relationship, it is significant that an alternative ancient Greek spelling of the word gematria, 'gametria' (ΓΑΜΕΤΡΙΑ), was a recognized variant also of the word 'geometria' (ΓΕΟΜΕΤΡΙΑ), from which the English word geometry is derived. In some instances, gematria was a system of notation used to record the secret forms and relationships of sacred geometry. Greek geometria contains many examples of geometrical usages, both extant in sacred buildings and encapsulated in esoteric lore. Both its Pagan and Christian users saw the Greek alphabet in general, and gematria in particular as encompassing the universal creative principles. This encapsulation of universal principles occurs also in the Hebrew, runic, ogham, Gothic and Westphallan alphabets.

Before Christianity was imposed on all Gentiles in the Roman Empire as the official and sole religion, there were many ancient and venerable schools of philosophy. The neo-

Platonists of Alexandria had their 'sacred succession', by which the inner teachings of the philosophy were developed and transmitted. The Mysteries celebrated at Eleusis and other sacred places of power likewise were based upon gradual revelation of esoteric secrets. Similarly, the Pythagoreans had a system of probation and progressive initiation into successively higher grades of adepthood, so that to become competent in the system, the candidate had to study for many years. The subtle esoteric interrelationship between symbols, numbers and letters was the means of transmitting wisdom, and, of course, the Greek alphabet was the vehicle for this. These schools of philosophy and sacred initiation existed and developed for many centuries, being the repositories for scientific and mathematical knowledge as well as the arts now considered more esoteric. But when Christianity was introduced as the established state religion, these schools and centres were closed. The adepts who escaped with their lives were compelled to transmit their arcane wisdom by other means. Pagan temples and other sacred sites of the elder faith were converted into Christian churches. But the arcane qualities of these places were not destroyed – they could not be – so they manifested themselves in terms of the incoming religious symbolism. This took the form of the use of Pagan altars in Christian churches, and the assimilation of local divinities as saints. The imagery of Athena was transferred to Saint Mary, the goddess of Victory became Saint Victoria, the Dioscuri transmuted into St Peter and St Paul, Helios transmogrified into St Elias, the qualities of Apollo and Mithras were assimilated into the Christ-figure, and so on. The Jews, however, excluded from the blanket Christianization of the Empire, escaped the systematic destruction of esoteric culture that befell the Pagans. Despite persecution, their very dispersal throughout the then-known world enabled the secret doctrines to live on, and become refined further. Thus it was that qabalistic knowledge emerged and crystallized finally in the key texts of that school of philosophy. But the Pagan traditions, which accessed the inner core of human and cosmic being equally as successfully as the Jewish or Christian mysteries did, became assimilated into esoteric Christianity.

'The Christian equivalent of the word Cabala', wrote the nineteenth-century English mystic William Stirling, 'was

Gnosis, knowledge, and from innumerable references in the writings of the Fathers [the Church Fathers] it is evident that the new sect, in the construction of the Gospel and ritual of the Church, perpetuated the same mystical tradition which they had received from the Hebrews'. The nature of this knowledge, Stirling tells us, was stated explicitly by Clement of Alexandria: 'And the Gnosis itself is that which has descended by transmission to a few, having been imparted underwritten by the Apostles'. A similar assertion was made by St.Basil: 'They were well instructed to preserve the veneration of the mysteries by silence. For how could it be proper, publicly to proclaim in writing the doctrine of those things, which no unbaptized person may so much as look upon?'

The evidence of these, and other, writers, is that the Apostolic succession, so jealously guarded by the churches, depended upon the receipt of the oral tradition, the Gnosis. Only through this oral tradition, comparable with the Mosaic unwritten Torah, could the Gospels be interpreted properly. Like the Jewish Qabalah, this Gnosis depended upon secrets mystically encoded within the very words of scripture. But, as befitting a Hellenized tradition, the working language and alphabet was Greek, not Hebrew. However, because of the origin of the Christian religion in Jewish practice, many of the techniques and actual words were taken over from the older tradition. Similarly, the gematria and symbolism of the Pagan Greek tradition was incorporated into the Gnostic system. As with the rabbinical practice, where it was considered that the inner knowledge was too powerful to be imparted to the masses, it appears that the Church Fathers held the same views. Although qabalistic numerology and astrology were condemned publicly, there is plenty of evidence that this was a political move intended to keep even the knowledge that there was an inner tradition away from ordinary folk. Adepts and priests, whether Pagan, Jewish or Christian have always kept inner teachings away from the uneducated and unititiated, lest they be misused, or fall into heretical hands, whence they will be perverted. From this doctrine comes the idea of 'casting pearls before swine', a concept considered élitist and outmoded by some modern occultists. Whether or not they were correct, for the greater period of human history, traditional doctrines have held such a view. By this means, certain truths have been preserved. Along with the written scriptural texts, oral tradition, transmitted necessarily from master or mistress to disciple has provided the means of interpreting them correctly.

The survival of this traditional knowledge through cataclysmic changes of official government religious doctrine can be seen in the practice of Greek gematria. The use of this technique was continuous and unbroken through the Pagan and the Christian observances, including the Gnostic version of Christianity. This claim to universality was because, like the Jewish qabalah, Greek gematria operates at a level beyond that of mere doctrinal or sectarian differences. The universal creative principles are approached in many ways through many religions. Greek gematria deals with these principles through symbolic numbers. The integral part of the Christian Gnosis with gematria is shown from the very word 'Gnosis', which in Greek is 'Η ΓΝΩΣΙΣ. This has a numerical value of 1271, the same value as the word Stauros (ΣΤΑΥΡΟΣ), the Cross.

Each of the letters of the Greek alphabet has an associated meaning which incorporates a full range of esoteric correspondences. They relate to specific divinities in the ancient Greek pantheon, and also have a Mithraic symbolism, which was assimilated later into the Christian tradition. Thus they link the Pagan and Christian world-views and their corresponding magical traditions. The letters of the alphabet are associated with the 'twenty-four Mysteries' of Gnostic tradition, which was a continuation and development of the earlier Pagan tradition. The Greek letters have the following meanings and correspondences:

α **Alpha,** the first character, has the literal meaning of a bull or, more generally, cattle. As with the corresponding Hebrew first character, this is interpreted basically as mobile wealth in all of its aspects, both materially and spiritually. When coinage was introduced, the value was expressed in terms of head of cattle, and from this comes the English word 'capital' (from the Latin, 'caput', a head). As with a herd of cattle, the esoteric nature of Alpha means that wealth should be nurtured and used wisely. Life is transitory, and, so that future generations can benefit, wealth should be managed in a way that is of benefit to all. Alpha makes an interesting parallel with Hebrew and runic, two other alphabets with symbolic equivalents, where the first character has the same meaning as cattle-wealth. In Hebrew, this is the letter Aleph, whilst in the runes it is Feoh, which has the phonetic value of 'F'. Yet, despite these differences, cattle wealth is seen as the primary basis of society, reflecting the origin of alphabets in a certain phase of human development. Numerically, Alpha is the number which symbolizes the first and most important, the primary concerns of existence, Gnostic symbolism tells of the 'triple Alpha', symbolic of the Holy Trinity. In gematria, the number of Alpha is 532.

β **Beta,** the second letter, has challenging, perhaps demonic connotations. Numerically 2, the second one, is always seen as the breaker of unity, and, in dualistic religions, it became identified with the demonic challenger to the unity of God. Often, this challenger is called the 'Other One', as in Sweden today, acknowledging the challenging aspect of the second that always threatens to become the first by rivalling or overthrowing it. In the Mithraic religion, the demonic god of wrongdoing, Angra Mainyu, also has the epithet, 'the second', a challenge to God and the destroyer of his unity. In Christian terms, this negative aspect was personified as the Devil. But also, the second brings with it the possibility of reunification. Without the second, the monad, complete in itself, is devoid of relationships, and therefore there can be no existence. All religions which see the universe as having a creator recognize this necessity, symbolized here by Beta. Some recognize that this second quality is not necessarily in diametrical opposition to the first principle. By gematria, the name Beta is 308.

Γ **Gamma,** the third character, has the number 3, and the meaning of godliness, the sacred. From out of the monad and the second comes naturally the third, as from the mother and father comes the child. Generally, the letter Gamma refers to the triadic godhead, which is found everywhere. For example, the Triple goddess is known throughout the Mediterranean region, as well as across Europe to the north. The Babylonians worshipped the triad of Anu, Enlil and Ea; the Egyptians revered Isis, Osiris and Horus; the Anglo-Saxons worshipped Woden, Frigga and Thunor, whilst the Vikings venerated Odin, Thor and Balder. In Christian terms, Gamma signifies the trinity of God the Father, the Son and the Holy Ghost. In symbolic terms, Gamma represents the threefold nature of process: creation, continuance and destruction, beginning, middle and end; birth, life and death. It is the third, waning phase of the moon, marking the future extinction of the light, and, by implication, the re-birth of the next cycle. This is the 'child', the third one that will outlive its two parents. More specifically, in the Greek context, Gamma is the letter associated with the Three Fates, Clotho, Atropos and Lachesis, their Roman counterparts Nonna, Decima and Morta, the Three Graces, and even the three Weird Sisters of Old English tradition. By gematria, Gamma is equivalent to 85.

Δ **Delta,** represents the classical four elements of Fire, Air, Water and Earth. For at least 7000 years, since the construction of the temples of the archaic Old European culture in the Balkans, four-sidedness has been associated with human artefacts. Four-sided structures, easier to make than round ones, represent the fourfold orientations of the body that all, human beings share: back, front, right and left. Delta is thus the first element of the human alteration of the world from its primal state. It is the number 4, the four directions, the four horses of the chariot known as the quadriga, and (in Christian eschatology), the Four Horsemen of the Apocalypse. It is a symbol of completion on the material level, the quality of wholeness. By gematria, Delta is 340.

E **Epsilon,** stands for the spiritual element which is contained within the material, and in some ways exists separately from it. It is the Aion, or ether, the fifth element known as the 'Quintessence' in alchemical lore (the equivalent to the 'Nwyvre' of the Bardic tradition of the Celts). Whatever it is called, this power of spirit is the subtle energy of life, the 'breath of life' known in Greek as 'Pneuma', upon which all living existence is based (whose esoteric number is 576). Traditionally, this element is represented by the pentagram, the five-pointed star. In magical writing, the pentagram is thus a substitute for the letter Epsilon. It contains within it the sacred ratios of the Golden Section, one of the three bases of sacred geometry, used in the design of the most sacred and beautiful of ancient Greek temples, such as the Parthenon in

Athens and the temple of Zeus at Olympia. Through this quality of mathematical ratio, Epsilon is linked mystically with Lambda, the eleventh character of the Greek alphabet. In Gnostic tradition, Epsilon represents the second heaven. Numerically, it is the number 5. By gemetria, Epsilon is 445.

Z **Zeta,** the sixth letter, means an offering or sacrifice. This is not to be taken as meaning a destructive offering, but rather the sacrifice of energy in the furtherance of the process of creation. Esoterically, Zeta is the seventh letter, the old sixth character Digamma (F) having been abandoned, except for numerical uses, before the Classical period. As the seventh-but-sixth, Zeta signifies the formative principle of the cosmos. In the biblical tradition, the universe was created in six days, with a seventh rest day for completion. Geometrically, too, the number six is the ruling principle of matter, the hexagonal lattice which underlies material structure. The six points of the hexagonal lattice are required in order that the seventh might be enclosed. The figure equivalent to Zeta is thus the pattern associated with the archangel Michael, six equally spaced dots around a central seventh. This magic sigil can still be seen today as a magical protection on old houses in England and Germany. Numerically, Zeta is equivalent to the number 7, and by gematria to 316.

H **Eta,** as the actual rather than the conceptual seventh character, represents the energy inherent in the qualities of joy and love. It is a character of balance, that quality of being in harmony with the world, being in the right place at the right time to achieve one's full potential. More specifically, as Eta this is manifested as the divine harmony of the seven planets and seven spheres of pre-Copernican cosmology. It can thus signify the music of the spheres. The Gnostic Marcus connected Eta with the third heaven: 'The first heaven sounds Alpha, and the one after that E (Epsilon), and the third Eta . . .' In Christian numerology, Eta represents the tendency towards perfection, regeneration and salvation. But numerically, Eta is the number 8, which is the basic solar number. By gematria, the letters of Eta are equivalent to 309, the number of the god Ares, the planet Mars.

51

Θ **Theta,** the eighth character, has the phonetic value of 'TH'. Theta symbolizes the eighth, crystal sphere, upon which, in the former cosmology, the fixed stars were believed to stand. Therefore, it is the symbol of balance and integration. As the eighth, Theta represents the eightfold division of time and space of traditional European custom. Numerically, however, Theta is the number 9, which signifies the esoteric linking between 8 and 9 which underlies the magic of sun and moon. Theta's number by gematria is 318, the number of the solar deity Helios.

I **Iota,** although the smallest letter, represents destiny, being sacred to the goddess of fate Ananke, and thus also to the Three Fates. Ananke is linked by gematria to the Great God Pan, the number of Ananke being 130 and Pan 131. Thus, although the smallest letter, it is a microcosm of them all, linking with the complex gematrial numerology associated with Pan. Thus, symbolically, the smallest part of the universe contains within it the whole in microcosm. The letter Iota is equivalent to the number 10, considered to be the fourth heaven of the Gnostic branch of the Christian faith. By gematria, Iota is 381, the number of Aiolos, the winds. As a character of destiny, the connection with the fickle winds of fate is very appropriate. It is also a symbol of insignificance, when something makes 'not an iota of difference', but when someone tempts fate by 'not caring a jot' about something that should be important to them, this seeming insignificance may show itself by backfiring upon the tempter and bringing disaster.

K **Kappa,** is said to be the bringer of bad luck, disease, old age and death. Appropriately, it is sacred to the god Kronos. In Mithraic tradition, as the tenth Greek letter, it is associated with the bad god Angra Mainyu, who is associated with 1000 ($10 \times 10 \times 10$) death-bringing demons. Angra Mainyu was said to possess 10,000 types of disease with which he visited the human race. On a more abstract level, Kappa is a letter of time, the bringer of inevitable, inexorable processes. In this respect, it is linked with the rune Ken, which represents the inexorable process of burning. Kappa is equivalent numerically to the score, the number 20. By gematria, Kappa is equivalent to 182.

Fig. 14. The Lambda as a geometric tool for making the Golden Section.

λ **Lambda** is connected with plant growth, and the mathematical progressions associated with the figure in classical geometry, upon whose principles organic growth proceeds. It is linked mystically with the geometric ratio known as the Golden Section. As the 11th letter of the Greek alphabet, Lambda represents the ascent to a higher level. Mathematically, this is demonstrated by the two progressions of Lambda, the geometric and the arithmetic, the fundamental sequences of ancient Greek mathematics. On a more abstract level, Lambda signifies the flow of numerical sequences that lie within all physical processes. In the runic alphabet, there is a direct continuation of this Greek letter through the character called Lagu, which also has the qualities of growth and the phonetic letter of 'L'. Similar characteristics are borne by the Hebrew letter Lamed. Numerically, Lambda signifies 30, with a gemetria value of 78.

M **Mu,** the 12th Greek character, represents the sacred number 40. It is connected with the trees, the most large, powerful and stable of growing things. The tree is symbolic of the cosmic axis. It is the link between the underworld, the middleworld and the upperworld. Its roots grow in the ground – the underworld of Hades. It passes through the surface of the middleworld upon which humans live, and then upwards towards the heavenly Empyrean of the gods and goddesses.

Thus, as suggested by its physical form, the letter Mu represents fixity and stability, enclosure and protection, and a link between the three states of being. With the gematria value of 440, this meaning is reinforced, as 440 is also the number of the house ('O OIKOΣ), the prime symbol of protection against the terrors and dangers of the world outside. Cosmically, as the 12th character, it suggests the 12 months of the year, the enclosing cycle of all things that live upon the Earth.

N   **Nu** is the 13th character. As the number 13, it has somewhat sombre connections, in this case with the hag aspect of the Great Goddess, Hecate. Hecate is the Greek goddess of nighttime and the underworld. There is also a connection here with the Egyptian goddess Nut, and the later Norse night goddess Nott. Like its runic counterpart, Nyd, Nu is a character of unpleasant necessity, the darkness that must exist in order for the light to be in being. Nu's number is 50, and its gematria figure 450.

Ξ   **Xei** is the 14th Greek letter. According to the esoteric interpretation of the alphabet, this character represents the stars, the 15th, the sun and the moon, and the 16th, Mithras himself. This 14th letter can thus be interpreted as the stars, more specifically the '15 Stars' those given magical sigils in medieval astrology. These stars and asterisms are important because they have been ascribed traditionally with certain qualities and influences. Above all others, these fixed stars were believed to exert known powers. To medieval magicians, the individual powers of the 15 stars were the basis of much talismanic work. In the creation of talismans, in addition to the prevailing qualities emanating from the astrological planets, the influence of relevant members of the 15 stars have to be taken into account. In standard astrology, too, these stars have their own peculiar qualities. Because of this, they are treated in exactly the same way as the better known planets. The stars are: The Pleiades, Aldebaran, Algol, Capella, Sirius, Procyon, Regulus, Algorab, Spica, Arcturus, Polaris, Alphecca, Antares, Wega and Deneb Algedi. This character's number is 60, the Babylonian astronomical number. Xei's number in gematria is 615.

O **Omicron** is the enclosed power of the sun, fountain of all energy on Earth, its various aspects symbolized by the gods Helios and Apollo. Its circular form reflects the apparent disc of the sun, and the eternal nature of its light within the darkness of space. As a later correlation, Omicron also symbolizes the Christ in his aspect of the bearer of the light. In another aspect, Omicron can represent the moon, the mirror of the sun. It is the fifth heaven of the Gnostics. It represents the number 70, and in gematria, 'Omicron' has the value of 1090.

Π **Pi** also symbolizes the sun in its glory, but this time not just the disc, but the round form surrounded by 16 rays of light, identified with the spiritual illumination associated with solar divinities including Apollo, Serapis and Christ. More specifically, it is associated with Mithras who was worshipped most fervently on the 16th day of each month in the Avestish calendar of Persia. The 16 rays of light from the sun occur much later in Christian art, where it is also associated with the name of God (for example, at King's College Chapel, Cambridge, see Fig. 8). Pi is equivalent to the number 80, and, by gematria, it has the value of 101.

P **Rho,** the 17th letter of the Greek alphabet, represents the creative female qualities that are present in all things, both female and male. More specifically, these are seen as being fruitfulness, the power of vegetative growth and reproduction. Rho expresses the qualities of infinite adaptability and fluidity that lead to the 'coming into being' that is creation in all of its aspects. This meaning prefigures the motion and fluid qualities ascribed to its later runic counterpart, Rad. Arithmetically, Rho is equivalent to the number 100, and the gematria value of 170, which, according to convention is equivalent to the number of 'O AMHN ('Amen') – 'so let it be'.

Σ **Sigma** is the Lord of the Dead, in the Greek pantheon personified as Hermes, the Psychopomp. As the 18th figure, it has connexions with the mysterious '18th rune' of Norse magic and also the esoteric '18 letter' of the Gaelic alphabet. In the Mithraic tradition, it signifies Rashnu, the second brother of

Mithras, who was god of the underworld. Its numerical equivalent is 200, and its gematria value is 254.

T **Tau,** represents the microcosm, more specifically, the lunar aspects of the human being. The Tau cross has often been taken as being the basic pictographic form of the human body. It appears to be derived from the ancient Egyptian Ankh sign that represents eternal life, used magically as an amulet against barrenness. In Christian iconography, Tau represents the cross. This can be the Tau bearing the brazen serpent of Exodus, Aaron's Rod, the Old Testament 'anti-type' that prefigures the 'type' of Christ's cross. Naturally, Tau also represents the cross of Christ, for the 'Tau' form is the true shape of crosses used for crucifixion. Many medieval and Renaissance representations of the Crucificixion show the crosses of Christ and the two thieves in this form. Esoterically, in Christian symbolism, its three arms symbolize the trinity. Tau's arithmetic number is 300, by gematria equivalent to the lunar goddess Selene (ΣΕΛΗΝΗ), whose number is 301. The gematria value of Tau is 701, corresponding by convention with the number of the 'Chrismon', the monogram of Christ, the Chi-Rho, whose value is 700.

Y The 20th character, Ypsilon, stands for water, and flowing qualities. Here, unlike the creative, generative, fluidity of Rho, the qualities are those connected with the element of water. Ypsilon represents those things which, although difficult to define, like running water, are essential to the continuance of life. In Greek mysticism the number 20 was also connected with water. In esoteric geometry, Plato's solid called the 'Icosohedron', representing the element water, has 20 surfaces. Gnostic tradition assigns Ypsilon to the Gnostic 'sixth heaven'. Its numerical equivalent is 400. By gematria, the name 'Ypsilon' adds up to 1260.

Φ **Phi** is the phallus, the male generative principle, Phi has a number of 500. By gematria, 500 signifies the mystic garment, (ΕΝΔΥΜΑ), the manifestation of the spiritual world in the world of form. It also represents the words 'to Pan' (ΤΟ ΠΑΝ), 'the all'. In Greek tradition, this is personified in the great god Pan, he who links all things together in their holistic unity. He bears the number of Phi and the Universe (gematria number 501). The gematria value for the word 'Phi' is 510.

X   **Chi,** the 22nd character, signifies the cosmos, and on the human level, private property. The number of Chi is 600, the number in gematria of the Greek word 'Kosmos' (ΚΟΣΜΟΣ), and also 'the godhead' ('Ο ΘΕΟΤΗΣ), the divine counterpart of the cosmos. Chi is the mark of possession, delimiting that which is already taken. It is also the gift symbol, which, looked at horizontally, links human to human, and seen vertically, links the Gods to humanity. In form, but not phonetics, as it represents 'CH', it is related to the rune *Gyfu* (written 'X', phonetically 'G'), as a gift from or to the Gods. By gematria, the word 'Chi' is equivalent to 610.

Ψ **Psi,** the 23rd, is the heavenly light embodied in the sky-god Zeus. It has the secondary meaning of daylight, most specifically the highlight of midday. Thus it is a character of illumination, of seeing clearly and precisely. It has a numerical value of 700, which is equivalent by gematria to the Christian monogram Chi-Rho, representing the heavenly light of the Christ. The gematria value of the word 'Psi' is 710, equivalent to the words 'piston' (ΠΙΣΤΟΝ), meaning 'faithful', and 'pneuma agion' (ΠΝΕΥΜΑ ΑΓΙΟΝ), 'the Holy Spirit'.

ω   **Omega,** the 24th and final character, stands for riches and abundance, a successful conclusion to business. As an apotheosis, it is the seventh heaven of the Gnostics. Its number is 800, which is the number of 'pistis' (ΠΙΣΤΙΣ), faith and 'kyrios' (ΚΥΡΙΟΣ), lord. By gematria, 'Omega' is 849, the number of 'schema' (ΣΧΗΜΑ), meaning 'the plan'. Thus, Omega is a representation of faith and the divine plan, both in the Pagan and Christian interpretations of 'the Lord', whether Zeus or Jesus.

GREEK ALPHABET TRADITIONS

As a series of universal metaphors to describe the world, it follows that specific letters of the Greek alphabet are related to specific parts of Nature. Thus, according to Hippolytus, it was revealed to Marcus the Gnostic that certain letters of the Greek alphabet related to the parts of the human body.

Hippolytus recorded them in *Book IV* of his writings, chapter 39:

> *The Tetrad, after having explained these things, spoke as follows: 'Now I wish also to exhibit to you Truth herself, for I have brought her down from the mansions above, in order that you may behold her naked, and become aquainted with her beauty; nay, also that you may hear her speak, and may marvel at her wisdom. Observe then first the head above, Alpha and Omega; the neck, Beta and Phi; shoulders, along with hands, Gamma and Chi; breasts, Delta and Phi; diaphragm, Epsilon and Ypsilon; belly, Zeta and Tau; pudenda, Eta and Sigma; thighs, Theta and Rho; knees, Iota and Pi; calves, Kappa and Omicron; ankles Lambda and Xi; feet Mu and Nu' . . . and he styles this element Man, and affirms it to be the source of every word, and the originating principle of every sound.*

The Greek alphabet, then, by accessing the basic structure of the universe which underlies everything, provides a link between the traditions of the Pagan world and that of the Christian. Equally, it links both of them with the world of scientific enquiry. There are also links with central and northern European Paganism through the Runes, some characters of which parallel Greek letters (see Chapter 3). This connection may be seen in the so-called 'Pergamum bowl', illustrated in Fig. 15. This is a 'divination-bowl' or pantacle that bears esoteric Greek inscriptions. It dates from around the year 200 CE. It is in the form of a disc bearing various sigils. The outer part of the bowl is divided into three concentric zones divided by eight radii. This makes 24 separate areas that contain letters, sigils and glyphs. These areas are related directly to the three 'Ogdoads' of the Greek alphabet and the three 'Aettir' of the earliest runic row, known as the Elder Futhark. The inner part of this remarkable disc is divided irregularly into seven sectors, representing the seven astrological planets. Sigurd Agrell, the Swedish expert on magical alphabets, saw this divinatory pantacle as a prime example of the magical ideas current in the late antique period of the Roman Empire that became assimilated into rune-magic. The numerical correspondences of the hieroglyphs and characters

Fig. 15. The Pergamum Bowl.

in this disc, he believed, were an example of a link between the Greek magical tradition and the alphabet-magic of central and northern Europe.

Greek letter-magic may be approached in a number of ways, all of which however demonstrate links between objects, concepts or beings. The links made through numerical values are a valuable means to understanding the subtle connection between things, and may be used as a worthwhile part of education. The modern concept of 'lateral thinking' is closely related to this ancient way of looking at things. To the ancient Pagan Greeks, number was the underlying basis of the universe. This concept was not abandoned when the Christian religion was introduced. In his *Introduction to Arithmetic*, Nichomachus of Gerasa explains this idea well:

Everything in the universe that has been arranged with systematic method by Nature seems both in part and as a whole to have been defined and set in order that conformity with number, and by the thoughtfulness of the mind of him that created all things.

GREEK GEMATRIA

In Greek gematria, similar concepts are set in order in conformity with number, often having the same gematria value. Linked physical and spiritual qualities are also connected. A good example of this is the number 1500, which is the number of light 'phos' (ΦΩΣ), and the eye 'ops', (ΩΨ). Sound, the voice, 'phone' (ΦΩΝΕ) is related by gematria through its number, 1358, to perfect knowledge, 'epignosis' (ΕΠΙΓΝΟΣΙΣ); the Great Knowledge, 'e megale gnosis' ('Η ΜΕΓΑΛΕ ΓΝΩΣΙΣ); and knowledge and truth, 'gnosis kai aletheia' (ΓΝΟΣΙΣ ΚΑΙ ΑΛΗΘΕΙΑ).

Naturally, the linking of concepts through number allows opposites to have the same number. Thus the number 46 represents justice, 'dikaia' (ΔΙΚΑΙΑ), and also 'adikia' (ΑΔΙΚΙΑ), injustice. This is an example where anagrams represent opposites. Of course, anagrams always have the same numerical value. The example of the number 1500 given above also contains its opposite. The eye and light have the same number as 'tuphlos' (ΤΥΘΛΟΣ), which means blind. The tradition of gematria allows a discrepancy of one between any two numbers. This is called *colel*. In this way, the god Hermes ('ΕΡΜΕΣ) has the gematric number 353, linking him, as god of roads, with the word for the road, 'odos' (Η ΟΔΟΣ), whose number is 352. Again opposites may be linked in this way. An example is 'delos' (ΔΕΛΟΣ), which means manifest, having the value of 312, and 'adelos' (ΑΔΕΛΟΣ), unmanifest, equivalent to 313.

The human perception of the world is often manifested through gematria, as with the number 430, which signifies 'arithmos' (ΑΡΙΘΜΟΣ), number. This number is also the gematria for 'nomos' (ΝΟΜΟΣ), the Law. Sometimes, gematria links things in another way. For example, the number 691, which means power, 'kratos' (ΚΡΑΤΟΣ) also stands for the powerful north wind, Arktos ('ΑΡΚΤΟΣ), its anagram. Another power number, the cosmic figure of energy and creation, 740, is especially interesting, for it is equivalent to the cycle or circle of existence, 'kuklos' (ΚΥΚΛΟΣ); creation, 'ktisis' (ΚΤΙΣΙΣ);

heat, 'thermotes' ('Η ΘΕΡΜΟΤΗΣ); the music of the spheres, 'aitheros melos' (ΑΙΘΕΡΟΣ ΜΕΛΟΣ) and the demigod Adonis (ΑΙΔΟΝΕΥΣ). Plato's name for the divine creator, 'O epipasi theos' ('Ο 'ΕΠΙ ΠΑΣΙ ΘΕΟΣ) is also 740 by gematria. The transmutational power over matter represented by Hermes Trismegistos ('ΕΡΜΗΣ ΤΡΙΣΜΕΓΙΣΤΟΣ), deified founder of the alchemical arts is linked with the ruler of the cosmos, 'kosmokrator' (Ο ΚΟΣΜΟΚΡΑΤΩΡ), for they both share the gematria number 1791. These connections operate at many levels, especially in personal names. There, unexpected links may emerge. For example, two demigods of Greek mythology, Orpheus and Achilles have a link through their numbers: Achilles ('ΑΧΙΛΛΕΥΣ) has the number 1276, and Orpheus ('ΟΡΦΕΥΣ) is 1275. Argos (ΑΡΓΟΣ), who built the Argonauts' ship, Argo, is identified through gematria with the love-god Eros (ΕΡΟΣ), as their numbers are 374 and 375 respectively. Eros also has a connection with the Great God Pan, through the 'Pan series' (see below).

Through the mystical medium of gematria, it is possible to trace connections which may not be immediately apparent. By colel, the abode of the gods, Olympus (ΕΛΥΜΠΕΣ), whose number is 890, is linked with the heavens, 'Ouranos' (ΟΥΡΑΝΟΣ), 891. The connections that gematria brings us is especially interesting with regard to the Cretan labyrinth myth. The labyrinth in which Theseus slew the Minotaur, 'labyrinthos' (ΛΑΒΥΡΙΝΘΟΣ, value 872), is shown by gematria to be a species of chaos (ΧΑΟΣ), 871, whose number is also that of foam, 'aphros' (ΑΦΡΟΣ). The name of the homicidal man-bull at the centre of the labyrinth, as spelt on the fourth-century labyrinth mosaic at Kato Paphos in Cyprus, is Meinotauros (ΜΕΙΝΩΤΑΥΡΟΣ). This has the gematria number of 1871, which is equivalent to 'tauros', the bull, 1071, plus the number 800, which is 'kyrios' (ΚΥΡΙΟΣ), 'lord'. Thus the Minotaur is by gematria, 'lord of the bulls'. The name of the Minotaur-slayer, Thesus (ΘΕΣΕΟΣ) is 489 by gematria. This, through colel, is equivalent to Troy (ΤΡΟΙΗ), which is 488. It is interesting to note that, all over northern Europe, where they are cut in turf or made from large stones, classical labyrinths are known as 'Troy', 'Troy-town' or the 'walls of Troy'.

Sacred geometry and architecture, too, are linked in the esoteric tradition of gematria. The following example is typical.

The macrocosm, 'makrokosmos' (ΜΑΚΡΟΚΟΣΜΟΣ), has the number 831. This is also the number of the mystic geometrical form, the pyramid, 'pyramis' (ΠΥΡΑΜΙΣ), and the phallus, 'phallos' (ΦΑΛΛΟΣ). These three demonstrate the esoteric link between three manifestations of the generative principle. Gematria provides numerical connections between divinities and their attributes. Their numbers were used to define the length, width and height of temples, and the dimensions of sacred objects used in the worship of the god or goddess. Symbolic carvings on the temples represented, through their equivalent numbers, the name or attributes of the deity worshipped there. Clearly, these alphabet-magic techniques can be applied to anything, making possible a highly cryptic symbolic art. In a painting or sculpture, seemingly extraneous objects, plants or animals may actually encode the names of principles, qualities or deities. The possibilities are limitless. Through gematria, the parts of a building symbolically represented related qualities. 'Pyle' (ΠΥΛΗ), the gateway, has a value of 518. This is also the number of 'oi kleito' (ΟΙ ΚΛΗΤΟΙ), 'the elect' and also on a more prosaic level, 'thura' ('Η ΘΥΡΑ), the door. Thus the gate of the temple is the door through which the elect may enter the sacred temenos of the gods. This number later became absorbed into Christian usage, being the number of words 'drink and live' (ΠΙΕ ΖΗΣΗΣ) once inscribed upon the chalices used in the Greek Eucharist. Appropriately, this Christian rite was seen as a means by which the elect entered into eternal life. The temple itself, 'naos' (ΝΑΟΣ), with the number 321, is 'kalos' (ΚΑΛΟΣ, 321), beautiful.

On a most basic level, the cosmos, (ΚΟΣΜΟΣ), with the number 600, is equivalent by gematria to 'theotes' ('Ο ΘΕΟΤΗΣ), the godhead, who is immanent in the cosmos. In turn, the cosmos is related to paradise, 'paradeisos' (ΠΑΡΑΔΕΙΣΟΣ), whose number is 671, the cosmos, with the definitive article ('Ο ΚΟΣΜΟΣ) being 670. Nous (ΝΟΥΣ), the divine intelligence, has the number 720, the same as that of 'topos' (ΤΟΠΟΣ), the abode of the deity, and 'iereus' ('ΙΕΡΕΥΣ), a priest of the temple of truth. This is an example of the sort of link that the ancient Greeks sought and found, demonstrating a complex and fundamental connection between language and experience. The names of Zeus (God), the Greek tetragrammaton, 'Dios' and Theos' (ΔΙΟΣ and ΘΕΟΣ) both add up to 284. The great mother goddess Cybele (ΚΥΒΕΛΕ), whose number is 455 has the epithet of 'Mother' (ΜΗΤΗΡ), whose number is 456. The goddess Artemis ('ΑΡΤΕΜΙΣ) has the same number, 656, as the saviour, 'messias' (ΜΕΣΣΙΑΣ). The number 1004 is associated with Dionysos (ΔΙΟΝΥΣΟΣ), whose name is an anagram of 'Nous Dios' (ΝΟΥΣ ΔΙΟΣ), the mind of God. It is also the number of 'the baptism', (ΤΟ ΒΑΠΤΙΣΜΑ) and the divine attribute, 'Sabao' (ΣΑΒΑΩ), a Greek version of a Hebrew word meaning 'armies' and hence temporal power. The name of the 'gentle goddess', Leto (ΛΕΤΩ), whose number is 1138, is equivalent to the womb, 'delphys' (ΔΕΛΦΥΣ). She is shown thereby to be she who represents the feminine essence of creation, worshipped as an embodiment of the matter of the universe. The marine divinity Poseidon (ΠΟΣΕΙΔΟΝ), has the number of 1219, which is that of the fish, 'icthus' (ΙΧΘΥΣ), his sacred symbol. The fish was appropriated later by the Christians as a symbol of Christ. Another name for Christ is the Cosmocrator, ('Ο ΚΟΣΜΟΚΡΑΤΩΡ) 'ruler of the Cosmos', with the gematria number of 1791. Not surprisingly, this is also an epithet of the divine being Hermes Trismegistos, '(ΕΡΜΗΣ ΤΡΙΣΜΕΓΙΣΤ ΟΣ), legendary founder of the science of alchemy. Alchemy gives its practitioners the power to rule the material cosmos through manipulation of the subtle aspects of matter, the power of the Pantocrator.

The great god Pan

The most important series of gematria correspondences focuses on the number of the great god Pan (ΠΑΝ). In Greek Paganism, Pan, the personification of wholeness, who links the divine with the human and animal worlds, has the number 131. This is the starting-point of a major series of gematria interpretations. The generative power of Pan, the phallic god, is emphasized by two correspondences. Pan and the serpent (drakon, ΔΡΑΚΟΝ, 245) produces the same gematrial value of Eros (375). The divine source of this generative power is explained by the addition of the number of creation ('Η ΓΕΝΕΣΙΣ, 481), and that of Pan (131), which makes 612, the number of the supreme god, Zeus. Pan and the number 800, which can mean 'the Lord', 'Faith', 'the Great Power' and also Pasiphaë, a by-name of the goddess Artemis, makes the number of Ammon ('ΑΜΜΩΝ), an epithet of Zeus, 931. Furthermore, when again added to 931, the 131

Pan makes 1062, by the convention of colel, the number of Apollo ('ΑΠΟΛΛΩΝ), 1061. Pan with the moon goddess Selene (ΣΕΛΗΝΗ, 301) makes the gematria value of 432, which is ΚΑΤΑΒΟΛΗ, conception. Pan with Nous, the conscious will, (131 + 720) makes 851, the number of substance (ΥΠΑΡΞΙΣ). Added to the number of Teleion' ('the perfect number', ΤΕΛΕΙΟΝ, 470), the number of Pan makes the number 601, which is ΤΟ ΟΝΟΜΑ, 'the Name', equivalent by colel to Cosmos and Godhead, 600. As befitting his universal status, the number of Pan with the Empyrean (ΠΑΝ + 'ΕΜΠΥΡΕΙΟΝ, 131 + 760) produces the number of the heavens, Ouranos (ΟΥΡΑΝΟΣ, 891). Finally, when the number of Pan and that of the garment of light, Endyma (ΕΝΔΥΜΑ, 500) are added together, the number of death, Thanatos (ΘΑΝΑΤΟΣ, 631) is produced. The panic of those who have seen brilliant apparitions of the great god Pan in his terrible aspect is well known, resulting in the death of the unfortunate persons!

CHRISTIAN GREEK GEMATRIA

These Pagan god-connections were continued, expanded and refined in the later Judaeo-Christian magical tradition of Gnostic gematria. As in early Christian art, where Christ was often depicted as Apollo, Orpheus or Dionysos, there are connections between the name of Christ and the earlier divinities and heroes. For example, by gematria, the number of 'Christos' (ΧΡΙΣΤΩΣ) is 1480. This is equivalent to the 1479 of Odysseus (ΟΔΥΣΣΕΥΣ). There are several gematria numbers associated expressly with Christ. These are 700, the 'Chi-Rho' monogram (see Fig. 16); 888, Jesus, (ΙΗΣΟΥΣ); 1480, Christos (ΧΡΙΣΤΩΣ); 1998, 'physis Jesou' (the nature of Jesus, ΦΥΣΙΣ ΙΗΣΟΥΣ), and 2368, Jesus Christ ('ΙΗΣΟΥΣ ΧΡΙΣΤΟΣ). These names are often composed of numbers that, when combined, express divine or cosmic qualities. Jesus, 888, for example, is composed of Ether and Empyrean ('ΑΙΘΗΡ and 'ΕΜΠΥΡΕΙΟΝ, 760 + 128 = 888).

The Greek tradition of bind-letters or monograms became highly developed to express the name of Christ. The best known of these sigils is the Chrismon or 'Chi-Rho' monogram. This is a binding together of the characters Chi (Ch, written X) and Rho (R, written P) to make a sigil composed of the first two letters of 'Christ'. It has the gematria value of 700. This

Fig. 16. Christian monograms in the Greek tradition: (*top row*) (i) standard Chi-Rho; (ii) Alpha, Omega and cross; (iii) IHS; (iv) variants of Alpha and Omega; (*second row*) (i) variant Chrismon, Jesus Soter (saviour) and Jesus Christ combined; (ii) Mother of God; (iii) variant Chi-Rho; (*third row*) (i) Alpha-Tau-Omega; (ii) Chrismon and Ichthys; (iii) Chrismon from Greek Orthodox communion wafer, Jesus Christ – Conquer; (iv) short version of the preceding sigil.

sigil is clearly a version of older, solar, symbols, such as the circle with a cross beneath it, which represents the rising sun. It is also closely related to the ancient Egyptian sign known as the 'Ankh' or 'Crux Ansata', symbol of eternal life. The monogram of Jesus Christ used the first three Greek letters of the name Jesus, IHΣ. Later, the Greek letter Eta (H), with a phonetic value of 'E', was mistaken as representing the Roman letter 'H', and so the meaning ascribed to the monogram became *In hoc signo* (In this sign). This recalled the celebrated dream of the Emperor Constantine. According to legend, in this dream the Chrismon sigil appeared to him, accompanied by a voice that said, 'In this sign thou shalt conquer'. Interpreting the dream as a divine prediction, Constantine therefore used the sign on his personal war banner, the Labarum. Victorious, he imposed Christianity on the Roman Empire. In its Roman misinterpretation, the monogram IHS has also come to represent *Jesus Hominem Salvator* (Jesus, mankind's redeemer). A German interpretation of this monogram is *Jesus Heil und Seligmacher* (Jesus, saviour and redeemer). The original Greek monogram IHΣ has a value of 218. By colel, this is part of the 'Pan series', where a number of the great god Pan is added to other significant gematria equivalents. Here, the name of Victory, 'Nike' 88, added to

65

131 makes 219, representative of ΙΗΣ. Symbolically, this can be interpreted as 'victory over all'.

Another Greek letter correspondence with Christ is through the first and last letters, Alpha and Omega. This comes from the book of *Revelation* 22.13: 'I am Alpha and Omega, the beginning and the end, the first and the last.' There, Christ is associated with the Greek letters Alpha, Α, and Omega Ω, the first and the last letters of the alphabet. Esoterically, this signifies eternal continuance, the first and the last encompassing all that is between them. They also represent the generative and regenerative power ascribed to the Christ. This is shown by the formula 'Alpha and Omega' (Α ΚΑΙ Ω), which has the gematria value of 832. By colel, this phrase is equal to 'Phallus' (ΦΑΛΛΟΣ, 831).

Even by themselves, the two letters Alpha and Omega demonstrate the wonderful versatility of Greek gematria. The numerical equivalent of ΑΩ is 801, made up of Alpha's 1 and Omega's 800. These letters are written sometimes in connection with the cross, for example, in the rite of consecretion of a church. When written with the letter Tau, as a representation of the cross, the number of ΑΤΩ monogram is 1101, by colel equivalent to the number of the name Simon, 1100. The use of this monogram was an esoteric sign used by those who believed that Simon of Cyrene died on the cross as a substitute for Jesus. Another important Christian symbol is the dove, 'peristera' (ΠΕΡΙΣΤΕΡΑ), sometimes used explicitly as a symbol for Christ as bringer of peace, whose gematria number is 801. Thus, through gematria, the dove symbolizes Alpha and Omega, which itself is a cipher for Christ. The connection between 800 and Christ is because it is the number of power and dominion, signifying omnipotence, 'autodynamis', (Η ΑΥΤΟΔΥΝΑΜΙΣ). It is also the number of 'lord', 'kyrios' (ΚΥΡΙΟΣ); and faith, 'pistis' (ΠΙΣΤΙΣ). Thus, Alpha and Omega together symbolize omnipotent power, lordship, faith and peace. Another common symbol of Christ is the fish, which is derived not by gematria, but by notarikon. Here, the Greek word for 'fish' is 'ichthus'. From this, by notarikon comes the sentence '*I*esous *CH*ristos *TH*eou *V*ios *S*oter (Jesus Christ, Son of God, the Saviour). The use of the fish as a symbol for Christ connects him with Poseidon, yet another link between Christ and the older gods.

The Greek Alphabet

Esoteric Greek tradition relates the 12 apostles of Christ to the 12 signs of the zodiac. By gematria, each of the names of the signs of the zodiac has a number, and similarly with the apostles. The correspondences of the zodiacal signs take the order of the apostles as listed in the gospel according to St Mark 3.16–19). Taking Simon Peter as the beginning of the zodiac, the sign of Aries, the correspondences are as follows:

Zodiac Sign	Greek name	Gematria value
Aries	ΚΡΙΟΣ	400
Taurus	ΤΑΥΡΟΣ	1071
Gemini	ΔΙΔΥΜΟΙ	538
Cancer	ΚΑΡΚΙΝΟΣ	471
Leo	ΛΕΩΝ	885
Virgo	ΠΑΡΘΕΝΟΣ	515
Libra	ΧΗΛΑΙ	649
Scorpio	ΣΚΟΡΠΙΟΣ	750
Sagittarius	ΤΟΞΕΝΤΗΣ	1343
Capricorn	ΑΙΓΟΚΕΡΩΣ	1209
Aquarius	ΥΔΡΟΧΟΣ	1514
Pisces	ΙΧΘΥΕΣ	1224
Total		10569

Apostle of Christ	Greek name	Gematria value
Simon Peter	ΠΕΤΡΟΣ	755
James Boanerges	ΙΑΚΩΒΟΣ	1103
John Boarnerges	ΙΩΑΝΗΣ	1069
Andrew	ΑΝΔΡΕΑΣ	361
Philip	ΦΙΛΙΠΠΟΙ	980
Bartholomew	ΒΑΡΘΟΛΟΜΑΙΟΣ	603
Matthew	ΜΑΘΘΑΙΟΣ	340
Thomas	ΘΩΜΑΣ	1050
James Alphaeusson	ΙΑΚΩΒΟΣ	1103
Thaddaeus	ΘΑΔΔΑΙΟΣ	299
Simon Canaanite	ΣΙΜΩΝ	1100
Judas Iscariot	ΙΟΥΔΑΣ ΙΣΚΑΡΙΩΘ	1835
Total		10598

The sum total of the 12 signs is 10,569,whilst that of the 12 apostles is 10,598, a very close parallel. The difference is 29. Symbolically, the zodiac has been synthesized with the apostles of Christ, and merged perfectly with their names through gematria. As with the 12 tribes of Israel, the apostles of Christ each represent some aspect of the yearly and thus also the universal cycle. The necessity of the renegade apostle, Judas Iscariot, is thus made apparent. Christ stands at the centre of this yearly circle, paralleling the position of solar deities in the Pagan interpretation of the cosmic order. A major motif in Princess Antonia's seventeenth-century qabalistic painting at Bad Teinach shows Christ at the centre of the zodiac circle of the 12 tribes of Israel, demonstrating the longevity of this image. As master of the 12 disciples and 12 months of the year, Christ can be seen as paralleling Mithras, whose number 360 is that of the degrees in the circle. Many Mithraic scriptures survive in which the deity is shown within a circle depicting the signs of the zodiac. This parallels closely the concept of the deity Abraxas, whose 365 shows him as ruler of the days of the year, with a gematria equivalent to 'Meson', the second of the five tetrachords of Greek musical harmony. Each of the components of Greek harmonics have their own names which are related by gematria to the names of related qualities and divinities. By this means, the Hermetic maxim 'As above, so below' operated throughout Greek science, art and religion alike.

The connection between the Eucharist words and the gateway has been mentioned already. Inscriptions in Greek on Christian tombs in the Roman catacombs of the word 'Zeses' (ΖΗΣΕΣ – 'may you live') is actually an encryption of the number of the Egyptian mother goddess, Isis, re-memberer of the slain god Osiris. Both words have the number 420. Here, as elsewhere, both the Pagan and the Christian interpretations are as one. This denotes the universal nature of reality underlying all belief, for there can be no religion higher than the truth. In Gnostic Greek gematria, a most important number is 481, for it represents the beginning, 'Genesis' (Η ΓΕΝΕΣΙΣ). It is the number of the Greek tetragrammaton used by Clement of Alexandria, ΙΑΔΥ, representing the name of God. The gematria number from the three letters of the Trinity, Π, Υ, Α, which signify 'pater' (ΠΑΤΗΡ), the Holy Spirit is 481. Further-

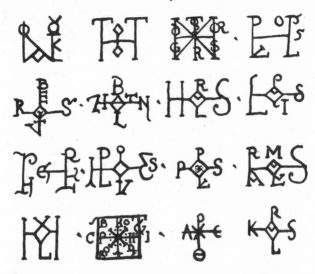

Fig. 17. Secular monograms in the Greek tradition. The Byzantine and Holy Roman Emperors, followed by other early medieval kings, dukes and church prelates, liked to use personal sigils derived from Greek letters: (*top line*) (i) Justinian; (ii) Otto I; (iii) Lothar III; (iv) Louis VI of France; (*second line*) (i) Robert of France; (ii) Zwentibold von Lothringen; (iii) Lothar I; (iv) Louis II; (*third line*) (i) Henri I; (ii) Louis the Pious; (iii) Philip I; (iv) Karlmann; (*fourth line*) (i) Hugo of Provence; (ii) Charles IV; (iii) Bishop Arethras of Caesarea; (iv) Charlmagne.

more, it is also the number of 'episkope' ('Η ΕΠΙΣΚΟΠΗ), the Lord's visitation, and the quality of overseeing, 'episkopeia' (ΕΠΙΣΚΟΠΕΙΑ), emphasizing both the attributes of the Father and the Holy Spirit. There are a number of other important links in this area of gematria. The number 1080, the Holy Spirit (ΤΟ ΑΓΙΟΝ ΠΝΕΥΜΑ), is a lunar number, associated with the Void (or abyss), 'Η ΑΒΥΣΣΟΣ (1081). The cross, 'stauros' (ΣΤΑΥΡΟΣ), has the number of 1271. This is also the number of 'the knowledge of God', the Gnosis, ('Η ΓΝΟΣΙΣ). This is also the number of 'the knowledge of God', the Gnosis, ('Η ΓΝΟΣΙΣ).

The number of the beast

The number 666 must figure large in any discussion of gematria, for it is only through this esoteric art that people have striven to unravel this great mystery. This number, like the others derived from the Hebrew Aiq Beker grid, is a multiple of the number 37, and is thus related to the number of Jesus, 888. In the Bible, 666 is described as 'the number of the beast' in the Revelation of St John the Divine: 'Here is wisdom. Let him that hath understanding count the number of the beast: for it is the number of a man; and his number *is* Six hundred threescore *and* six.' (*Revelation* 13.18). This has led to the number being given an evil connotation. This superstitious fear has been played upon by certain magicians, such as Aleister Crowley, who actually called himself the Great Beast and used the number 666 as a kind of personal sigil. It is gleefully celebrated by certain practitioners of modern Heavy Metal rock music, but usually only for theatrical effect or sensationalist purposes. Those who fear this number, or use its supposed negative qualities do so because it is seen as the number of the Antichrist. According to Christian eschatology, the Antichrist is the negative reflection of the divine, positive, qualities of the Christ. But is is a mistake to connect a number, which, at the deepest level, is neutral, solely with the qualities of evil. Numbers cannot have a dualistic interpretation. Like any other number, it possesses certain physical and spiritual qualities whose effect depends on its use. Also, despite its bad press, this number may not be what it at first appears to be. In the original Greek, the phrase from Revelation 'and his number *is* Six hundred threescore *and* six' has the gematria value of 2368, the number of Jesus Christ. The number 666 within this phrase is a necessary part of the entire computation, indicating that the 'number of a man', the gematria of the entire sentence, is that of Jesus Christ.

By Greek gematria, 666 is the number of Teitan, a Greek opponent to the gods of Olympus, generally held to signify the power of opposition and destruction of the established order. However, according to Victorinus, Bishop of Petau at the end of the third century: 'As they have reckoned from the Greek characters, as they find it among many to be TEITAN, for Teitan has this number, which the Gentiles called Sol and Phoebus'. The masonic writer William Stirling saw this as associating it with the 'ark of the sun', which contained the figure of the Microcosm. In his books *The View Over Atlantis* (1969) and *City of Revelation* (1972), John Michell corroborated this view that 666 itself is predominantly a solar number. It also corresponds with the Ptolomaic-period Egyptian deity Serapis, who combined some of the characteristics of Osiris and Zeus. In his books 'against heresy', the second century CE writer Irenaeus speculated on the meaning of 666; he suggested three names.

> *The first was Teitan. A second contender was the unexplained Evanthas. The name Evanthas contains the required number, but I make no allegation regarding it. Then also Lateinos has the number six hundred and sixty-six, and it is a very probable solution, this being the name of the last kingdom (of the four seen by Daniel).*

In Iraneus's eyes, Lateinos, meaning the Latin One, meant the Roman Empire, the most powerful manifestation of earthly power and oppression. Later, anti-Catholic commentators have seen this as indicating the Pope, the Latin One, to be the beast of the Apocalypse: 666 is the number of ΤΟ ΜΕΓΑΘΕΡΙΟΝ (the Great Beast). This anti-church interpretation is reinforced by the fact that in Greek, 'E Latein Basileia' (the Latin Church), and 'Ekklesia Italika', (the Italian Church) also have the gematria value of 666. But there are many other interpretations of the number 666. By colel, it is equivalent to ΦΛΟΓΓΟΙ, the number describing the 18 notes of the Greek musical scale, symbolically an image of wholeness. This is one of the numbers connected with the great god Pan (131): added to 'Eureka!' (ΕΥΡΗΚΑ, 534), the number 665 is formed. Thus this key number can be interpreted as the realization of the quality of wholeness implicit in the Pan whose totality links the worlds of gods, humans and beasts.

But since early times, it has been popular to identify 'the beast' with the current arch-tyrant or popular enemy. Thus, in Hebrew, the words Neron Caesar, the Emperor Nero, scourge of early Christians, add up to 666. In medieval times, Christian apologists saw Mahomet as adding up to 666, and during the Reformation, Catholic commentators made Martin Luther fit the numerology of 'the beast'. More recently, others have been connected with the number – Napoleon Bonaparte is one of them. John Michell has even shown how if A = 100, B = 101, C = 102 and so on, then the number of Hitler is 666. Written

Fig. 18. The Pagan sage Apollonius of Tyana (*c*.1–90 CE), with the Greek-order alphabet ascribed to him, 'Apollonian'.

in Greek with the definitive article, the name of another notorious twentieth-century dictator, Stalin, has the number 666. The 'number of the beast' is certainly flexible in its application, and it is certain that in the future, tyrants not yet born will be assigned this number by esoterically minded commentators.

The esoteric tradition of the Greek alphabet has continued in use in the modern era. In mathematics, various Greek letters are used to denote standard constants or irrational numbers, such as Π (Pi, the value of 3.1416) times the diameter of a circle for the relationship between the circumference and the diameter. In magic, too, Aleister Crowley's mysterious Thelemic '93 Current' used the number that denoted the Greek gematria for ΘΕΛΗΜΑ (Thelema), which is 93. This is the same as, ΑΓΑΠΕ (agape), love. Crowley was using the classical technique whereby a single number can stand for two or more related concepts. As with all of the other magical alphabet traditions described in this book, the Greek tradition is alive and well, and still capable of valid development.

THE ETRUSCAN SCRIPT

The Etruscan or North Italic script is another of the alphabets derived from the Phoenician. In this it parallels the early forms of Greek and Roman alphabets, and, indeed, several of the characters resemble them closely. But, unlike the Greek and Roman scripts, which continue in use today, the Etruscan alphabet went out of use. At the height of Etruscan civilization, Etruscan traders travelled northwards to the shores of the Baltic Sea in search of amber. So it was that these traders carried the letters far and wide into central and northern Europe. But during the struggles for the mastery of Italy, the Romans progressively defeated the Etruscans, and finally subdued them. Much of Etruscan magic and geomancy was absorbed into Roman usage, but the Etruscan alphabet was not. However, its use in trade is likely to have influenced the evolution of the runes, and some of the earliest forms of runes are almost indistinguishable from this North Italic script. Although it is known that magic was an everyday part of life in the Etruscan civilization, the meanings of the letters of the alphabet are not known. This is unfortunate as these would give us the key to the relationship between the Runic and the Etruscan alphabets.

Fig. 19. The North Italic or Etruscan alphabet. Compare this with the rune-rows illustrated later (Figs. 20, 23, 24, 26).

3
The Runes

You will discover runes and imaginative staves –
Very great staves, very strong staves –
Which a powerful thule painted, and great gods created,
Carved by the prophet of the gods.
                    HAVAMAL (THE WORDS OF THE GOD ODIN)

Runic is the major magical alphabet of central and northern Europe. Like Greek letters, the runes are far more than just characters designed for the transmission of information. As with Greek letters, they encapsulate symbolic meanings that go far beyond modern materialistic considerations of information theory. The importance of the runes today lies in the revival of interest in the runes which has taken place during the twentieth century. The combined application of scholarship and esoteric techniques has made the runes into a major field of esoteric study and practice. Some academic runic scholars have deplored this modern development. Their viewpoint is that there is insufficient evidence for the magical or symbolic use of the runes in former times for them to be reinstated today. But as they represent a certain modern, materialistic world-view which denies the validity of other, alternative views of reality, it is difficult for them to come to terms with concepts outside their experience. Even if they were correct, this does not invalidate modern esoteric research and practice.

The connotations of the word rune itself shows that even in ancient times, the runes were part of a mystery in its spiritual meaning, connected intimately with the inner secrets of magic. This meaning is apparent in northern European languages, where it connects directly with words meaning 'to whisper': the Old Celtic word 'run'; the Middle Welsh 'rhin'; the Old English verb to 'rown', and the modern German 'raunen'. In modern

Fig. 20. The 24 characters of the Elder Futhark.

Irish, the word 'rún' means 'secret', or 'a resolution', 'rúndiamahair' is a mystery, whilst a 'rúnai' is a secretary and a 'rúncléireac' is a confidential clerk. As the modern Irish words show, traditionally the runes were used for divination and decision-making. The counsellors of Anglo-Saxon England called their discussions 'runes'. In such meetings, the runes would have been consulted when problems arose. The traditional Scottish system of farming, known as Run-Rig, used lots (runes) to determine which peasant should farm which 'rig' or lot of land.

The origin of the runic alphabet, or more correctly, Futhark, has long been the cause of keen contention amongst students of ancient European culture. Theories have come and gone with the fashions of the times, and scholars have derived the runes from the Phoenician, Samian, classical Greek, Latin, Etruscan and Gothic scripts. In some cases, chauvinistic nationalists and even racists have used runic theories to bolster their claims to the supposed superiority of their causes. In these cases, the runes have been presented as having sprung indigenously, without precedent, from whichever ethnic or national group to which the claimant belonged. Even today, despite a considerable amount of research and speculation, there are still a number of viable contenders. It has been established to many peoples' satisfaction that as an alphabet the characters of the runes were derived from the North Italic script, used by the Etruscans. Historically, it was used by Etruscan merchants who carried it from Italy across central Europe to the Baltic when trading for amber. Also, there is archeological evidence for a link between the North Italic script and the runes. An excavation at Negau in Austria-Hungary in 1812 revealed 26 brimmed helmets of bronze, dating from the fourth century BCE. Engraved on the helmets were inscriptions in Germanic words, including the name of a war deity. But what is significant about these helmets is that the words were written in North Italic script. However, despite this evidence, some students consider the runic alphabet to be a direct modification of the Roman one. Statistically, it can be seen that ten letters of the Etruscan alphabet are identical in form and sound value to the letters of the Elder Futhark, whilst eight Roman letters fulfil this criterion. But the argument is clouded by five further letters of the Roman alphabet which are similar but not identical with runes. But, equally, several letters in the Greek, Etruscan, Old Latin, Roman and Runic alphabets are almost identical with one another, showing their common derivation from the Phoenician Ahiram alphabet of *circa* 1000 BCE. As this book shows, there are variant forms of letters in any alphabet we may choose to examine. It is a matter of opinion to define the point at which there are so many variants in an alphabet that then it must be classified as a 'new', different, one. Doubtless the arguments will rage as long as people are interested in runes!

Throughout the history of alphabets, magical and otherwise, individual scholars, mystics and rulers have played an important part in formalizing new alphabets. Some researchers consider this to be the case with the runes. It can be surmised that they were formed when some of the sigils previously used in rock carvings and divination magic became identified with certain transalpine alphabetic characters. This act of synthesis is recorded in the myth of Odin's self-sacrifice. According to this, the revelation of the runes for human use came about as the result of a self-torturing ritual. In the Norse *Hávamál*, stanzas 138 and 139, we read:

I know that I was hanging on the wind-blasted tree,
Through nine days and nine nights,
I was wounded with a spear, and given to Odin,
Myself dedicated to myself,
On that tree, which nobody knows,
From which roots it grows.

Neither with bread,
Nor with the drinking horn
did they assist me.
I accepted the runes.
Screaming, I took them,
Then I fell back from that place.

This myth recalls the practices of shamans in the northern parts of the world. From Scandinavia and Central Asia to North America, this archaic magico-religious tradition was practised as an essential part of human culture. In the myth of the discovery of the runes, Odin, the counterpart of the Greek Hermes, likewise is the god of magic, poetry, divination and inspiration, who undertakes shamanic practices. In former times, shamans practised ecstatic methods of gaining altered states of consciousness, travelling, they believed, to the worlds beyond this material one. Their techniques included journeys to wild places, fasting, the taking of natural hallucinogenic plant substances and physical self-torture. The myth of Odin's shamanic grasp of the runes appears to have involved self-crucifixion on a tree for the traditional magical period of nine days and nights. After this ordeal a tormented flash of insight enabled Odin to realize the full potential of the runes for human use. This appears to have been the amalgamation of the intuitive, oracular, use of the pre-runic sigils with the rational, phonetic alphabet. This was a rare moment of agony and ecstacy where the two sides of the brain – intuitive and rational – were influenced in their response to a single sign.

The concurrence of certain characters in ancient European rock carvings and Mediterranean alphabets makes it plain that many of the runes were derived initially from two basically separate sources. The creator of the runes, an earthly Odin, amalgamated the two systems. This was accomplished using a deep understanding that gave access to the common, under-lying levels of the two hitherto separate systems. Just as the written characters may have more than one source so, similarly, the individual meaning of each rune may also be derived from and amalgamate the two sources. Greek, from whose early form came the North Italic script, has a complex series of meanings as detailed in Chapter 2. Because of this, it is very probable that the Etruscan and Celtiberian alphabets also possessed similar esoteric correspondences with each letter. Regardless of from which source some of the runic characters were derived, collectively the runic letters, as we know them, were not just taken *en masse* from any other script. Unlike the other alphabets derived ultimately from Phoenician scripts, the runic letters were arranged in a different order F, U, Th, A, R, K. Because of this order, the runic alphabets are often called Futharks. But the new arrangement, seen by many as the prime evidence for a single creator of the script, is not irrational as many have felt. When the meanings of the runes are taken into account, this order is rational, and related to the cycle of the year. It is the incorporation of Mediterranean, Alpine and northern European sigils into a new system that is the most important aspect of the runes' genesis. As long ago as 7000 years, pottery of the Vinca culture in the Balkans bore signs, some of which are identical with the form of runes from over five millennia later. Also, many sigils which are known now as runes already existed as forms used by rock carvers. In various parts of Europe, most notably during the late Bronze and early Iron Ages (1300–800 BCE), pictographic rock carvings were made at various locations. The general type is often known as Hällristningar from those in Scandinavia, although similar examples are known from Britain, Ireland, Spain and those Alpine regions now administered by Germany, Switzerland, Italy and Austria. These Hällristningar contained a variety of sigils which can be recognized in the earliest runic alphabets.

This collection of pre-runic signs, sigils and symbols is sometimes called by the alternative name of the Rune-Hoard. Even in their most developed form, many of the runes have a pictographic nature. The first rune, Feoh, which has the meaning of cattle, is said to resemble the horns of the cow, whilst the second, Ur, is shaped like the strong bodily form of the wild ox. The third rune, Thorn, is shaped like a thorn. Similarly, the sixth rune, Kennaz or Cen, is in the shape of an early form of lighting, the *kienspanhalter*. The eighth rune, Wyn, is shaped like the weather vane of its name. The rune Nyd, which means 'need' resembles a fire-bow used to kindle the sacred need-fires of old, whilst the attribute of ice, Is, the letter 'I', is shaped like an icicle. Elhaz or Eolh refers to the Elk, whose antlers are echoed in its form. Ehwaz resembles the

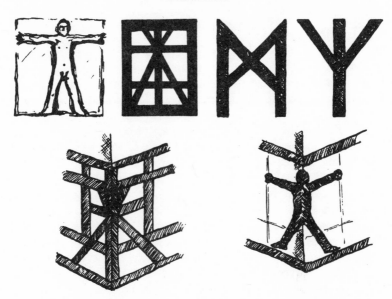

Fig. 21. The rune Man, as it appears in traditional German *fachwerk* timber-frame buildings. Runes show Elder Futhark and later version of the Man character, and its structural relationship to the human being and the building form.

body of the horse which is its name. Lagu is shaped like the leek or overflowing water that it symbolizes, whilst Odal is in the shape of an enclosure. Yr is in the shape of the bow which is its correspondence. Stan is in the form of a stone or playing piece used in a board game, whilst Wolfsangel is in the form of the 'wolf-hook' used in former times. The rune Ziu represents the thunderbolt of the eponymous sky-god. Erda, like Odal, encloses the Earth, Sol is the solar disc with a ray of light.

We know from three extant ancient texts that each of the runes had a specific meaning from the earliest times. These Rune Poems – Anglo-Saxon, Norwegian and Icelandic – tell us that certain specific objects or concepts were used to describe each individual stave or character. Because of this, each rune is a precise concept in its own right, each rune encapsulates a certain aspect of existence which expresses part of the fundamental nature of the inner structure of reality. In this way, like Hebrew and Greek, each rune stave is a symbolic storehouse of knowledge and meaning which becomes apparent when it is studied in depth. According to this concept, every individual rune is an expression of a quality that is revealed to the world of our experience as the specific things or processes that are characterized by the rune. But, unlike many ancient magical disciplines, whose concepts were formulated rigidly in the distant past, rune lore is still developing. This characteristic makes rune lore a very dynamic and creative area. Essentially, the meaning of each of the runes is fixed, as described in the rune poems. But because, with each new day, new things are made, new experiences are gained, new developments take place and new relationships are formed, these seemingly fixed runic meanings will take on a fresh significance in relation to the new circumstances. No time or place can ever be identical to any other, and correspondingly the action of the runic archetypes must be with reference to the specific conditions operating then and there.

Due to the specific relationship of each rune to some thing or quality, by using combinations of runes, every aspect of existence can be described or investigated. In their symbolic use the runes are seen as analogues of reality in which each character describes a set of events. It is because of the eternally fluid nature of existence that it is impossible for anyone to make a definitive statement about the meanings of the runes. In the light of this flexibility, the complex of concepts and correspondences that make up the essence of the runes have been developed by modern rune masters into a detailed and precise system. This is a process which is continuing today. Unfortunately, this aspect is shunned by most academics, who believe, wrongly, that runic development ceased in the medieval period, and consequently is a closed book. Dr Stephen Flowers, who has written several excellent books on traditional and modern rune lore, is a notable exception to this deplorable tendency. A few other writers, in both the German and English languages, have made valuable contributions and opened up new vistas in rune research both on the physical and spiritual levels. Rune lore is a living system, reclaimed, restored, reinstated and refined into a vital body of knowledge which sets it on a par with any other magical system in use today.

Historically, there have been a considerable number of runic alphabets, some of them closely linked to one another, but others considerably different. There are also some runic

Fig. 22. Runestone from Denmark. The lines symbolize the world axis-tree Yggdrassil. The runes are read from the bottom to the top, then down the right-hand panel, and finally up again on the left.

characters that were never included in formalized rune rows. In addition, in the twentieth century, with the resurgence of runes, have come several new variants based on one or other of the earlier alphabets. The oldest complete version of the rune alphabet known is called the Elder Futhark or Common Germanic Futhark. The earliest complete rune row of this futhark is carved on a Gothic stone from Kylver, on the island of Gotland, Sweden. It dates from the early fifth century. This rune row has 24 characters. Traditionally, these are collected into three groups of eight, which is paralleled by the Greek practice of dividing the alphabet into the three Ogdoads which reflect the three parts of the universe. Each group of eight runes is known as an *aett*, a Norse word which has a number of meanings to do with place, direction and lineage. In its most fundamental meaning it describes the eight directions and is cognate with the Scots word *airt*, and the Irish word *aird* (meaning a direction, more specifically, one-eighth of the horizon). *Aird* has the additional meaning of 'attention'. According to modern rune researchers, each of these three runic aettir is ruled over by a god and a goddess from the pantheon of the Northern Tradition. The first aett, which begins with the rune Feoh, the letter 'F', is dedicated to or ruled by the deities of fecundity and increase, Frey and Freyja. The second aett, which begins with the rune Hagal, the letter 'H', is connected with the watcher-god Heimdall and the underworld guardian goddess Mordgud. The third aett, which begins with the rune Tyr, the letter 'T', is sacred to the old north European sky god, Tîwaz, (Tyr or Ziu) and his consort, the goddess Zisa.

The order of the Elder Futhark, although different from that of the Graeco-Roman alphabets, is fixed. The precise order in which the runes are arranged can be seen as significant when one examines the runic meanings in detail. Then, the whole rune row can be seen to be a coherent sequence. To alter the order would be to disrupt and render the pattern meaningless, for there is a precise sequence directly related to the cycles of time. The only exception to this fixed order of runes is with the final two characters, the 23rd and 24th, Odal and Dag. Sometimes, Dag comes before Odal.

Historically, the runes did not remain fixed in number. Although their order remained almost unaltered, the Frisian

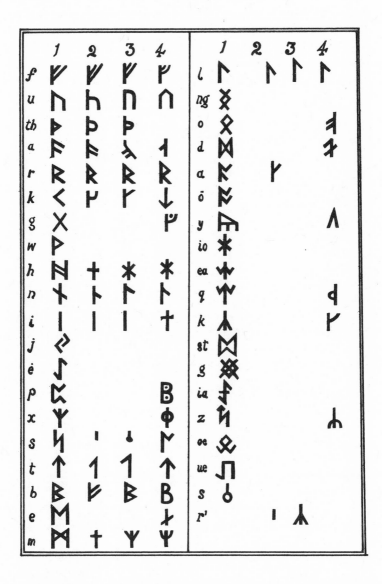

Fig. 23. Runic parallels: 1. The Elder Futhark and additions; 2. Runes from the stone at Rök, Sweden; 3. Danish 'mixed' runes; 4. 'Dotted' runes, c. 1300–1600.

people, in what is now north-east Holland and north-west Germany, found it necessary to create four additional runes. This 28-character runic alphabet was formulated *c.* 550–650 CE. Several Frisian runic staves are known including one, dating from *c.* 800 CE, inscribed with a runic formula to give its owner power over the waves of the sea. The Frisian Futhark was enlarged in England by the addition of a further rune. Finally, it was expanded into the runic alphabet developed in ninth-century Northumbria, which was the longest, having 33 characters. In the Anglo-Saxon rune rows, the final aett contains runes which show some Celtic influence. As well as these characters, there are later, additional, runes, which although used, do not fit into these systems.

In England, with the strong influence of the Church, the Roman alphabet became the norm, and the runes were no longer used officially. But, of course, they survived in the rural tradition. Throughout the history of the runes, there has been continuous development; runic has not been a static alphabet, fixed at a certain time in history. Alphabets have developed according to the needs of the time and place in which they have been used. Historically, the runes underwent their most radical development in Scandinavia, parts of which remained Pagan until the twelfth century. There, they were in everyday use for

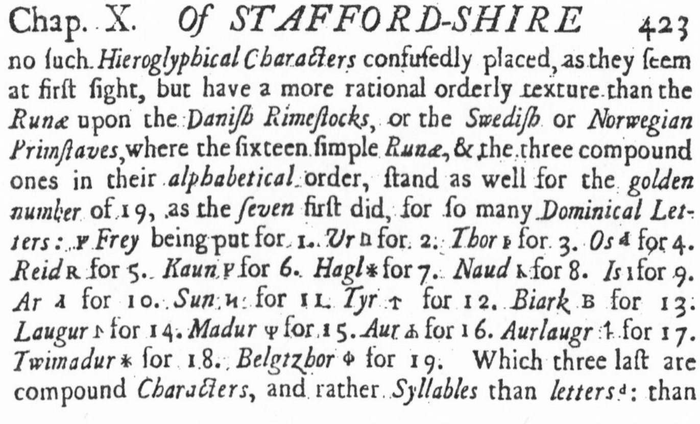

Chap. X. *Of STAFFORD-SHIRE* 423

no fuch. *Hieroglyphical Characters* confufedly placed, as they feem at firft fight, but have a more rational orderly texture than the *Runæ* upon the *Danifh Rimeflocks*, or the *Swedifh* or *Norwegian Prinftaves*, where the fixteen fimple *Runæ*, & the three compound ones in their *alphabetical* order, ftand as well for the *golden number* of 19, as the *feven* firft did, for fo many *Dominical Letters* : ᚠ *Frey* being put for 1. *Ur* ᚢ for 2. *Thor* ᚦ for 3. *Os* ᚬ for 4. *Reid* ᚱ for 5. *Kaun* ᚴ for 6. *Hagl* ᚼ for 7. *Naud* ᚾ for 8. *Is* ᛁ for 9. *Ar* ᛆ for 10. *Sun* ᛋ for 11. *Tyr* ᛏ for 12. *Biark* ᛒ for 13. *Laugur* ᛚ for 14. *Madur* ᛘ for 15. *Aur* ᛦ for 16. *Aurlaugr* ᛐ for 17. *Twimadur* ᛣ for 18. *Belgtzhor* ᚤ for 19. Which three laft are compound *Characters*, and rather *Syllables* than *letters* : than

Fig. 24. Extract from Dr Robert Plot's book. *The Natural History of Stafford-shire*, 1690, explaining the use of Scandinavian runes as calendar-numbers.

all kinds of purposes, ranging from farmers' and tradespeople's marks, the *Bumerker* and *Merkelapper*, to church inscriptions and magical formulae on talismans and amulets. The runes also became an integral part of calendar-making. Scandinavian alphabets first shed eight of the original 24, but later, old ones were reinstated and new ones were added. These runes, which remained in everyday practical use until the late eighteenth century, have a different order from the Elder Futhark and its extensions. In the calendar, the necessity for marking the 19-year solar-lunar cycle produced a special calendar rune row. Three new runes, two with the phonetic value of 'x' and one with 'y', were added to the customary Scandinavian 16.

There are thousands of surviving examples of ancient runic usage. Over a period from around 250 CE until the eighteenth century, many everyday objects exist bearing runic inscriptions. Some state the function of the object; others bear the name of the maker or owner, whilst others have magical inscriptions. Rune magic was very important in the northern martial arts of the first millennium, and there are many surviving artifacts. Single runes were found cut on the shafts of arrows found in a bog at Nydam in Denmark, dating from around the year 400 CE. It was customary to give names to armour and weapons of all kinds. These names had magical meanings, and were engraved in runes. A number still exist. The earliest extant runic weapon inscriptions are on spears. A spear bearing the name Raunijar, 'the Tester', from Øvre-Stabu, Denmark, dates from around the year 150 CE. Another spear found at Dahmsdorf, Brandenburg, Germany, dating from a century later, bore the related name Rannja, 'the Assailer', and another of Alemannic origin, discovered at Wurmlingen, south Germany, dating from around the year 600 CE, had the runic name Dorih, meaning 'powerful in courage'. Other known runic spear names include Gaois, believed to mean 'the barker' or 'the roarer'. In Viking and Norman times, the battleaxe was the most formidable of weapons, and so these, too, received names to be inlaid in runes. Among those recorded are 'Fiend of the Shield', 'the Wound's Wolf', 'Battle-Witch'. 'Fiend' and 'Witch' were the most popular names for battleaxes.

More than any other weapon, the sword has always had a mystique, and in the earliest writings sword names are in evidence. The ancient Anglo-Saxon poem, *Beowulf*, names one:

> *Not the least or worst of his weaponry*
> *Was the sword Hrothgar's herald lent him*
> *In his hour of need – named Hrunting –*
> *An ancient heirloom, trusty and tested;*
> *Its blade was made of iron, with engraved design*
> *Tempered in the blood of many battles*
> *Never in combat had it failed the hand*
> *That drew it, risking the dangers of war,*
> *The enemy's onslaught. Not the first time then*
> *That its edge must be ventured in deeds of valour.*

Sword names expressed the quality of the weapon on both a physical and magical level. The meaning of some of them is lost now, being part of the as yet undeciphered magical cryptology of runes. Thus, the sword owned by the two kings named Offa, symbol of Saxon and Mercian kingship, was called Skrep. The names of several famed swords are recorded in the Norse sagas, *Magnus Barefoot's Saga* recounts that King Magnus 'was girded with a sword called Leggbitr [Leg-biter]. Its guards were of walrus ivory, and its hilt was sheathed with gold. It was one of the best weapons'. *Kormac's Saga* tells of the misuse of the famed sword known as Sköfnung. A passage in *Egils Saga*, which reports the Battle of Brunanburgh, fought in northern England in the year 937, tells of the runic sword names: 'Thorolf had a wide and thick shield, a very strong helmet on his head and a sword which he called Lang [Long One], a large and good weapon . . . Egil had the same equipment as Thorolf, he had a sword which he called Nadr [Adder], which he had obtained from Kurland; it was an excellent weapon . . .' Sword names recorded in Sagas include the following, all of which are kennings, some of them runic: Odin's Flame, the Ice of Battle, the Fire of the Shields, the Sea-King's Fire, the Battle-Fire, Torch of the Blood, Serpent of the Wound, Snake of the Byrnie, the Byrnie's Fear, Harmer of War-Knittings, the Dog of the Helmet, Tongue of the Scabbard. This runic sword tradition continued well into the Age of Chivalry. For example, a sword found in a stone coffin at Korsoygaden, near Oslo, has no writing on the blade, but the upper fillet on the grip, made of bronze, has a runic inscription, which may be as late as 1300, and the sword itself is probably thirteenth century.

It was not only weapons that had runes carved upon them. Excavations conducted in 1980 by F. Wallace at the Norse site at Fishamble Street in Dublin revealed other runic objects. One was a sliver of wood bearing a rune row known as the Dublin Futhark, two slightly variant versions of the Scandinavian Younger Futhark of 16 characters. Another important find was a deer antler with the runic inscription 'Hurn Hiartar' – 'the horn of the Hart', probably a magical invocation to the material which was made before it was used. Another inscription on the antler, 'La Ausar' remains undeciphered.

Despite its widespread use as a means of communication and record, runic is best known as a magical alphabet. Of course, it is used for magical purposes today, but there are many ancient examples of rune magic still extant. They range from the magic formulae of Pagan times, through Christian uses to the dual faith Pagan-Christian inscriptions of some medieval magic. The runic Canterbury charm against infection in wounds, dated 1073, contains the words 'Thor hallow you'. An interesting mixture of religious traditions – Islamic, Christian and Pagan – exists in the intriguing coin discovered in an eleventh-century grave on Bornholm in the Baltic. It was a Cufic coin from Samarkand, dating from between the years 907–13, over whose Islamic Arabic inscription runic formulae had been engraved. This magical runic inscription was a Christian formula in Latin, for the eternal life of the buried person.

Love amulets were another way in which rune magic flourished. Excavations at the Aebelholt monastery in Sjaelland, Denmark, have yielded lead love amulets bearing runic inscriptions, and an ancient stick from Viborg, North Jutland, carved with a mixture of crosses and runes has long been known as the Viborg 'love stick'. Centuries later, this magical application still flourishes today! But one of the most spectacular survivals of medieval rune magic is the 'healing stick' from Ribe in Denmark. This is a square-section pine stave about a foot long which is inscribed with a runic spell against 'the Trembler' – malaria. Dating from around the year 1300, it contains the dual faith invocation: 'Earth I pray guard, and the heaven above, Sun and St. Mary and Himself the Lord God.

That he grants me hands to make whole and healing tongue, to cure the Trembler when treatment is needed'. The formula first invokes the power of the divine – the Lord God and the Mother Goddess, as St.Mary, the solar power of the heavens, and the Earth. After this comes an exorcism, a formula to terrorize and banish the demon of sickness: 'A stone is called Swart, it stands out in the sea. On it lie nine Needs. They shall neither sleep nor wake warm until you are better of it'. Finally, the runic formula ends with 'Thoet se' – So must it be!

Magical formulae continued to use runes throughout the middle ages, especially in Sweden. The tombstone of Bishop Gisike at Lösen has an inscription in runes, dating from 1310 or 1311. Lund cathedral, in Skåne province, contains a later runic inscription carved around 1500. It was made by Adam Van Düren at the base of a sculptured pillar, stating in Low German 'Got help' (God help [us]). Even after the official use of runes by the Scandinavian Church had expired, runes cont'nued to be used for correspondence. In 1543, the Danish admiral Mogens Gyldenstjerne wrote his personal journal in runes. During the Thirty Years War (1618–46), a Swedish general, Jacob de la Gardie, used runes as a 'secret' code. In Iceland, however, the runes were outlawed in 1639 as 'witch-

Fig. 25. Consulting the runestocks in sixteenth-century Scandinavia.

craft'. For writing in runes, people were burnt alive. The magical runic formulae known as Kotruvers, invocations of saints and kings to help the player win at chess or backgammon, were included in this proscription. The laws were enforced with severity. For example, in 1681, Árni Pétursson was burnt at the stake in the presence of the Icelandic Althing (parliament) for having used Kotruvers. But elsewhere in Scandinavia runes continued to be used in calendars until the late part of the eighteenth century.

Today there is a renewed interest in the runes which has spread them throughout the world, and to a larger number of practitioners than ever before. In their modern usage, they operate at a deep symbolic level – at the level of the archetypal underlying reality which is active in all our lives, whether or not we recognize the fact. The Elder Futhark and its developments, the Anglo-Saxon and Northumbrian, describe almost all of the runes whose names are known. There are also a number of others which will be described below which are no longer part of the repertoire of the rune-user. The following details these meanings:

The first rune of all runic alphabets is Feoh, the primary rune of the first aett. As the first character, this rune has the meaning of 'cattle', with the phonetic value of 'F'. It has the same meaning as the first characters of the Hebrew and Greek alphabets, though in runic its phonetic value is 'F'. Literally, 'cattle' refers to movable wealth. In traditional nomadic and agrarian societies, the main sign of wealth of an individual, family or clan, was the cattle owned. In the ancient European tradition, unlike the homestead, which was inheritable property which could not be sold or bartered, cattle represent negotiable wealth. Symbolically, the cattle rune signifies wealth that can be traded or exchanged – negotiable property. Consequently, in modern English, the rune name appears in the word *fee*, a payment.

Traditional society relied heavily upon the cow, for milk, meat, hide and horn. This basic nature of the cow is fundamental in Indo-European tradition. The Norse creation myth tells of the primal cow, named Audhumla, whose formative function was to lick the cubic block of crystalline salt which contained the progenitor of humankind, the primal being

Buri. In runic terms, the rune Feoh represents that primal coming into being from which we all originate. In the classical Mediterranean tradition, too, the steer marks a starting-point. To the ancient Egyptians, the bull's horns symbolized the beginning. Virgil's account of the birth of man commences: 'The white bull with his gilded horns opens the year', and the devotees of Mithras asserted that the bull was the first thing in organic creation.

Materially, the rune Feoh represents the accumulation of power. It signifies the ability to control. This is a two-fold power, physically in terms of controlling the cattle herd itself, and economically through its exploitation. This symbolism of control contains within it the responsibilities that ownership brings. Ownership and management of cattle, indeed any manifestation of wealth demands that the owner should show responsibility. Appropriate stewardship is called for if the value is not to be lost. To manage the herd or other wealth in a wasteful or greedy manner will soon bring disaster and poverty. In the modern-day context, the rune Feoh signifies money and the ability and opportunity to attain worldly success and wealth, and the intelligence to keep it. The old renderings of the rune warn us against avarice and the consequences to society of miserly conduct. The Norwegian rune poem warns that with stresses the problems of wealth may become greed and envy. This can cause divisions within the family, clan or nation, resulting in the downfall of all: 'Wealth causes friction between relatives, while the wolf lurks in the woods.' Similarly, under the rubric of the first rune, the Old English rune poem tells us that 'Wealth is a comfort to everybody, yet all of us must give it away freely, if we want to gain favour in the sight of the lord.'

The second rune in all systems is Ur, phonetically the letter 'U'. Originally, it represented the enormous European wild steer known as the Aurochs, (*Bos primigenus*). Both its English and Latin name means 'the Primal Ox'. Although in ancient times it was widespread in northern and central Europe, by the medieval period it became an endangered species, and it was finally hunted to extinction in Poland in 1627. From extant skeletons, it is plain to see that the Aurochs was a formidable animal. 'The Aurochs is bold with horns standing high, a fierce horned fighter who stamps over the moorlands, a striking creature!', the Old English rune poem tells us. Ur symbolizes the impersonal raw, tameless power of wild cattle. This contrasts strongly with the personally oriented, socially controlled power of property expressed by Feoh, the first rune. Ur denotes the limitless power of the universe, the awesome embodiment of unlimited creative potential. Ur's irresponsible might ensures that it can never be restricted to an individual level, under the control of one person. When applied to human endeavours, Ur refers to the power of the collective will, 'our' power. Ur's magical influence brings good fortune, collective strength and personal success measured in terms of the common good.

The third rune is called Thorn or Thurisaz, phonetically 'th' as in '*th*orn'. This rune denotes the resistant and protective qualities of the thorn tree. The thorn is a protective structure which can operative passively or as a deterrent against attack. It also has the meaning of a giant, demon or troll, all of which are beings ascribed with the power of effective offence and defence. The Old English rune poem tells us that 'The thorn is very sharp, an evil thing to grip, very grim for anybody who falls among them'. Thorn hedges are a practical means of preventing access to a field, and customarily, sacred enclosures in northern Europe were surrounded by hedges of hawthorn and blackthorn. Mythologically, Thorn signifies the defensive powers of Mjöllnir, the Hammer of Thor. Mjöllnir means 'the crusher', and protective amulets in the form of this hammer are popular amongst followers of Asatru today. The form of the Thorn rune resembles the stylized form of Thor's hammer. Here, Thorn is the power that resists everything that threatens the natural order of things. Finally, Thorn also symbolizes the creative energy of the masculine gender, the wilful application of the generative principle.

Thorn is the only rune that survives in everyday use. It can be seen all over England in its later form as the character 'Y' in 'olde worlde' names such as 'Ye Olde Tea Shoppe'. Until the eighteenth century, it was used in England along with Roman alphabet characters to denote the first 'th' of words like 'the', 'that', and 'this'.

The fourth rune of the Elder Futhark is As, also known as Asc, Asa and Ansuz. This is the 'god rune', signifying the divine force in action. Phonetically it is 'A' and is the Sanskrit 'primal sound' which brought on the manifestation of this cycle of the universe. It is equivalent to the Greek ΛΟΓΟΣ (logos), with all that implies. As a rune, As is represented by the ash tree, one of the most sacred trees in the Northern Tradition. In Norse mythology, the world tree Yggdrassill, the cosmic axis, is an ash. As is the divine power that oversees the maintenance of order in the cosmos: 'The Ash, beloved of humans, stands high. It holds steadily to its place in a firm position, though many foes come forward to fight it', the Old English rune poem tells us.

The fifth rune is Rad, Raed or Rit, which has the phonetic value of 'R'. The Old English rune poem tells us that 'For a hero inside the hall, riding is soft, but it is more arduous when he is astride a great horse riding the roads' long miles'. The rune represents all forms of formalized directed activity. The poem refers to both types of 'riding': sexual intercourse and horsemanship. Its name, however, also indicates the wheel (the German *rad*) and the road upon which the riding takes place. In esoteric terms, this rune represents the 'vehicle' which we must employ in order to achieve anything. Rad signifies the necessity to channel our energies in an appropriate manner if we wish to achieve the results we desire. The emphasis of Rad is thus the necessity to be in the right place at the right time to perform the appropriate act. In this way, Rad signifies the ritual nature of activities. In a ritual, there is a transformation of energies, a transference of spirit, matter or information from one place to another. But the main emphasis is upon personal transformation. Rad therefore symbolizes our conscious attempts at controlling the facts which affect our well-being. It is our positive, conscious interaction with our position on the wheel of fortune, a situation with which we must interact harmoniously if we are to live successfully.

The sixth rune is called Ken, Cen or Kennaz, which has the phonetic value of 'K'. Its early form is an angular version of the Roman letter 'C', but in its latter form it represents the *kienspan*, the chip of pine wood which was burnt to illuminate houses in former times. The Old English rune poem tells us that 'The torch is living fire, bright and shining. Most often, it burns where noble people are resting indoors'. The later form of the rune is in the form of the *kienspanhalter*, the stand into which the burning pine chip was inserted. These devices were used in country districts of southern Germany until the nineteenth century. As a rune, Ken therefore represents illumination. Its form is of a branch from a straight stave, representing the active principle. It is the polar opposite of the eleventh rune, Is, a single stroke which signifies the static principle. Symbolically, Ken is the rune of the mystery of transformation, Ken represents that mystical creation achieved by the union and transmutation of two separate entities, making a third which did not exist before. With the *kienspan*, the resinous pine wood is destroyed, but is transformed into heat and light. Ken thus brings light in the darkness. On all levels, it symbolizes those things that permit us to see. Thus Ken is the bringer of the inner light of knowledge. The rune name Ken is cognate with *cen*, a Celtic word which means 'powerful'. In Scots and some English dialects *ken* means 'knowledge'. Esoterically, it signifies regeneration through death.

The seventh rune is Gyfu or Gebo, which has the phonetic value of a hard 'G', and the meaning of a gift. Shaped like the Roman letter 'X', Gyfu's form is the 'sacred mark', used to denote things dedicated to the gods. With regard to this rune, The Old English rune poem tells us that 'To people, giving is an ornament of value, and to every outsider without any other, it is substance and honour'. Gyfu refers to a gift and the act of giving/receiving. Symbolically, it describes the gift of one's own ability or talent in the service of another. Ability itself – talent – is viewed as a gift to the individual from the gods. When anything is given, a relationship is established between the giver and the receiver. Gyfu signifies the unifying effect that a gift makes between the donor and the recipient of the gift. Gyfu expresses the qualities of linking seemingly separate people in a common bond, or even the human with the divine. In modern usage, Gyfu is the sigil used to represent a kiss on lovers' letters. Esoterically, Gyfu is the quality personified in the Norse goddess Gefn or Gefjon, the bountiful giver, the equivalent of the goddess Abundantia, formerly worshipped in central Europe.

The eighth rune is Wyn, Wunnaz or Wunjo, with the phonetic value of 'W'. This is the last rune of the first aett. In the form of the wind-vane, Wyn represents joy. It signifies the ability to remain in harmony with the flow of events, as the wind-vane moves with the changing breezes, winds and gales. The Old English rune poem expresses it thus: 'Joy is for someone who knows little of sadness. Without sorrow they will have bright fruits and happiness and houses enough'. Wyn thus signifies the happy medium, that point of balance that we need to seek in order to lead a sane and happy existence. Wyn is liberation from the twin tyrannies of shortage or excess. But in this, Wyn represents the fulfilment of our wishes and desires in a sane way, the transformation of life for the better. As this can best be achieved in concord with others, Wyn is the rune of fellowship, shared aims and general well-being.

At the beginning of the second aett comes Hagal or Haegl, a rune with the phonetic value of 'H'. Hagal's name literally means 'hail', that frozen water which falls from the sky in granular form. Hail is water transformed for a short while into ice, during which time it can fall from the sky and destroy crops or property. When it has done its damage, it melts, changing back into harmless, even beneficial, liquid. Symbolically, Hagal is the icy primal seed of structure and transformation, patterned in accordance with the primal sacred geometry whose forms underly the universe. In this manner, Hagal signifies the processes which are necessary for anything to be accomplished, and because of this it is sometimes interpreted as indicating or bringing a delay. Obviously, Hagal's element is ice, the fifth element in the Northern Tradition.

Hagal is a link between the upper world and Middle Earth, upon which we live. It is the rune of the number nine, the most sacred number of the Northern Tradition, and, as such, is the Mother Rune. Hagal is associated with the guardian deities of the passages which link the world of human consciousness with other planets. These divinities are Heimdall, the watcher god who links Middle Earth on which we live with the upper world by way of the Rainbow Bridge, Bifröst; and Mordgud, the goddess who guards the bridge to the underworld. Ice crystals in the sky sometimes cause rainbow-hued haloes, such as those seen around the moon on icy nights. Similarly, the chilling bridge to the cold underworld is icy in nature. The rune is also associated with Urd, the elder Norn, 'that which was'. It is the rune of Samhain, the modern Halowe'en.

The ninth rune represents those patterns of being which, although originating in the past, still remain active and affect the present state of things. It signifies powerful if subtle influences, accordingly representing the power of evolution within the framework of present existence. Hagal is the rune at the root of things, both on a physical, material, level, and in time. It is one of the major runes of Wyrd: those patterns of events in our past life which make the present what it is today.

Rune readers often ascribe a bad significance to Hagal, viewing its presence in a shoat as a disruption in life. The bad aspects of the rune may occur as the result of physical accidents or, more diffusely, as generally unforeseen 'bad luck'. But whatever they are, the events indicated by the rune may come suddenly and unexpectedly. In addition, they cannot be avoided, for these events are outside human control or intervention. However, they are not random, for they proceed according to already established rules, such as in a court of law. So the outcome of the event will be impersonal and inexorable, not subject to human emotions or preferences. In this aspect, Hagal signifies the action of a mechanical process rather than the results of human creativity.

Hagal is the rune of the personal unconscious mind and of the formative process of thought. More specifically, it is a disruptive agency working in the unconscious, causing a much needed change. Hagal tells us that these problems must be dealt with now if we are to progress. But, once recognized, this awareness is powerful. Hagal shows us that the best way of living is to come into harmony with nature – with the natural cycles of the seasons, with our own true nature. Whatever happens to us, the way we deal with it is within our own free will. If we follow the traditional teaching which tells us that the most important knowledge that we can acquire is knowledge of ourselves, then we can begin to live creatively within our own Wyrd.

The tenth rune is Nyd or Not, phonetically the sound 'N'. This rune means 'need'. This is need in all of its forms. It can refer to the usual perception of need, the kind of need that is occasioned by the scarcity or absence of some requirement. The Old English rune poem describes this variety of need: 'Need is a tight band across the chest, but often it can be transformed into a help-bringer, if attended to early enough'. It expresses the maxim that the ability to be released from need exists and can be found within the need itself.

Nyd calls for caution in action, and the old adage 'know thyself' is particularly applicable to this rune. This can be seen as not striving against our Wyrd, but using it constructively. In Norse legend, Nott was the goddess of night. She had had three husbands. By the first, Naglfari, she bore a son, Aud; by the second, Annar, a daughter, Jörd, the Earth goddess; and by her third, Dellinger, a son, Dag (day). Thus the rune Nyd (Nott) is the mother of the 24th rune, Dag. The shape of the rune is taken from the fire-bow and block which was used customarily to ignite the needfire. In this way, the object is the mother of firelight.

The 11th rune is Is or Isa, phonetically the letter 'I'. Its meaning is ice, referring to the principle of static existence.

Ice is the result of a change in state from liquid to solid, after a loss of energy. Fluid water becomes resistant ice. As the principle of inertia and antropy, it is the polar opposite of the rune Ken. But, according to the esoteric tradition of the North, in conflict with fire, ice brings forth matter. But within ice there is the potential of melting, and again becoming fluid. It can also move, as in a glacier, exerting a painfully slow but, nevertheless, irresistible, force. As an iceberg, Is is deceptive, for only one ninth of the true mass is visible above the surface. The rune Is thus signifies cessation of progress or the termination of a relationship, according to powerful, inexorable forces. It is sometimes associated with death. The Old English rune poem tells us that: 'Ice is very cold and slippery. It sparkles like glass, jewel-like. A field covered in frost is beautiful to see'.

The twelfth rune is called Jera, Ger, Jara or Jer. Phonetically, it is 'J', or soft 'G'. This rune has the esoteric meaning of 'year' or 'season'. It refers to the cycles of time, the processes within time and their culmination points. More specifically, Jara symbolizes the fruitful results of doing things in the correct order and at the fitting time. This is the appropriate completion of any process. More specifically, Jara signifies the bountiful harvest that may be repated through the application of careful husbandry. It demonstrates that when human activities are conducted according to the correct principles, that is when they are done in harmony with the natural order, then the result will be beneficial. The result will be 'a bright abundance for both rich and poor'. Jera is the rune of completion, marking the end of one cycle and the commencement of a new one. This is appropriate for the 12th character of the runic row, representing the 12 months of the complete year. In both its older and younger forms, this rune mirrors the mystic marriage between earth and the cosmos, or the cycle of the seasons.

The 13th rune is known as Eihwaz or Eoh. This represents the yew tree, and has the phonetic equivalent of 'EO', or 'Z'. In The Old English rune poem, it is described as follows: 'On the outside, the Yew is a rough tree, strong and fast in the Earth, guardian against fire, a joy to the home'. All over Europe, from ancient times the yew tree has been revered. It is the longest-lived of European trees, and as such signifies longevity. A phenomenon of some ancient yews is that they may regenerate. Old trees which have almost died and which have rotted away partially, can be regenerated by their own daughter trees growing inside them. Magically, the yew is revered as being a 'bleeding' tree, for trees may be found in which red resin oozes incessantly from a wound like blood. These characteristics, recognized in ancient times, set the yew aside as a tree of death and rebirth – hence its use in the churchyard as a symbol. Traditionally, the yew has the dual function of protecting the dead and of giving access to the otherworld. This access to other states has been accomplished by means of traditional shamanic practices. Yew products, such as incense made from the resin, leaves or bark, which are extremely dangerous, and could prove lethal, are part of these rites. These have made Eoh the rune of death. Because of this, Eoh is the 13th character of the runic alphabet. But as a rune, its power is generally considered in a positive way, affirmative of continuity and endurance.

The most significant traditional use of yew wood was for the longbow. It brings in another death aspect to this rune, as a means of death in hunting and in warfare. Before firearms were invented, anyone who carried a longbow threatened possible assailants, making yew a magically protective wood. Also, many ancient wooden staves carrying runes were made of yew. A number of ancient yew staves survived from sixth- and seventh-century Frisia. The best known are the Britsum stave of the sixth century, and the yew wand from Westeremden, dating from *c*. 800.

The 14th rune is known as Peorth, Peord or Perthro. This rune's meaning is perhaps the most contentious of all. Many runic writers refer to it as a 'dice cup', the 'shaker' in which dice are tumbled before being rolled on the gameboard. Occasionally, it is seen as a mechanized refinement of the dice cup, a mechanism for casting lots. Another, related, interpretation is of Peorth the pawn or gamepiece, whose play upon the gameboard, like the dice, can be seen as a metaphor for the vagaries of human existence. When Peorth is seen as a gamepiece, then it is reflecting the dynamic relationship between the action of conscious free will and the constraints of existing circumstances. In any board game, the possible movements of the pieces are defined by the rules of the game. Beyond these inherent limitations, however, the actual movements in any given game are not fixed. They are the result of the conscious skill of the players and their interaction during the game This is a good description of how we lead our lives, where we have free will within our own Wyrd. These most common interpretations of Peorth do not tally well with that given in the Old English rune poem. This text describes Peorth: 'Lively music brings laughter and play where brave people sit together in hall, beer-swilling soldiers together.' Here, Peorth is seen as lively music, perhaps a dance, which bears some relationship to the gamepiece moving across the board. Finally, Freya Aswynn's intuitive analysis of the runes, *Leaves of Yggdrasil*, tells us that this rune can refer to the womb of the Great Goddess, the All Mother. Here, Peorth represents that which brings into existence, as a fertile womb brings a child into the world. It manifests that which formerly was concealed. Through all of the several interpretations of this rune, Peorth represents the potency of fate or destiny functioning in the material world, bringing forth the hitherto-concealed patterns into existence.

The 15th rune is Elhaz or Eiwaz, with the phonetic equivalent of 'X' or 'Z'. In its form, it resembles the Elk, the defensive 'warding sign' of the splayed hand, and the water plant known as the 'elongated sedge'. This plant is hardy and resistant. According to the Old English rune poem: 'Elk-Sedge grows mainly in the fenlands. Flourishing in the water, it grimly wounds, running with the blood of anyone who tries to grasp it'. Expressed as either the elk or the sedge, this rune denotes protection. It is considered the most powerful rune of protection against those influences or forces which we find in conflict with ourselves. Esoterically, Elhaz denotes the human aspiration towards divine qualities.

The 16th rune goes by the names of Sigel, Sig or Sowilo, whose phonetic value is 'S'. As the 'sun' rune, it represents the power of the holy solar disc, expressing vital qualities of daylight. Sigel denotes the overwhelming brilliance of the light of the sun. Symbolically, this represents clear vision and the ready attainment of one's aims, manifested on either the physical or spiritial planes. The Old English rune poem explains it: 'When they navigate across the fishes' bath, to sailors the Sun always means hope, until the horse of the sea brings them to harbour'. In symbolic terms, the rune Sigil represents the conscious magical will acting in a beneficial manner throughout the world. It denotes a certain selfless spiritual quality which has the strength to resist the powerful forces of death and disintegration. This rune celebrates triumphantly the ascendancy of light over darkness, invoking the power of the sun for guidance and healing. It is thus the rune of victory.

The 17th rune is called Tyr, after the central and northern European sky god, also known as Ziu, and Tîwaz who is considered to be the counterpart of the Roman Mars. Its phonetic value is 'T'. Tyr is the first rune in the aett of the same name, ruled by the God of Justice. The Old English rune poem describes this rune: 'Tyr is a special sign in which nobles have faith. It is always on its way and never fails in the darkness of the night'. Tyr represnts the quality of steady, reliable, positive regulation. As with the legend of Tyr, who gave up his right hand in order to bind the Fenris-Wolf, this rune accepts that in order to rule justly, one must accept self-sacrifice. It denotes the unity between the successful accomplishment of something, and the sacrifice which must be made in order to succeed. In its shape, 'like an arrow', it signifies that to have the greatest effect, we must target our energies in the correct place.

The 18th rune is known as Beorc, Birkana or Bar, whose phonetic equivalent is 'B'. The meaning of this character is the birch tree. This tree is the symbol of purification and regeneration. The Old English rune poem tells us that: 'The Birch bears no fruit, yet it grows without seeding, has shining branches high in its decorated helmet, laden with leaves, scraping the sky'. Here, it is a symbol of regeneration, the domain of the great Earth Mother goddess Nerthus. This aspect is emphasized by the rune's shape, which resembles the breasts of the goddess. Beorc is connected directly with the primary ogham character, Beth, the tree that symbolizes the springtime regeneration of the sun's vigour. In both the runic, ogham and Gaelic traditions, the birch is the tree of purification, whose twigs are used by witches to form the brush part of their broomsticks. The birch is also the traditional tree cut to make maypoles. Being the 18th rune, Beorc's number is double the sacred nine of Hagal. This denotes new beginnings.

The 19th rune is Ehwaz or Eh, with a phonetic value of 'E'. This rune has the literal meaning of a horse. 'The horse is the peers' joy, stepping out with pride when discussed all around by wealthy riders, and to the restless, always comforting', says the Old English rune poem. In its shape and its poetic meaning, Ehwaz is a rune of combination. It is usually associated with twins, brother- or sisterhood and the intuitive bond between a horse and its rider. The underlying quality of Ehwaz is thus of trust and loyalty. Ehwaz represents the motion that we require to undertake any task, more specifically referring to the 'task of life' to which our destiny has brought us.

The 20th rune is Man or Mannaz, with the phonetic value of 'M'. Man is seen as the human being, not just the male gender. It represents the basic reality of our human nature, that quality which is present in every human person, whether they are male or female. Man signifies the shared basic experience of every person who is conscious of their being. The Old English rune poem states this reality: 'In happiness, a man is beloved of his relatives, yet each must depart from the other, because the gods will commit their flesh to the earth'. In its shape, the man rune reflects the archetypal human being as that ancient concept of man the microcosm. The human being in her or his small way, is seen as the reflection of society, the world, and the cosmos. The rune expresses the full range of human experience, without which the total potential of our lives is not realizable.

The 21st rune is Lagu, with the phonetic value of 'L'. It signifies water in all of its many aspects, and the vegetable known as the leek. Pre-eminently the rune of fluidity, Lagu represents the ever-changing nature of existence. Lagu represents the stupendous waxing power of growth. The leek is known for its enormous power when pushing its way through the soil, and the rune expresses this aspect of irresistibility. This irresistible power of growth is a fundamental charcteristic of matter. The Old English rune poem tells us that: 'To landlubbers, water seems troublesome if they put to sea on a tossing ship, the waves terrify them, and the horse of the sea refuses its bridle.' This represents the dangerous aspect of flow, the power of the sea. As water, Lagu is the medium by which passage may be gained, but not without risk. But, as with all things, there are two aspects to Lagu. Although human life cannot be sustained without water, yet we cannot live in water for more than a short period. This balance, the law of the unity of opposites, is manifested in the way that growth proceeds in cycles. This is evident in the growth rings of seashells and tree-rings, manifested in Lagu as the ebb and flow of the tide.

The 22nd rune, representing the god Ing, is Ing or Ingwaz. Its phonetic equivalent is 'Ng'. In the Northern Tradition, the god Ing is the male consort of the goddess of fertility and nurture, Nerthus. Ing is the god of male fertility who guards the hearth-fire, the inglenook, and consequently this rune has long been used for the protection of households. On a more general level, Ing is a symbol of light. It is the fire beacon that transmits a message far and wide. Ingvi is a by-name of the Norse fertility god Frey, clearly identical with the god Ing. In Pagan times, on certain holy days, the image of Yngvi was transported around his sacred enclosures in a consecrated wagon. This is recorded in the Old English rune poem: 'Originally, the eastern Danes saw Ing, departing across the sea with his wagon. So the Heardings called this champion.' On a general level, the rune Ing represents potential energy. The form of the rune demonstrates its capability of limitless extension. As an aspect of the ithyphallic god, Frey, it signifies the male orgasmic force and its consequences. It is an energy which must build up gradually for a period of accumulation before being eleased as a single burst of enormous power.

The 23rd rune is called Odal, Odil Ethil or Ethel, with the phonetic value of 'O'. Literally, Odal means ancestral land, more specifically the property of the family – the homestead. In the Frisian language, this rune is called 'Eeyen-eerde': 'own earth' or 'own land'. The Old English rune poem calls it 'home', and tells us: 'All human beings love home, if they can prosper in peace there and enjoy frequent harvests'. Odal represents the qualities of belonging, togetherness, ancestral heritage and the indefinable yet real family qualities that are handed on from generation to generation. On a less personal level, this rune signifies the innate qualities of anything, its material and spiritual heritage. It is a symbol of resistance against the intrusion of the arbitrary rule of human governments: it signifies integrity, wise husbandry of resources and the liberty of the individual and clan within the framework of natural law.

The 24th, and final, rune of the Elder Futhark is Dag or Dagaz. This has the phonetic equivalent of 'D'. Literally, Dag means 'day'. 'Day is the messenger of God, the light brings consolation and happiness to rich and poor alike'. Dag is the rune of the bright light of day, especially at its zenith. Thus it is the rune of midday and midsummer. Overall, Dag is a beneficial rune, of light, health and prosperity. In the spiritual realm, it represents cosmic consciousness, the divine light as the source of strength and joy. As the rune of midday and midsummer, the high points of day and year, Dag denotes the end of one cycle, and the beginning of the next. In its shape, the rune Dag symbolizes the balance between polarities, especially those of light and darkness. Dag has a Gaelic counterpart, 'Doir' the oak tree, and Ogham character 'Duir'. In Ogham tree calendar, as in the runic year circle, it signifies the period around midsummer. This is the 'door' that lies at the meeting-point of the half of the year when the light is rising, and the half in which it is declining. This 'door' aspect is also the runic counterpart of the Hebrew letter Daleth.

The first rune of the fourth aett is Ac. It has the phonetic equivalent of the short 'A'. Sometimes, this aett is called 'the aett of the Gods', sacred to the Norse group of gods known as the Aesir. Developed in Britain, this group of runes has a number of tree connections, which may be taken as indicating Celtic influence. Literally, this rune means the oak tree, which is sacred throughout Europe to the Thunder God, whatever name he may go by: Zeus, Dispater, Jupiter, Thor, Taranis, Dagda, Perun or Perkunas. Esoterically, this rune represents the acorn, symbol of great potential: 'mighty oaks from little acorns grow'. This oak-fruit is a natural representation of the cosmic egg which encapsulates the primal potential of coming-into-being and growth. Because of this, the rune Ac signifies the potential of powerful growth and continued, unfailing, support.

Os must be dealt with as the next rune, although it never appears in this position. It does not exist in the 24-rune Elder Futhark, but appears in the longer rune rows of 29 and 33 characters. In these alphabets, it occupies the place of the fourth rune. It then becomes the 26th rune. Phonetically, Os is the sound 'O'. The meanings of As and Os are close to one another. Os means 'speech' or 'mouth', and is specifically the rune of inspiration, connected with Odin as god of eloquence. The sound of Os is taken to be the primal vibration of existence, the logos (ΛΟΓΟΣ) of the Greek tradition. This rune therefore represents the creative power of words and thus wisdom itself. On another level, it symbolizes the concept of information. It is through information that all of the structures and processes of life take their being. In human terms, it signifies culture, that corpus of identity-defining information that is expressed in poetry, song, saga and literature.

The 27th rune is called Yr. This has the phonetic value of 'Y', and the meaning of a bow from which arrows are shot. In northern Europe, the best bows were fashioned from the wood of the fateful yew tree. In addition to its use as a weapon for hunting or warfare, the bow can be used as an instrument of divination. As well as or instead of using the famous 'Y'-shaped Hazel branches, traditional rhabdomants were known to use a tensioned bow of yew as a dowsing rod in their search for underground water. In its form of the bow, Yr represents the creative crafts. It is through the action of the knowledgeable skills upon materials taken from the physical world that human artefacts come into being. In this way, the rune Yr signifies defence, the individual's protection *at the expense of others*, and correct location – being in the right place at the right time, and spot on target!

The 28th rune is Ior, which, in its shape, is similar to the Hagal of the Younger Futhark. It has the phonetic value of 'Io'. Ior means 'a sea animal'. Whilst some commentators link this with the beaver, an animal now extinct in Britain, a more appropriate ascription is the mythological beast known as the Sea Serpent. This beast appears in Norse mythology as the Midgardsorm, the World Serpent whose name is Jörmungand. Like the dual nature of amphibious animals – earthly and watery – Ior symbolizes that dual nature which exists within many things. In the myth of Jörmungand, the world serpent is depicted naturally as a most dangerous animal. Although, periodically, its movements threaten to destabilize the world, nevertheless it is an essential part of it. If it were removed, then that would lead to a permanent change. This would be more disastrous to human life on Earth than would be its continued presence. The Midgardsorm and its rune Ior thus symbolize those problems and hardships with which we must all come to terms if we are to continue to live a tolerable life. The occasional paroxysms of nature symbolized by the orm are integral parts of the human natural order. Norse legend explain this in the myth of Thor. Fishing with an ox-head that represents Ur, the rune of strength, Thor catches the Midgardsorm. But the moral of this story is far from demonstrating the cleverness of the Thunderer. It is shown as a foolhardy attempt to override the balance of Nature, something that even a god cannot do without dire consequences. Fortunately, before Thor can pull the orm from the ocean bed, Hymir, Thor's giant companion, severs the line, and Jörmungand sinks back into the abyssal depths of the ocean. Whilst dangerous, the forces represented by Ior are recognized as being essential components of life. The response of modern society to these dangerous forces results in an attempt to extirpate them completely. But in the Northern Tradition, there is a fundamental recognition of the law of the unity of opposites. Like the Thor myth, the concept underlying Ior shows us that if we attempt to eradicate one of the polar complementary parts of something, it must be doomed to failure. The experience of modern medicine demonstrates the principle that when one disease has been eliminated, then another has evolved to fill the place vacated by the older one. However, the irony of such a situation is that new diseases are more virulent than older ones because they are so new and there is little resistance to them. The motto of Ior is thus 'leave well alone'.

The 29th rune is Ear, whose phonetic value is 'Ea'. This rune has the meaning of 'dust', from which our bodies are made, and to which we return at death. Symbolically this is the grave and it represents the end of one's life. But it is not to be seen as a bad rune, for without an end there could never have been a beginning. The very existence of life requires that there be death. Ear denotes this unavoidable end, the inevitability of the return of individual, living, human beings to the undifferentiated material on which our bodies are made. To signify the end, Ear is the last character in the Anglo-Saxon runic alphabet of 29 staves.

Around the year 800, the Anglo-Saxons of Northumbria (the part of England north of the River Humber) added further letters to the 29-character rune row. This made the longest runic alphabet, of 33 characters. This had the effect of making an additional complete aett, with one further rune which had the symbolism of the central point. The first exclusively Northumbrian rune is Cweorth, number 30 in the rune row. This has the phonetic value of 'Q'. Cweorth signifies the ascending, swirling flames of ritual fire. This can be the celebratory bonfire, the supplicating need-fire, or the fire of the funeral pyre. Whichever fire is meant, the rune Cweorth embodies the concept of ritual cleansing by means of fire. All fires are microcosmic reflections of the sacred hearth.

The 31st rune is Calc, with the phonetic value 'K'. This is another rune whose meanings are not as clear as some of the others. Usually, it is said to mean a ritual container or offering cup. Alternatively, its name means 'chalk', the soft rock used in building and as a means of writing on slate. When seen as a cup, it can be visualized as an inverted, drained one. Although it was full once, it is empty now. Its contents have been used or spilled. Perhaps the drink has been drunk or spilled out onto the earth as a sacred libation to the gods. As both an offering cup and as a marker, Calc can signify the recall of absent friends or the dead in an act of remembrance. The shape of the rune is an inversion of Elhaz, the 15th rune, a rune of protection. Because of this, Calc can be interpreted as representing the individual's death. Esoterically, the mystery of Calc denotes that which is full, yet empty. Like Ior, it is the encompassing aspect of the unity of opposites. On a spiritual level, Calc denotes that aspect of the sacred which may appear to be readily accessible, yet cannot be touched – the unattainable. In medieval myth, Calc is the rune of the Holy Grail.

The 32nd rune is Stan, which has the meaning of 'stone'. This can be taken as describing stone in any of its aspects. It can mean 'the bones of the earth', the bedrock. Generally, it can mean an individual boulder, pebble or stone. But it can also refer to a special stone such as a megalith or a dressed stone for building. Also, it can be the 'stone' or gamepiece used in a board game, for the rune is shaped like traditional forms of playing pieces used in board games like Tawlbort (for details of this and other games, see my book *Games of the Gods*, Century, 1988).

Whatever form the stone of Stan takes, it signifies the link between the power of the Earth, human beings and the heavenly powers. Just as a rock can block the road, or a gamepiece can block another's move on the board, the rune Stan can either provide protection, or act to hinder our progress. Stan has the phonetic value of 'St'.

Gar is the final, 33rd, rune, of the Northumbrian rune-row. It has the phonetic value of 'G'. The meaning of this character is 'a spear'. Mythologically, this refers to Gungnir, the spear of Odin. Traditionally, spears used staves made of ash wood. As *Beowulf* records: 'Their stout spears stood stacked together, Shod with iron and shaped of ash.' Unlike the previous 32 runes, Gar cannot be assigned to any of the four conventional aettir. As the spear of Odin, which is a microcosm of the world ash tree, Yggdrassil, Gar serves as the central point around which all of the other runes circle. Additionally, in the Northumbrian system, Gar is seen as a rune of completion. But, in addition to the above 33 runes, with their near standard order, there are some other runic characters whose meanings are known, but which are rarely used. This is probably because they are not part of any standard rune row. But perhaps they are, with Gar, the fragments or nucleus of a fifth aett.

The most widely surviving of these additional characters is the rune Wolfsangel, which has the phonetic rendering of 'Ai'. This is the 'wolf-hook', a rune in the form of a device used in medieval times to capture and torture wolves. Because of this, Wolfsangel has the meaning of capture and binding. In its form it is close to the yew-rune Eoh, and, similarly, it has a woeful quality. The Wolfsangel was a pattern sometimes used for the wall-anchors in north German and East Anglian vernacular building. It also appears in north German civic heraldry. It can be seen between the artist's initials on the 1541 painting by 'Der Meister H.G.' of the martyrdom of St Katharina (in the Staatsgalerie in Stuttgart). As a wolf-catcher, it stopped the animal from doing harm to humans, and as a wall-anchor, it prevented the collapse of the building. Primarly, then, Wolfsangel is a rune of blocking and restraint.

Another important non-standard rune is Ziu, with the phonetic value of 'Z'. This can be taken as a bind rune of Tyr and Sigel, but its name indicates an earlier provenance, for Ziu is one of the ancient names of the sky-god Tîwaz or Tyr, a version of Zeus. The old name of the German city of Augsburg, holy place of this god, was Ziusburg. As the rune of the sky-god, Ziu represents the thunderbolt which is the attribute of the deity. It is a rune of concentrated power and energy, above all in the pursuit of justice. In medieval symbology, this stave had the meaning of the past taking revenge upon the present, namely the working out of justice over a long period.

Erda is a rune with the phonetic value of 'Oe'. It represents the Earth as the goddess through which she is personified. Erda is thus a rune of enclosure and protection, as befits its form, which is close to Odal. However, the two additional 'tails' which distinguish Erda from Odal represent a tying-in of the protective enclosure to the wider universe. This rune is composed of eight equal-length straight lines, and is thus another rune symbolic of stability and wholeness.

The rune Ul is that of the Frisian sky-god Waldh or Ualdh, related in some ways to the Norse deity Ullr, god of winter-time. It has the phonetic value of 'Ue'. Ul is a rune of personal strength, representing all those qualities signified by the words 'to be strong'. It also signifies turning-points, the 'ul' element in yule, the 'yoke of the year', the winter solstice, and the mystic place called Thule, 'the place where one is forced to turn back'. Overall, it is an embodiment of strength, and the power to come through turning-points unscathed and even empowered by the experience.

Another 'fifth aett' rune is Sol, which may be taken as a version of Sigel, although of a completely different form, being a circle within a vertical stave above it, signifying the rising sun. This rune has the phonetic value of 'Ss'. It represents the Norse sun goddess Sól, the provider of benevolent warmth and light to the world. Sol is a powerful rune of healing and benevolence, an embodiment of gentle growth and the power of nurturing.

As with all alphabets, there are many variant forms, ancient and modern, and this applies to the rune names. The *Abecedarium Nordmannicum*, a ninth-century manuscript from St Gallen in Switzerland, gives the names of the Danish staves thus: 'Feu first, Ur thereafter, Thuris the third stave, Os there-above, Rait at the end write Chaion cleaves thereto, Hagal, Naut has Iss, Ar and Sol, T, Bria and Man in middle, Lagu the light-filled, Yr ends all.' The Norse calendar runs, derived from the Danish runes, have somewhat different names (their Elder

Futhark equivalent names follow in brackets): Frey (Feoh); Ur (Ur); Thor (Thorn); Os (Os); Reid (Rad); Kaun (Ken); Hagl (Hagal); Naud (Nyd); Is (Is); Ar (As); Sun (Sigel); Tyr (Tyr), Biark (Beorc); Laugur (Lagu); Madur (Man); Aur (Yr); Aurlaugr (bind rune of Aur and Laugur = Yr and Lagu); Twimadur (bind rune of Aur and Madur, Man and Yr); and Belgtzhor (Jara).

In modern times, the majority of rune work has been done with either the Elder Futhark of 24 characters, or the Armanen system (see Fig. 26). Modern rune masters and rune mistresses have produced their own versions of the runes, specific forms and orders which suit some personal requirement or vision. Since 1980, runic talismans and amulets have become popular. Inexplicably, those sold by the Archaeological Trust at York

Fig. 26. The Armanen system of 18 runes, as propagated by Guido von List.

109

included invented runes for the letters D, X and Z. But whilst these variants caused some recrimination amongst rune users, their existence is clear evidence of the modern vitality of the runic scene, and the continuing development of the runes today. The present author favours the extended rune rows, such as the Northumbrian, but it is really a matter of personal preference, as with practice practitioners will find that system with which they can work best.

The most important of these modern variants is the 'Armanen' system of runes, widely used in German-speaking countries. This system, which has 18 charcters, is derived from the Scandinavian rune rows, with two added runes. It was devised by, or revealed to, the Austrian mystic Guido von List at the beginning of the 20th century. Lying in darkness, eyes bandaged after an operation, the secrets of the runes came to him. Whatever their origin, these runes have a geometrical basis on the rune Hagal, which, in this alphabet, is in the form of the six-branched 'star'. All of the other runes fit into the hexagonal lattice derived from this 'Mother Rune'. Most of them have forms similar to or identical with the Scandinavian runes. The Armanen runes have a specific order, and the number correspondences 1–18. They are Fa (F), Ursache (U), Thor (Th), Os (O), Rit (R), Ka (K), Hagal (H), Not (N), Is (I), Ar (A), Sig (S), Tyr (T), Bar (B), Laf (L), Man (M), Yr

Fig. 27. Figures in runic postures from a horn found at Gallehus, Denmark. These illustrations provided the impetus for the development of modern Runic Yoga.

(Y), Eh (E), and Gibor (G). A whole school of rune magic, divination and runic exercises has grown up within this system. An important part of this runic system is runic yoga, in which the practitioner stands in a pose resembling the rune, called *stödhur*, and calls out the sound that it represents. This technique, depicted on two ancient Danish horns from Galle-hus, was evolved by Siegfried Adolf Kummer and Friedrich Bernhard Marby, and later developed further by Karl Spiesberger, is practised widely among German rune users today.

THE GOTHIC ALPHABET

The true Gothic alphabet has nothing to do with the variants of the Roman alphabet used in the late middle ages, such as Black Letter. Along with the pointed-arch architecture, these scripts were wrongly called 'Gothic' by eighteenth-century commentators who saw them as barbarous in comparison with Graeco-Roman classicism. Unfortunately, this erroneous epithet has remained as the description for high medieval art. The true Gothic alphabet, however, is a script used by the 'barbarian' nation of the Goths, which originated on the Baltic island of Gotland, and spread, through conquest, through east Prussia, Lithuania and Poland, to the northern shores of the Black Sea. From there, the Goths migrated west, ultimately to conquer Italy, southern France and Spain. When they were in their homeland, the Pagan Goths used the runes. The oldest known inscription of the whole runic alphabet, the Kylver stone on Gotland, was carved by a Gothic runester. The parallel script was devised in the fourth century CE by Bishop Ulfilas, who undertook the conversion of the Pagan Goths to the Arian sect of the Christian religion. To make the new alphabet, Ulfilas took some Greek cursive characters and modified some existing runes so that they could be written with brush or pen rather than carved on wood or stone. After the creation of this new Gothic alphabet, both the new alphabet and the runes were used in parallel with one another. The Visigoths in Spain and the south of France used them until both were suppressed as Pagan by a ruling from the Council of Toledo in 1018. Despite the fact that the parallel Gothic alphabet was devised by a Christian bishop, this Church edict caused the immediate destruction of many important books written in the Gothic scripts that until then had been kept in the cathedral library at Toledo and other places.

Even if it were not recorded historically, it would be clear from the names and order that the Gothic script is the younger of the two. The origin of the Gothic alphabet in the runes is demonstrated by its letter order, which is that of the runes, and not that of the Greek or Roman alphabets. As with the runes, the Gothic alphabet begins with the letter Fe, which is equivalent to the Gothic rune Faíhu. Following that is the letter 'U', Uraz (rune Uras); 'Th', Thyth (Thauris); 'A', Aza (Ansus); 'R', Reda (raida); 'K', Chozma (Kusma); 'G', Gewa (Giba) and 'W', Winne (Winja). This completes the first aett. The second aett begins with Haal, the letter H, with its rune equivalent Hagl. Following this is 'N', Noicz (Nauths); 'I', Iiz (Eis); 'G', Gear (Jer), followed by 'Z', Waer, in the form of the Greek Theta (Θ), the rune Aihus. Next comes Pertra, the letter 'P', in the form of the Greek Pi (Π), with its runic equivalent, Pairthra. Ezec (X), follows, with its rune Algs, then

Fig. 28. The Gothic alphabet and the Gothic runes.

'S', Sugil (rune Saúil); 'T', Tyz (Teiws); 'B', Bercna (Gothic rune Bairkan); 'E', Eyz (Egeis) and 'M', called Manna both as a Gothic letter and as a rune. Manna is followed by the letter 'L', Laaz, rune Lagus. Then comes the equivalent of 'Ng', Enguz, and its rune-equivalent Iggws. The final three characters are Utal, representing 'O', with its rune Othal; Daaz, the letter 'D', with rune Dags, and Quertra, 'Q', which has no runic counterpart in the Gothic system. Each character of the Gothic alphabet thus has the same meaning as its runic counterpart, and was used magically in a manner identical to the runes. But it also contains 11 Greek letters in their cursive and standard forms. These are Aza, Bercna, Gewa, Daaz, Eyz, Ezec, Chozma, Laaz, Noicz, Pertra and Tyz. The esoteric meanings are inherent in these Greek characters in addition to their runic equivalent meanings. In this way, the Gothic alphabet contains within itself a wealth of meaning which lies untapped in modern esoteric practice. The techniques of runic divination apply equally to Gothic.

Runes in magic

In former times, when runes were used for magical purposes, they were known as Ram runes, that is, strong or bitter runes, which were categorized by their function. First were the Mal runes. This word comes from mal or maal, which signifies speech. Mal runes are thus speech runes. They were used in gaining legal redress against injuries, to be inscribed upon the pillars, seats, etc., of a place where a trial was to be held and judgement pronounced. Next were the Sig runes, the runes of victory, to be used to gain advantage in all contests. These would be drawn on the individual's clothing, armour and weapons to ensure success. In making Sig runes, the name of Thor had to be invoked twice. The third type were the Lim runes, used in healing. These were carved on the south-facing bark or leaves of certain appropriate medicinal trees. Fourth, were the Brun runes, or Fountain runes. These were carved on the stern, steering-oar or rudder of a ship in order to ensure a safe passage. Next were the Hug runes, the runes of the mind. Inscribed on the breast and 'secret parts', these runes assisted the user in excelling in mental agility. The sixth kind was the Biarg rune, that invokes the Mother Goddess to procure a safe birth, and generally to protect women and their babies. The

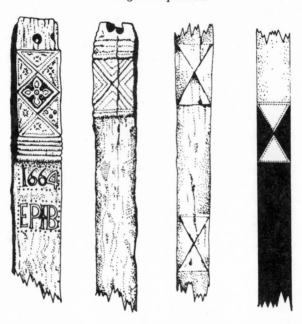

Fig. 29. Runic protection (Ing and Dag runes), 'witch posts', England and Germany.

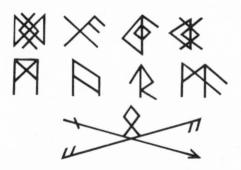

Fig. 30. Magical bind-runes: (*top row, left to right*) long lasting; good luck; love rune, man for woman; love rune; woman for man; (*middle row*) I am; Alu (power); success in legal action; mind-power; (*bottom row*) bind-rune from Soest, Germany, *c*. 625 CE.

114

seventh category was that of the Swart runes or necromanic characters, used in invoking spirits of the dead. Connected with these were the Troll runes, used for divination and enchantment. Ale runes were used by men to counter the allurements of any strange woman. They were to be cut in the vessel from which she drank, and on the back of the man's hand, with the rune 'Nyd' cut upon his finger-nail.

Wend runes were runes written in reverse, from right to left, and inverted, for magical purposes. Bind runes or Band runes were characters which incorporated two or more runes in a single figure, creating a magical sigil for a specific purpose. This technique was very similar to the ligatures of letters used sometimes in Roman inscriptions, Greek 'chrismons' of the name of Christ, and the more complex monograms used by monarchs of the Byzantine and Holy Roman Empires. Allied to this, cryptic runes were an important part of rune craft. Each of the types of cryptic rune had its own name. Kvist runes (branch runes) and Tjald runes (Tent runes) were two varieties of cryptic runes. Branch runes were based on a simple numerical principle. The Futhark is divided into its three aettir, which are given numbers. These may be given in a straightforward or in an encoded sequence. Then each rune of each aett is given a number, again in a straightforward or an encoded way. Each letter is then represented by two numbers: the aett number, and the rune number within the aett. This is written as an upright with side branches. The branches on one side stand for the aett from which the letter comes, and on the other side for the number of the character within it. As an example, we might find a branch rune bearing one stroke to the left and five to the right. Using the most straightforward system, where every aett and rune are numbered sequentially, this will represent the fourth rune of the first aett, which will be Rad. Using such a system, whole words and sentences can be built up. Tent runes work on a similar principle, but they are based on X-shaped forms, and read clockwise, beginning at the left. Other cryptic forms are the 'Iis runes', similar in principle to the Branch and Tent runes, but using single strokes unconnected with a basic support stave. These used short strokes to represent the number of the aett, and longer ones for the character numbers. 'Lagu runes' are another similar form, using sequences of the Lagu rune, sometimes written backwards to represent aett and character. Finally, Klap runes or Klop runes were a kind of forerunner of the Morse Code, in which a series of claps or knocks on wood represented specific runic characters. The details of this sytem are lost, but it is most probable that the principle was the same as that used in the Branch runes and other runic cryptography.

Finally, there is the type of encryption where the meaning of a rune is incorporated in a passage of prose or poetry arranged so that the letters spell out a hidden word or words. The Anglo-Saxon poem *Elene*, written by Cynewulf late in the eighth century, incorporates just such a runic encodement. It comes in a passage in Chapter 15 (author's interpretation in brackets):

Until then, the man had always been assailed by waves of sadness: he was a burning torch [Ken, C], though in the Mead-Hall he was given treasures, apple-shaped gold. He lamented the evil [Yr, Y], he the brother of sorrow [Nyd, N]; he suffered affliction, cruel secret thoughts, though for him the horse [Ehwaz, E], measured the mile-paths, ran proudly, adorned with ornaments. Joy [Wyn, W] is reduced, and pleasure too, as the years go by; youth has gone and former pride. The glory of youth was once ours [Ur, U]. Now, with time, the old days have departed, life's joys have slipped away, even as water [Lagu, L] drains away, the shifting floods. Wealth [Feoh, F] is transitory for all people under heaven: the ornaments of the earth disappear beneath the clouds like the wind when it blows loudly . . .

This Anglo-Saxon passage is typical of the means by which the ancient northern bards and skalds encoded messages for those sufficiently educated to encode them. Here, the runic equivalents spell out the Cynewulf.

RUNES AND TREES

Modern rune research has rediscovered the correspondences between the runes and trees, each of which expresses some quality of the rune. This is an important parallel with the Celtic ogham and Gaelic alphabets, in which most character names and qualities are based on relevant trees. These systems of correspondences have been collated by several runic experts, including Edred Thorsson, Freya Aswynn and the present author. In a few cases there are alternatives, but as the runes show their different aspects under different conditions, this should not be surprising. There is no cosmic law that restricts correspondences to a one-to-one scheme. The following are those most commonly encountered:

Feoh's tree is the elder, (*Sambucus nigra*), whilst that of Ur is the 'primal tree', the birch, (*Betula pendula*). Thorn's sacred trees are the oak, (*Quercus robur*), the blackthorn (*Prunus spinosa*), the blackberry or bramble, (*Rubus fruticosa*), and the hawthorn or may tree, (*Cratagus monogyna*). Both As and Os correspond with the ash tree, (*Fraxinus excelsior*). Rad's ruling trees are the oak, (*Quercus robur*) and the often-ignored wayfaring tree, (*Viburnum lantana*). The trees associated with the rune Ken are the deal or pine, (*Pinus sylvestris*) and the bilberry, also known as the whortleberry or blaeberry, (*Vaccinium myrtillus*). Gyfu has two related trees: the ash, (*Fraxinus excelsior*) and the wych elm, (*Ulmus glabra*). Similarly, Wyn has the ash as its tree. Hagal's tree is the longest-lived European species, the yew, (*Taxus baccata*). It also has the ominous bryony, (*Bryonia alba*), the northern European mandrake, as its herb. In traditional lore, both tree and herb are seen as linking the underworld and the upperworld by

Fig. 31. Alrauns, medieval magical figures with runic inscriptions.

means of shamanism and death. Nyd's trees are the beech, (*Fagus sylvatica*) and the mountain ash or rowan, (*Sorbus acuparia*). The tree of Is is the alder, (*Alnus glutinosa*), and its herb is the henbane, (*Hyoscyamus niger*). The oak, (*Quercus robur*) is the tree of Jera.

Eoh's name means 'yew', of which it, with Yr and Wolf-sangel, are the yew-runes *par excellence*. Eoh is also linked with the herb mandrake, (*Mandragora officinarum*), whose root has many well-known magical properties. It is also connected with the poplar, (*Populus canescens*). The rune Peorth is a direct parallel of the Celtic ogham character Peith, whose correspondence is the guelder rose, (*Viburnum opulus*). As a rune, Peorth corresponds with two trees. One is the beech, (*Fagus sylvatica*), and the other is the aspen, (*Populus tremula*). As with Hagal and Eoh, Elhaz has the yew, (*Taxus baccata*) for its sacred tree. But, a second, rarer, ascription is the wild service tree, (*Sorbus torminalis*), which is traditionally a tree of protection against wild things. The herb of Elhaz is the sedge, (*Carex elongata*), whose form resembles the rune's shape and its Anglo-Saxon name, *Eolc-Secg*. The next rune, Tyr, corresponds with the oak, whilst the following one, Beorc, has the tree sacred to the Great Mother Goddess, the birch. Enwaz has two sacred trees, the oak and the ash. The sacred trees of man are the alder, (*Alnus glutinosa*), holly, (*Ilex aquifolium*) and the maplin tree or field maple, (*Acer campestre*). The herb corresponding with man is important, for it is the madder, (*Rubia tinctorum*), from which comes the magic pigment known as 'tiver', used traditionally for colouring runes. Lagu, whose element is water, has as its sacred tree the type of willow known as the osier, (*Salix viminalis*).

Ing's sacred tree is the apple, (*Malus spp*), and the tree of Odal is the hawthorn (*Crataegus monogyna*). Dag is sacred to Heimdall, and has the Norway spruce, (*Picea abies*), as its tree. Its herb is a type of sage, (*Salvia horminoides*). Ac is the namesake of the oak, whilst As or Aesc is the ash and Yr is the yew. Yr's herbal connections are with the underworld root plants. These are the bryony, (*Bryonia alba*) and mandrake, (*Mandragora officinalis*). In Britain, the root of bryony is often used in folk magic as a substitute for the non-indigenous mandrake. The trees of Ior are the Linden, (*Tilia platyphyllos*) and the ivy, (*Hedera helix*). The tree of Ear is the yew, (*Taxus*

118

baccata), and its herb is hemlock, (*Conium maculatum*). Cweorth's trees are the bay, (*Laurus nobilis*) and the beech, (*Fagus sylvatica*), Calc's trees are the maplin, (*Acer campestris*), from whose wood sacred cups were turned, and the rowan, (*Sorbus acuparia*). Stan's trees are the Blackthorn, (*Prunus spinosa*) and the witch hazel, (*Hamamellis mollis*). Gar, is connected with its namesake, the evil-warding herb garlic, (*Allium sativum*). Its trees are the ash, (*Fraxinus excelsior*) and the spindle, (*Euonymus europaea*). The tree of Wolfsangel is the yew, (*Taxus baccata*), befitting its connection with Eoh, whilst Ziu, rune of the sky-god, has the oak, (*Quercus robur*). The tree of the Earth-Goddess rune Erda are the elder, (*Sambucus nigra*) and the birch, (*Betula pendula*). That of Ul is the sea buckthorn, (*Hippophaë rhamnoices*), whilst the tree associated with the rune Sol is the juniper, (*Juniperus communis*).

Divination with the runes

The Roman author Tacitus (*c.* 120 CE) provides us with the earliest known reference to runic divination. In his account of the Germanic nations of northern Europe, *Germania*, he wrote that the people there had the highest possible regard for divination and casting lots. They would break off a branch from a fruit tree and cut it into slivers upon which they cut runes. These wooden slivers were then cast onto a white cloth. If the divination was of public importance, the interpretation was made by a state priest, but if it concerned a private matter, it was made by the head of the family. Three slivers were picked up, one at a time, and the meaning interpreted through the runes carved upon them. Of course, Tacitus was observing as an outsider without the inner knowledge necessary to give more than a basic outline of the procedure. However, several viable methods of rune casting have survived in oral tradition, passed down from ancient times to the present day. Modern rune casting is done in a similar manner, using the stone, wooden or plastic runic tablets manufactured by various producers. Of course, it is preferable magically to use runes made by the user.

Although it is possible to pull a single rune stone out of a bag, or to draw a card from a rune card deck, it is preferable to conduct a rune-casting ceremony if one is to be in the right frame of mind to benefit from a reading. The ceremonial method of casting runes is known as 'Raed Waen'. Literally, this means 'riding the wagon' that is, placing oneself in the position of the deity on the sacred wagon from which all things, past, present and future, may be viewed. Raed Waen is a ceremonial act, in which the actual casting takes place and, although associated with the runes, it can be applied equally to the Greek and Celtic alphabets. When performing Raed Waen, the matter of geolocation is considered first. This is the orientation of the room or space outdoors at which the rune casting is to take place. Indoors, the axis of the room is the first thing to be determined. This is a line across the room or ground where the energies of the earth and heavens are at their optimal potency for rune casting. Determining this alignment is largely an intuitive matter, being a dynamic interaction between the prevailing local conditions and customary rules, but there are simple rules-of-thumb which can be used. In a building or room correctly oriented to the cardinal directions (i.e. with the walls facing the four directions of North, East, South and West), the axis should lie parallel to the longer wall and divide the floor space in two. Indoors, the *shoat* (the area in which the runes will be cast) should be made towards the east in daylight, and to the west during darkness. Thus the cast of the runes will be at right angles to the 'presence', the place of the gods in the north, which will lie to the left of the runemaster in daytime, and to the right at night. The cast is always undertaken at right angles to the presence, as its outcome is a matter of human, and not divine, concern. Out of doors, the shoat should be towards the sun. According to the East Anglian tradition, the direction of terrestrial energy flow is always towards the sun. Ideally, the work should be aligned towards the sun herself. This direction can be determined by direct observation of the sun, or by the use of a magnetic compass.

The position of the shoat area along this axis can be determined now. This is often a white cloth whose dimensions are defined by the rune caster's own length from feet to fingertips at full stretch above the head, and in width the distance between the outstretched arms. (The shoat is the body space of the runecaster in space and time.) Indoors, it is

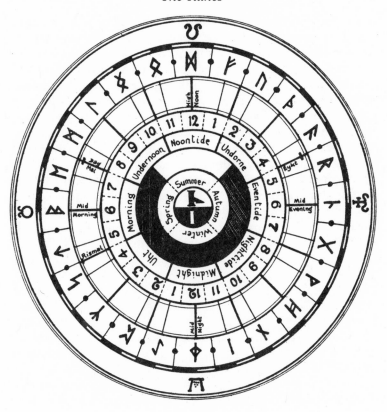

Fig. 32. Wheel of time, showing time correspondences in the Elder Futhark.

arranged so that the 'Nowl' or 'navel' point, the exact centre of the shoat, is located one third of the way along the axis. The wall in front of the runecaster is known as the 'positive' wall, and that behind, the 'negative'. Various ceremonial objects are arranged on the cloth prior to the rune casting. These are the 'stol', a cushion for the runecaster to sit upon. This is placed at the negative end. A small ceremonially embroidered white cloth may be laid at the opposite end. On this is laid a personal talisman. At each of the four corners are located consecrated symbols of the four elements. When the paraphernalia have been located correctly, the runecaster goes through appropriate personal mental cleansings before charging the runes by symbolically passing the stones through each of the elements in turn. Finally, the runes are cast along the shoat towards the positive end. There are several ways of casting the runes, and there is a considerable literature on runic divination. One popular method is to take a handful from the bag and to throw them along the shoat. Then, the runecaster examines what has turned up, literally, as only those runestones which fall face up are taken into account. When the Elder Futhark runes are used, these have 'reversed meanings'. If they appear inverted, then the meaning, generally, is reversed. This applies also to the Anglo-Saxon 29-rune system. But with the 33 runes of the Northumbrian system, or the 38 runes of the extended system, there is only one reading for each rune. The combinations of possibilities and complex interpretations make the runes an ideal system of divination or problem-solving.

4
The Celtic Oghams and Bardic Alphabet

Ogham is the name given to the ancient bardic alphabet used in Ireland and the western parts of ancient Britain. It is possible that the script dates back as early as 2200 BCE, although this is by no means certain. This dating is based upon the markings on some small chalk slabs found by Alexander Keiller during excavations at Windmill Hill in southern England. Seventeen of these inscribed pieces of chalk were unearthed, and the scratches on them have been interpreted as an early form of ogham. But some academics do not accept this. The ogham expert, Professor Brendan O'Hehir of the University of Berkeley, California, believes that the earliest dateable ogham inscriptions come from around the second century CE. Whatever their origin, there are several hundred known ancient ogham inscriptions, on rock faces, stones, crosses, portable artefacts and in manuscripts. In the 1940s, R. A. S. Macalister published 385 known inscriptions from the British Isles. Most are in Ireland (82 per cent, with 52 per cent of them from County Cork and County Kerry). The majority of the others are in Scotland and Wales, whilst a few are known from England, and mainland Europe. Although most of the ancient surviving inscriptions are on memorials, just giving names, it is clear that the ogham alphabet also had a magical element. But when the Roman alphabet and the runes were introduced into Ireland, they took over the function of memorial writing, and the use of ogham was marginalized. There are monuments upon which both ogham and Roman letters co-exist, but once the Roman alphabet was established, the use of ogham became restricted to the secret and magical realms, where it remains today.

The mystical basis of the oghams is in the trees. The fifteenth-century manuscript known as *The Book of Ballymote*, which is the main source of information on traditional ogham, recounts the origin of the Irish oghams, the 'Ogaim na nGadhel'. In the question-and-answer method typical of customary teaching it asks:

> *From whence, what time, and what person, and from what cause did the ogham spring?* [It answers,] *The place is Hybernia's Isle, which we Scots inhabit; in the time of Breass, the son of Elathan, then king of all Ireland. The person was Ogma, MacElathan, the son of Dealbadh, brother to Breass; for Breass, Ogma and Dealbadh were three sons of Elathan, who was the son of Dealbath.*

The originator was thus one of three brothers, like the Norse Odin with his brothers Vili and Vé reproducing the triadic order of things so common in the Northern Tradition. *The Book of Ballymote* continues:

> *'Ogma, being a man much skilled in dialects and in poetry, it was he who invented ogham, its object being for signs of secret speech known only to the learned, and designed to be kept from the vulgar and poor of the nation . . . It is called ogham, from the inventor, Ogma. The derivation is ogham, from "ghuaim", that is the "guaim" or wisdom through which the bards were enabled to compose; for by its branches the Irish Bards sounded their verses. "Soim" was the first thing written in ogham. On a Birch it was written, and given to Lugh, the son of Etlem . . .'*

In the Irish language spoken today, the word 'ogham' means the ancient alphabet. But the related word 'oghum' in the Gaelic language refers to the occult sciences. The Irish name for the month of June, which contains the summer solstice, is Ogmhios, for the name Ogma is associated with an old Celtic sun god.

It is clear that in former times the knowledge of the oghams was seen as identical with the knowledge that a ruler needed to govern his or her subjects. For example, MacLonan, the chief bard of Ireland, who died in the year 918, wrote:

Cormac of Cashel and his champions,
Munster is his, may he enjoy it long;
Around the King of Raith Bicli are cultivated
The letters and the trees

Ogham is unlike any other European or Near Eastern alphabet. Instead of having separate characters, the symbols of ogham are arranged along a line. This is the 'principal ridge' or 'stem line', which is known as the 'druim'. The characters are all in contact with this line, being scribed above, below or through it. Conventionally, ogham was usually written vertically, from below to above. When written horizontally, as on some ancient artefacts, the upper side of the druim is counted as the left-hand side, and beneath it, the right-hand side. Conceptually, then, the ogham script is written from left to right. When written on a standing stone, they are inscribed across the corner between flat surfaces, known as the arris. On stone, the vowels are formed by indentations or dots.

Like other alphabets, the oghams are arranged in a specific character order. But the actual arrangement is like no other. Today, there are five basic divisions, each with five characters, making 25 in all, but originally there appear to have been only four divisions, making 20 characters. This is apparent in *The Book of Ballymote*, which asks, 'How and what are the divisions of ogham? Four: B and her five; H and her five; M and her five; and A, her five.' The fifth division appears to be a later edition to the ogham row, bringing in diphthongs. *The Book of Ballymote* explains the basic form and derivation of the oghams:

From whence come the figures and namesakes in the explanation of B, L and N ogham? From the branches and limbs of the Oak Tree: they formed ideas which they expressed in sounds, that is, as the stalk of the bush is its noblest part, from them they formed the seven chief figures as vowels, thus: A, O, U, E, I, EA, OI . . . and they formed three others, which they added to these as helpers, formed on different sides of the line, thus: UI, IA, AE . . . The branches of the wood give figures for the branches and veins of ogham, chief of all. The tribe of B from Birch, and the daughter, that is the Ash of the wood, is chief; and of

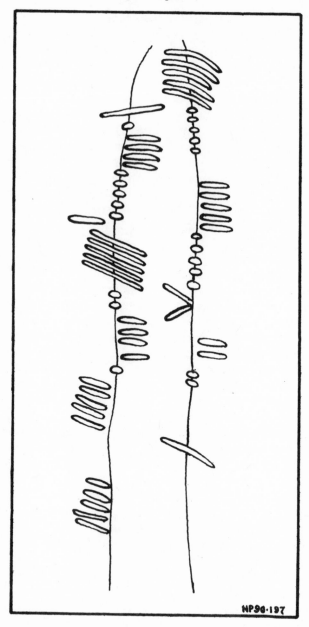

Fig. 33. A typical Ogham inscription: at Kilmakedar, County Kerry, Ireland.

*them the first alphabet was formed; of L, from Luis, the
Quicken Tree of the wood; F from Fearn, the Alder, good
for shields; S from Sail, a Willow from the wood; N in
ogham from Nin, the Ash for spears; H from Huath,
Whitethorn, a crooked tree or bush, because of her thorns;
D from Dur, the Oak of Fate from the wood; T from Tine,
Cypress, or from the Elder Tree; C from Coll, the Hazel of
the wood; Q from Quert, Apple, Aspen or Mountain Ash;
M from Mediu, the Vine, branching finely; G from Gort,
Ivy towering; NG from Ngetal or Gilcach, a Reed: ST or Z
from Draighean, Blackthorn; R, Graif [not explained
here]; A from Ailm, Fir; O from On, the Broom or Furze;
U from Up, Heath; E from Edadh, trembling Aspen; I from
Ida or Ioda, the Yew tree; EA, Eabhadh, the Aspen; OI,
Oir, the Spindle Tree; UI, Uinlleann, Honeysuckle; IO,
Ifin, the Gooseberry; AE, Amancholl, the Witch Hazel;
Pine Ogham, that is the divine Pine from the wood, from
whence are drawn the four 'Ifins', or Vineyard, thus #, per
alios, the name of that branch.*

Today, Tinne is generally accepted by practitioners of ogham
to be the holly, and not the cypress. However, in Irish, the
name of the holly tree is Craobh Chuilinn, giving a letter-name
of Cuileann. Also, in the Gaelic alphabet, where it is the 16th
and penultimate character, it has an obvious and direct
meaning, *Teine*, which in Gaelic means fire.

The most widely accepted modern interpretations of the
ogham characteristics are those described by the seventeenth-
century Irish bard Roderick O'Flaherty in his book *Ogygia*. His
information came, he claimed, from Duald MacFirbis, the clan
bard of the O'Briens. Some ogham scholars, like R.A.S.
Macalister, have claimed that the ascriptions of the ogham
characters given to them by O'Flaherty and others were late
artificialities having little bearing on the 'original' meanings. Of
course, this is important to those scholars who attempt to
determine the earliest meanings of alphabets. But, even if this
is a correct view (and there is no way of telling if it is), then it
still does not negate the use of ogham characters for divination
at the present day. We should not fall into the trap of
imagining that the older a system is, then the more 'pure' it
must be. This is fundamentalism, the belief that the modern

world is but a degenerate reflection of a former golden age. Everything must evolve from age to age, keeping itself in tune with the spirit of the age, otherwise it becomes useless and obsolete, and is lost. Although we study the past, we should remember that it is the repository of errors as well as truths, and enlightened people of the present day can make a contribution to the understanding of divination through alphabets as well as many a practitioner of former times.

O'Flaherty listed the ogham characters with their names as: B, Boibel; L, Loth; F (V), Forann; N, Neiagadon; S, Salia; H, Uiria; D, Daibhaith; T, Teilmon; C, Caoi; CC, Cailep; M, Moiria; G, Gath; Ng, Ngoimar; Y, Idra;; R, Riuben; A, Acab; O, Ose; U, Ura; E, Esu; I, Jaichim. Two versions of this alphabet are given by Lewis Spence in his book *The Mysteries of Britain* (1928), where alternative written characters are given. Spence's alphabets are not ogham at all, but Bobileth and Beth-Luis-Nion, which appear to be medieval magical alphabets based upon the old Celtic letter order.

According to the thought of the time, the oghams were seen as relics of ancient Druidism which had been transmitted orally by the bards down to the time of O'Flaherty. In later years, with the adoption of Christianity and the associated Roman alphabet, ogham had been used only for divination and not for writing. This is corroborated in modern Irish, whose words for people who deal with writing are all based on the root rún-, such as 'rúnaí', a secretary and 'rúncléiréac' (rune-clerk), a confidential secretary. The root rún- means a rune, the writing used in Norse-founded Dublin a thousand years ago. Even by then, the oghams were no longer used for everyday writing.

As used today in magic and divination, the standard names of the letters in the ogham alphabet, like those of the Gaelic alphabet, are based upon archaic tree names. In modern usage, the *first* tree letter of the ogham alphabet is the birch, (*Betula pendula*). Its name is Beth, which in modern Irish is Beith (pronounced 'Be'), and in Welsh, Bedw. Its phonetic equivalent is 'B'. Beth corresponds with the second letter of the Gaelic alphabet, Beath, which, like its ogham counterpart, denotes the white tree of purification sacred to the Great Mother Goddess. In every way, the birch is a pioneer tree. It was the first tree to recolonize the treeless wastes left after the

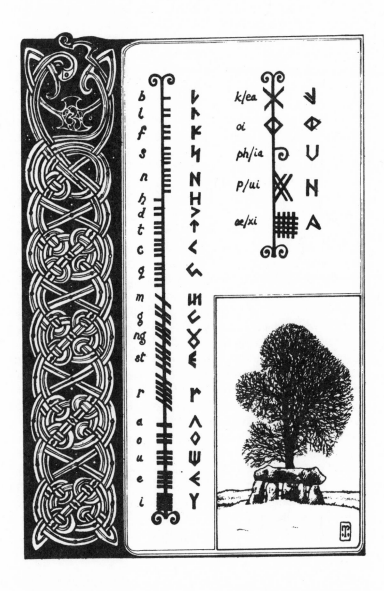

Fig. 34. The standard Irish Ogham characters, compared with their Welsh Coelbren counterparts.

retreat of the glaciers at the end of the last Ice Age. Each year, it is the first deciduous woodland tree to put out leaves in springtime. In Scandinavian country lore, the appearance of the first birch leaves marks the time for farmers to begin sowing their spring wheat. To the Irish ogham tradition, a birch tree provided the first wood upon which an ogham word was inscribed. Accordingly, it is classed as the first peasant tree, with the sacred colour of white.

Beth is one of the month oghams, of which there are 13. This 13-month year is a relic of the old way of reckoning time according to the phases of the moon, later fixed into a year defined by the solar phenomena of the solstices. The Beth moon begins on 24 December in the modern calendar and runs until 20 January. This fixes its beginning as just after the modern winter solstice, on a former midwinter's day, a time of purification and renewal. In Celtic symbolism, hats made of birch are associated with the dead. This is a very ancient tradition. When the sixth-century BCE burial mound of a Celtic lord at Hochdorf, near Stuttgart in south-western Germany, was excavated, a wonderfully worked conical hat of birch bark was found on the head of the buried man. The old English ballad 'The Wife of Usher's Well' also refers to the birchen hats of her three dead sons.

Esoteric Irish numerology ascribes the number five to the letter Beth. One of these numerical systems ascribes number equivalents to 17 ogham characters. Another, referred to in the system known as Ogham Consaine, an ogham alphabet which has only consonants and no vowels, gives 12 of the 13 numbers. Other correspondences of Beth are the birch colour, ban (white) and the bird-ogham correspondence, besan, the pheasant, 'the best bird that flies'. Symbolically and magically the birch and its corresponding ogham character Beth serve to protect one against all harm, physical and spiritual. It allows bad things to be dealt with and cleared away so that a new beginning can take place, unhindered by left-overs, on-lays and unfinished business.

The second ogham character is Luis, whose phonetic equivalent is 'L'. It is the rowan or quickbeam tree, (*Sorbus acuparia*, the modern Irish, *caorthann*, the Welsh, *criafol*). Traditionally, this tree, which also may be called the mountain ash, quicken and 'tree of life', is a magical plant. It is the second peasant tree, a tree of hedgerows and woodland. This ogham corresponds with the magical ninth letter of the Gaelic alphabet, which is also called Luis. The ogham character serves to protect its user against psychic attack and to develop the individual's powers of perception and prediction. In a divination, it can warn that one is subject to interference on the psychic level, but also indicates that, if one takes the appropriate precautions, one will not be harmed by the experience. In country tradition, when planted outside the front door of a house, rowan is believed to ward off harmful spirits, energies and onlays. According to a traditional Scottish rhyme:

Rowan tree and red threid
Gar the witches tyne their speed.

Translated into standard English, this is:
Rowan tree and red thread
Make the witches lose their speed.

In this post-medieval rhyme, the word 'witches' refers to all harmful psychic forces, and not to ancient Pagan practice, of which it is a part, or the modern religion of Wicca. In former times, sacred groves of rowan existed at places of sanctity as magically protective and oracular trees. One notable rowan grove grew on the Baltic sacred island of Rügen, and as late as 1777, in his *Flora Scotica*, John Lightfoot noted that this tree was prevalent in the vicinity of stone circles in Scotland. Another magical attribute is in the switches or whips of rowan wood that horsemen used to subdue 'bewitched' horses. Rowan was also considered to have an affinity for metals, and was used for metal dowsing.

In bird-ogham, Luis is *lachu*, the duck, which swims on land in this season of floods. In Celtic paganism, the duck was the sacred bird of river goddesses. An image of Sequana, goddess of the River Seine in France, depicts her riding in a duck-headed barge, and the duck appears in several ancient Irish manuscripts, upon crosses and monuments. In former times, rowan-berry jelly was eaten with duck.

Luis's esoteric number correspondence is 14. Its Celtic tree month covers the part of the year from 21 January until 17

February. In this period is the religious festival of the coming spring, the festival of Imbolc, Brigantia or Candlemas, 1–2 February. This festival marks the 'quickening of the year', when the days are noticeably longer after the darkness of winter, and the promise of springtime becomes a possibility. One of its colour correspondences is 'liath', grey, that in-between colour containing white and black, the mixing of light and darkness, echoing the grey skies of this part of the year. But *The Book of Ballymote* describes Luis's poetic name as 'Delight of the eye, that is Luisiu'. This colour is flame, the modern Irish *luisne*, a red glare, with the additional meaning of a sheen or lustre. Magically, this is a very powerful character, used for the development of the power of second sight and protection against enchantment.

The third ogham letter is Fearn, with the phonetic rendering of 'F'. This character corresponds withe the alder tree, (*Alnus glutinosa*, the modern Irish *fearnóg* and the Welsh *gwernen*. It parallels directly with Fearn, the sixth letter of the Gaelic alphabet, whose meaning is also the alder tree. But in the Gaelic alphabet, the letter 'R', Ruis, is also associated with this tree. In British mythology, the alder is the sacred tree of the Celtic god-king Bran, whose mummified oracular head was carried across Britain and finally buried at Bryn Gwyn – the sacred White Mount of Trinovantium, now occupied by the Norman White Tower of the Tower of London. Robert Graves asserted that the 'singing head' of Bran was the topmost branch – the 'head' – of the alder tree. This 'head' can be seen in winter as, after leaf fall, the Alder retains its black cones and next year's unopened catkins, giving the tree a purple-tinged, dense crown.

Fearn is connected with the spirit known as the 'Fear Dearg' (anglicized as Far Darrig), the 'Red Man' (the Irish word *fear* or *fir* means a man). According to legend, these beings are reputed to help human beings to escape from the Otherworld. But, like many Irish sprites, the Fear Dearg is also a prankster, and in wintertime will ask permission to warm hmself by the fire. Bad luck will dog anyone foolhardy enough to refuse. Fearn's esoteric number correspondence is eight, which is the Celtic number of man, in a human rather than a gender sense. This letter is also related to the word *fearsad*, which can mean a shaft, an axle, the ulna bone or a narrow sea passage. In its first meaning as a shaft, it refers to the alder piles which were used traditionally all over Europe for the foundations of buildings in wetlands. This use is universal, as alder wood is the best timber for this purpose. The foundations of the cities of Venice and Rotterdam, cathedrals like Winchester, water-mills and the island crannogs of Scotland and Ireland were built upon piles of alder. On a smaller scale, the wood was used for making milk pans and other containers used in the dairy, and clogs for the feet. This tree is connected also with sword-making. The smiths of this craft prized alder wood for giving the best charcoal for metal smelting, and in later times it was prized for gunpowder production. *The Song of the Forest Trees* describes alder as 'The very battle-witch of all woods, the tree that is hottest in the fight'. This second chieftain tree of Irish tradition has the corresponding colour of *flann*, blood-red or crimson. This is because when an alder tree is cut down, its sap turns red like blood. Like the yew, the alder is a 'bleeding tree'. Because of this, to cut down a sacred alder tree was held to be a sacrilege which would bring fire upon one's dwelling in retribution. In pre-industrial times, the alder was used for dyeing fabrics. The tree was prized for the three dyes which could be prepared from different parts: red from the bark, brown from the twigs and green from the flowers. These dyes were the bases for the ancient coloured plaid patterns of Scotland which evolved into the modern tartans we know today.

Fearn is a tree of fire used to free the earth from water. In its use as piles in traditional building, alder symbolically bridges the space between the lower world in the earth and the upper world of the air. Symbolically, its month parallels this by bridging the dark and light halves of the year, for Fearn rules the Celtic month which runs from 18 March until 14 April. The alder's first blooming is around the beginning of this month which includes the vernal equinox. In bird ogham, its correspondence is *faelinn*, the seagull. The gull's calls were imitated by sea-witches in their magical summoning of the wind, and similarly, alder can be used for making magic whistles used in whistling up the wind. Magically, this character is best used for personal protection in conflicts, and for freeing oneself from magical binding of any kind.

The next tree-letter is Saille, phonetically, 'S'. It is the Sally tree or white willow, (*Salix alba*, in modern Irish, *sáileach*, the Welsh *helygen*). This tree, whose narrow crown is silvery-grey in colour is associated with the growth of the lunar power, rooting in water. The character corresponds with the 15th letter of the Scots Gaelic alphabet, Suil. In Irish, its name is allied with the word *saill*, which means 'fat', referring to its month, which begins on 15 April and ends on 12 May. It includes the May Day festival of Lá Bealtane. Its bird-ogham character is *seg*, the hawk, mentioned in one of Amergin's poems referring to this month: 'I am a hawk on a cliff'. Saille is an ogham of linking, a watery symbolism which brings itself into harmony with the flow of events, most notably the phases of the moon. It gives indications of the states of the tides, and, in traditional medicine, provided protection against the diseases of dampness. In divination, its power is greater at night than in daytime, except when the moon is visible during the day. Its power fluctuates with the cycle of the moon's phases. The pliable, flexible nature of the osiers made it the preferred wood for basket-making. In building it was also used as a binding-material in thatch and wattle-and-daub walling. Esoterically, this eminent flexibility demonstrates Saille's harmonious amenability to the conditions to which it is subjected. The willow is the third peasant tree, whose colour is 'sodath', 'fine' or 'bright'. *The Song of the Forest Trees*: 'Burn not the willow, a tree sacred to poets'. Numerically, its equivalent is 16.

Nuin or Nion is the fifth letter of the oghams. It has the phonetic value of 'N'. Its tree is the first chieftain tree, the grey and the black ash, (*Fraxinus excelsior*). This is the Welsh, *onnen*, and the modern Irish, *fuinnseog*. This ogham corresponds with the 11th character of the Scots Gaelic alphabet, Nuin, whose meaning is identical. Nion is the third month of the Celtic calendar, which extends from 18 February until 17 March, a time when the budding of trees and the fresh growth of herbs becomes apparent. The ash is the tree of rebirth, linking that which is above with that which is below, the worlds of the spirit and of matter. It is the passage between the inner world and the outer world. In the Norse tradition, it is beneath the sacred ash tree Yggdrassil, the cosmic axis linking the underworld with the middle and upper worlds, that the three

Norns weave the fates of humans. The bunches of fruits that resemble keys signify the power to unlock the future. But, just as the seeds in these keys germinate only in the second year after falling to the ground, unlocking of the future may take a considerable time. The colour associated with Nion is *necht*, 'clear', and its esoteric numerical equivalent is 13. In bird-ogham, it is *naescu*, the snipe.

The sixth character of the ogham alphabet is Huath, sometimes rendered as Uath. It has the phonetic value of 'H'. Huath is the Goddess's tree of sexuality, the whitethorn or hawthorn, (*Crataegus monogyna*, in modern Irish, *sceach gheal*, the Welsh, *ysbyddaden* or *draenenwen*). Another name for it is the May tree, and Huath's month runs from the middle of the merry month of May, 13 May until 9 June. The ogham's name means 'terrible', referring to the 'hag' or destroying aspect of the Threefold Goddess. Traditionally, it is unlucky to bring May blossom into the house. It was on a thorn bush at Bosworth Field that the crown of the slain king Richard III was found in 1485. In folk tradition, this tree is considered a 'fairy' tree, and hence unlucky to anyone who is foolhardy enough to tamper with one. In Ireland, it was believed universally that the destruction of such a sacred thorn tree or *sceog* would bring bad luck to the individual who perpetrated the act. The most recent example of this was the obliteration of such a tree to make way for the ill-fated DeLorean car factory in Northern Ireland. Local people ascribed the disastrous collapse of the business to the ill luck attending the removal of this holy tree. The death of one's children or livestock and the loss of all one's money is the traditional fate of one cavalier enough to destroy a sacred thorn. Vaughan Cornish's work, *Sacred Thorn Trees in the British Isles* documents these sacred May trees, many of which are, sadly, now destroyed. But it is still customary, as part of the reverence due the holy thorn, to tie rags to their branches as votive offerings to the Goddess. In Christian times, this rite became assimilated into the cult of St Monica, whose name superseded that of the Pagan goddess of the thorns. Magically, Huath is the ogham of protection against all ills, invoking the power of the Otherworld. The bird ogham correspondence of Huath is *hadaig*, the night-crow. It is classed as the fourth peasant tree whose colour is *huath*, 'terrible' or more modernly, purple, the forbidden colour of the hag aspect of the Goddess. As a daunting ogham of the Otherworld, esoterically it has no numerical value, and no correspondence in the Gaelic alphabet.

Duir, the common or pedunculate oak, (*Quercus robur*, the modern Irish, *dair* and the Welsh *derwen*), is the seventh sacred tree of the oghams. This ogham corresponds directly with the fourth letter of the Gaelic alphabet, Doir. It has the phonetic value of 'D'. All through the European spiritual tradition, the oak is considered to be the most powerful tree, being sacred to the major European sky-god who goes by the names of Zeus, Jupiter, Taranis, the Dagda, Perkunas, Thunor and Thor, among others. In this aspect, Dur is related to the Irish words *dúr*, meaning hard, unyielding, durable, and *dúranta*, mysterious. Duir is the third noble or chieftain tree, whose colour is *dubh*, black. In Druidic times, the oak was grown in sacred groves. To the Druids, every part of the oak was sacred, there being ritual uses for its boughs, twigs, bark, leaves and acorns. Its sacred month, which extends from 10 June to 7 July, incorporates the summer solstice, the high point of the year, known esoterically as 'the door of the year'. Appropriately, the name *Duir* is cognate with other words for 'door' in various European languages: the Irish *doras*, the English 'door', the Greek *thura*, the German *Tür*, etc. The Nordic equivalent of Duir, the rune Dag, has the same meanings. Duir marks the central point of the summer, the cross-over point at which the longest day also marks the beginning of the shortening of the light and the ultimate onset of autumn and winter. It marks one of the two major turning-points of the year, the other being the winter solstice. The sacrifice of the Oak King at midsummer, later assimilated into the Christian calendar as the day of the similarly executed St John the Baptist, is commemorated by this letter. According to tradition, the Oak King was burned alive on the summer solstice, his place being taken by the Holly King. This ogham's bird is *droen*, the wren, smallest of the birds indigenous to northern Europe, one of the most sacred birds of the ancient Druids. Magically, this important ogham signifies strength. It can be used as a doorway to inner experiences. Traditionally, it is the ogham that enables one to see the invisible, and to become invisible; to allow entry of those who should enter and to exclude those who should not. In a magical way, it can also refer to things of great strength that are hidden from view at present, like the bog oaks buried beneath the peat in Ireland and the fens of East Anglia. Duir's Ogham Consaine numerical correspondence is 12.

The eighth ogham letter, Tinne, has the phoentic value of 'T'. It is usually associated with the holly tree, (*Ilex aquifolium*), although *The Book of Ballymote* gives alternative ascriptions. There, the Cypress, (*Cupressus sp.*) or Rowan, (*Sorbus acuparia*), are mentioned. But rowan is identified with Luis, (*caorthann*), and most ogham users prefer to use the holly. But the modern Irish word for holly is *cuileann*, cognate with the Welsh, *celyn*. But, conversely, the letter's magical name is related to the Irish words tine, meaning fire, and *teann*, strong or bold. It is this fiery meaning which is ascribed to its counterpart in the Scots Gaelic alphabet, Teinne, the 16th letter. Magically, the character Tinne brings strength and power, but in a balanced manner. It has a strong male element, more specifically connected with fatherhood and the consequent ability for souls to be reborn. It is the ogham of unification. Tinne's bird ogham is *truith*, the starling, a bird which forms enormous flocks. The holly is the fifth peasant tree, whose colour is *temen*, a word interpreted as meaning grey-green or dark grey. Its esoteric consonantal number is 11.

The ninth tree letter is Coll, with the phonetic value of 'K' or a hard 'C'. It signifies the hazel tree, (*Corylus avellana*), the fourth chieftain tree. Its ancient name is the same in modern Irish, whilst in Welsh it is *collen*. In the Gaelic alphabet it is Caltuinn, the third letter, also corresponding with the hazel. Its month runs from 5 August until 1 September. In Bardic numerology, Coll is the magic number nine, 'by the power of three times three', related to the three of its Gaelic counterpart. According to country lore, the hazel fruits first after nine years' growth.

Hazel is associated with finding out things. The druidic heralds of pagan Ireland carried white hazel wands as symbols of office, representing their ability to use words. In Viking times, hazel poles were used to delimit the sacred enclosures known as the *hoslur*, or 'hazelled field' in which formal combat took place. Both in single combat, *holmganga*, and in full-scale formal battles between armies, the area for battle was distinguished from the normal world of everyday life by hazel posts which formed a magical boundary around it. In warfare, hazel was used as a magical shield. According to the ancient Irish legend of *The Ancient Dripping Hazel*, this magic tree dripped venom, and when made into a shield by Fionn MacCumhaill, poisonous gases emanating from it slew his enemies. Fionn's Shield is a poetic kenning for magical protection. It alludes to the optical illusion binding knots of Celtic interlace-patterns known as *luaithrindi* carried by Celtic warriors. It also means a satirical poem which carries a curse on the subject of the satire.

The medieval text known as *The Book of St Albans* tells of a magical technique for invisibility, which involves the use of a rod of hazel, one-and-a-half fathoms in length (9 feet), with a green hazel twig implanted in it. Before the recent use of metal wires virtually superseded it, the forked hazel twig was the traditional wand of the water diviner. Here, hazel was another meaning of 'finding out'. Its colour is *cron*, nut-brown, the same word in Irish as its bird ogham correspondence, *cron*, the crane.

Quert, the crab apple tree, (*Malus sylvestris*), is the tenth ogham, the final character of the second rubic. It has the phonetic value of 'Qu'. Quert is a magical name, as the profane name of the apple is *aball* in modern Irish, and *afal* in Welsh, the seventh peasant tree. It has no Gaelic correspondence. European symbolism tells of the apple as the tree of rebirth and eternal life. The Greek tradition tells of the Golden Apples of the Hesperides, the Norse speaks of the goddess Iduna and the apples of immortality, whilst Celtic tradition has the Isle of Avalon, to which King Arthur is taken after his last battle, to heal his wounds. Quert thus celebrates the eternity of life. The five strokes to the left of the stem of the ogham letter reflect the five-fold petals of the apple flower, the five receptacles for the seeds within the fruit itself. Unlike the cultivated species of apple, the crab apple bears thorns, making Quert a protective tree like the hawthorn and blackthorn. Quert's colour is given variously as apple-green and *quiar*, mouse-coloured. Its bird ogham bird is another version of brown, *querc*, the hen.

Muin or Min is the 11th tree of the oghams, with the phonetic value of 'M'. This ogham is usually ascribed to the grape vine (*Vitis alba*). However, in the Irish language, the vine is *finiúm*. Also, this plant is not indigenous to the British Isles, but equally it may have been introduced by the Celts from mainland Europe. However, in the Irish language, *muine* means a thicket of any thorny plant, so the correlation of this ogham with the vine may be a late connection. As a thorny thicket, it is nearer to a tree than a vine, for Muin is the fifth noble, or chieftain, tree. This meaning is ascribed to the tenth character of the Gaelic alphabet, Muin. The thicket-month incorporates the autumnal equinox, being current from 2 September until the 29th of that month. Its bird ogham is *mintan*, the titmouse, a bird of thickets, and Muin's colour is *mbracht*, variegated. Its number correspondence is six. Magically, it signifies the ability to range over a wide area and gather together those things that might be needed. Once gathered together, these things are assimilated, leading to inner development.

Gort is the 12th ogham character, with the phonetic value of 'G'. In the modern tree-based interpretation of the oghams, it represents the native vine, the Ivy (*Hedera helix*), most particularly in its flowering season. In Welsh, the name of this 'tree' is *eiddew, eadhnéan* in modern Irish. But the Irish word *gort* means a tilled field, not ivy. This corresponds almost exactly with the meaning in the Scots Gaelic alphabet for the letter G, the seventh letter, Gart, which signifies a garden or vineyard. As an ogham of the flowering season, its appearance in a divination indicates the second harvest, that of fruits, as its time correspondence, 30 September until 27 October, indicates. Because the name of this ogham is also related to the Irish *gorta*, which means hunger or famine, in an unfavourable position in a divination, Gort may be an indicator of scarcity, the failure of the tilled field to produce an adequate harvest. *Gorm*, blue, is the colour associated with Gort, and its bird is *géis*, the mute swan. Its esoteric number is ten, the number of completion of the cycle. Symbolically and magically, Gort represents the changes that are necessary for growth, and the requirement that all things be related to the Earth. Just as it is necessary to till the fields in order to reap a harvest later, so it is necessary to do the 'groundwork' in anything, and to remember that in all things we must think of Mother Earth. Although it grows upon other plants or on the walls of buildings, the ivy must remain rooted in the ground in order to survive. But it is a tree of transformation, starting as a small, weak, herb-like plant, which finally, after centuries of growth, becomes an enormously thick, woody, sepentine tree in its own right.

Ngetal is the 13th ogham. It has the phonetic equivalent of 'Ng'. Like the previous character, Ngetal's 'tree' is not a tree according to modern botanical definitions. It is the reed, *giolcach* in Irish, the Welsh *cawnen*. Ngetal has no corresponding letter in the Scots Gaelic alphabet. According to the bardic tree classification, the reed is the first of the kiln or shrub trees. It appears that the reed was classified as a tree because the scribes of ancient Ireland used the hard, resistant stems of the reed to make pens. The modern, scientifically based definition of what is and what is not a tree is relatively recent. As in many other areas of biology, the scientific definition differs from the traditional. In former times, any plant with woody stems, such as a reed or ivy was called a tree. The reed was also the material from which a sort of paper or papyrus, known to the Welsh scribes as *plagawd* was made. The reed was a traditional rod of measure, used to delimit sacred enclosures. In bardic numerology, it signifies the number 1. This ogham is equivalent phonetically to the Nordic rune Ing, which refers to the divinity Ing, whose sacred enclosure was delineated by the image of the god being carried around it. The traditional use of reeds was in enclosing space in covering the roof of the house with thatch, and the patterns of the rune Ing are used in thatching to this day. Another use was as a floor covering, especially in winter, when reeds served as insulation. Ngetal's month extends from 28 October until 24 November. Ngetal is the thus the ogham of Lá Samhain, the festival of the dead and the beginning of the new year in the Celtic calendar. Traditionally, reed for thatching and other weavings is cut in November. Its bird ogham correspondence is the goose, the bird that winters in the reedlands, its old Irish name being *ngéigh*.

The greatest power of Ngetal is as a preserver. As a pen, the reed preserves memory and knowledge, as a rod, it preserves measure, and as roofing it preserves the house. Above all else, Ngetal is the ogham of written communication, and thereby signifies conscious precision and the maintenance of order in chaos. The many uses of the reed in traditional society are reflected in its symbolic meanings As well as representing preservation, Ngetal signifies flexibility. That is the flexibility one must possess if one is to come to terms with the prevailing circumstances without sacrificing one's integrity. From its use in thatching and basket-making, and as the covert in which birds take refuge, it is the container and protector of things, just as writing is the container and protector of thought and culture. Its colour is *nglas*. This is another colour where traditional colour perception differs from modern colour descriptions. It is usually thought of as 'glass green', a clear yellowish-green.

The 14th ogham, with the phonetic value of 'St', is Straif. This is equivalent to the blackthorn or sloe tree, Prunus spinosa, the seventh peasant tree. The modern Irish name of this plant is *draíon* or *draighnean*, the Welsh *draenenwen*. Blackthorn is a shrub that produces suckers which can make a single plant the nucleus of an impenetrable thorny thicket. It is one of the major trees of magical power, a tree whose name has the connotations of 'punishment' and 'strife'. Staves made from its wood, carried by witches, warlocks and wizards, have always been renowned for their magical power. It is no coincidence that the Irish word for a wizard is *draoi*, and that of a druid, *draí*, both related to the mantic turning power of the sloe tree. On a physical level, the thorns of the blackthorn have proved a valuable defence in hedging; walking-sticks, shillelaghs and cudgels made from the wood are hard and durable. In magic and divination, Straif signifies power in both the visible and invisible worlds. It provides the strength one needs to resist and defeat adversity, and to control or ward off supernatural and paranormal powers. Straif is perhaps the most powerful ogham for overthrowing all resistance to one's will. The once sacred alcoholic beverage made from the blackthorn's fruit, sloe gin, is a reviver and protector on another level. In bird ogham, this character is *smolach*, the thrush, a bird reputed to impale snails on the thorns of the blackthorn bush. Its corresponding colours are *sorcha* – 'bright coloured' and purple-black, the colour of the blackthorn's fruit, the sloe.

141

The next ogham character, the 15th, is Ruis, with the phonetic value of 'R'. This is symbolized by the elder or bourtree, (*Sambucus nigra*), in modern Irish, *trom*, the Welsh *ysgaw*. In all of northern Europe, it is another tree of great mantic power, the second kiln or shrub tree. Ruis is cognate with the Irish word rúisc, which means a violent attack, a blow, or a throw, which expresses the protective but dangerous nature of this holy tree. The bark and flowers have healing properties, but the vapours emanating from plantations of elder are reputed to produce disease and even bring death to those who might linger nearby for too long. King William II (Rufus) was shot by an archer who lurked beneath an elder tree. East Anglian folk tradition warns against burning elder wood in the house, for bad luck will surely follow. But branches of the flowering elder were known to be good for keeping flies away from stables and byres. The elder is sacred to the dark aspect of the Mother Goddess, the Hag. In connection with this, Irish witches were reputed to ride upon elder sticks in place of the more common broomsticks, hurdles or straws.

Symbolically, Ruis signifies the three aspects of time present in the Threefold Goddess, the Fates, the Parcae, the Norns and the Weird Sisters. It represents the ever-present threefold aspects of existence: beginning, middle and end. As Ruis, it denotes the acceptance of all three aspects that is necessary if one is to lead a balanced life. It is an ogham of timelessness, or, rather, the unity of all time. Like the blackthorn, the elder is the origin of two other sacred alcoholic beverages which ward off the cold and illness: elderflower wine, brewed in June and July from the creamy-white flowers, and elderberry wine, fermented from the purply-black fruits that ripen in August and September. The colour ascribed to Ruis is *rocnat*, one of the many forms of red formerly recognized, described in tartan ogham as 'roebuck red'. Its corresponding bird is the rook.

Ailm, the elm tree, (*Ulmus minor*), is the 16th ogham, the first character of the fourth rubric, whose strokes are drawn right across the stem. Ailm is the third kiln or shrub tree, being most usually the so-called 'Cornish elm' (*Ulmus minor*, var. *stricta*), which grows in Cornwall, Devon and south-western Ireland. Unlike most elms, this is a wayside tree that is not found in woodland. Ailm has the phonetic value of 'A'. But elm, although clearly the correct ascription, is less commonly used. Because, in Irish, *ailm* means palm tree, which is not indigenous to northern Europe, the modern interpretation of this ogham, based on the work of Robert Graves and Colin Murray, is to associate it with the European silver fir, (*Abies alba*). This is the tallest European native tree, the *tannenbaum* of German-speaking peoples. However, this identification produces more problems than it solves. This fir tree is not indigenous to the British Isles, and the Irish word for a fir tree is *giúis*. However, in the Gaelic alphabet of Scotland, the first letter is the Fhailm, elm, cognate with this ogham character. Therefore, I am convinced that the appropriate ascription for ailm is the elm tree.

Although the 16th character in the Irish ogham order, this letter 'A' corresponds with the first characters of other important alphabets; the Aleph of Hebrew and Alpha of the Greek. It also corresponds with the extremely powerful 'god-rune' of the Runic Futhark. Ailm represents the god-like strength that one needs to rise above adversity, like the elm tree, to create a viewpoint from a higher level: the god-like capabilities of healing and perception of future trends. Regeneration, like the elm, can re-grow from new shoots sent out from the roots. When an elm is cut down, and seemingly dead, new stems grow from the still-living roots. Its corresponding colour is usually given as blue (but, according to Frank McGaugh, the tartan ogham researcher, it is black and white). Its corresponding bird is the lapwing.

On or Ohn is the 17th ogham, being the second vowel. It has the phonetic value of 'O'. Its corresponding 'tree', the gorse or furze (*Ulex europaeus*), is the seventh chieftain tree. The modern Irish word for the gorse is *aiteann*, cognate with the Welsh *eithin*. It corresponds with Oír, the 12th character of the Gaelic alphabet. This is a plant which can be found in flower in almost every month of the year. Thus it is an ogham of continuous fertility. It represents the carrying on of one's activities despite the surrounding conditions, in this aspect of 'standing out' against the background, as does the gorse bush. The word 'on' also means a stain or blemish. The gorse grows only in open country, not in woodlands. Magically, On represents the collecting together and retaining of one's strength through adversity. The collection and dispersal of the gorse seeds by ants, expresses the necessity for gathering small and separate things together. Ohn's liturgical colour is that of the pea-like gorse flowers: golden-yellow, saffron, dun or sand, according to various descriptions. Its corresponding bird is a sea-bird, the cormorant.

The third vowel, with the phonetic value of 'U', is Ur. This is the heather (*Erica sp.*), the 18th ogham and the last of the eight peasant trees. The meaning of this ogham is problematical, for its corresponding character in the Gaelic alphabet is Uhr, one of the two yew tree connections there. Another problem with this ogham is that the Irish word for this plant is *fraoch*, and the Welsh *grug*. Ur has the literal meaning of 'fresh', 'new', or 'moist', with the associated meaning of the morning dew. Magically, Ur brings this luck and freshness to any venture to which it is applied. It becomes the entrance-point to the inner worlds. In everyday folk tradition, the heather is considered to be an extremely lucky plant. To this day it is sold in the streets by gypsies as a luck bringer. Its traditional corresponding colour is purple, the colour of its flowers, associated with the dark goddess; a subsidiary colour, used in the tartan ogham system, is light green. Its corresponding bird is the skylark. The late British druid Colin Murray linked this ogham with the mistletoe as well as the heather. This he saw as a complementary aspect of the ogham, the healing of all and fresh fertilization on solid foundations.

Eadha is the 19th ogham letter, the fourth vowel, phonetically 'E'. This corresponds with the aspen or white poplar, (*Populus tremula*), the fifth kiln or shrub tree. Scots Gaelic calls this character Eubh, whose tree is also the aspen. The modern Irish name for this tree is *pobail ban*, and the Welsh, *aethnen*. The aspen is very hardy, living in a range of habitats from low-lying wetlands to exposed mountain ledges. It thus has the quality of hardy resistance to a variety of seemingly inhospitable conditions. Magically, it is seen as a preventer of death. It is a facilitator of the individual's curative powers, providing access to the real essence that underlies the sometimes misleading outer form. It is the spirit that animates the flesh. At its most powerful, it signifies the power of one's will overriding destiny, the possibility of the power of the mind overriding the inertia of matter, overcoming death. Its corresponding colour is silvery-white, though in the tartan ogham system, it is ascribed light yellow. Its bird is the whistling swan.

The 20th ogham, Ioho, Idho or Iubhar, has the phonetic equivalent of 'I'. Ioho is the yew tree (*Taxus baccata*). after the Scots pine, this sixth kiln or shrub tree is the other conifer tree indigenous to the British Isles. In modern Irish, the name of the yew tree is *eo*, in Welsh, *yw*. Its correspondence in Scots Gaelic is Iubhar, the second yew of that alphabet. This character has a direct connection with the rune Eoh of the Elder Futhark, which is the magic double-ended stave of death and life. Throughout Europe, the yew is the longest-lived tree, green throughout the year. Because of this continuity, it is a tree of eternal life, sacred to various divinities and saints of death and regeneration, for example, Hecate in the eastern Mediterranean. The ogham Ioho has the meaning of the unity of death and life, the rebirth which comes, figuratively or physically, as the result of death. Ancient Irish tradition called for the yew 'the coffin of the vine', for it was from yew wood that wine-barrels were made. The connection of the yew with the bow has already been mentioned in the previous chapter. European yew-magic is concerned with the mysteries of life and death: Ioho expresses those qualities. It represents the magical staff or sliver of yew, cut at the appropriate hour, which guards against all evil. Shakespeare's *Macbeth* tells of the '. . . slips of Yew, sliver'd in the Moon's eclipse' which is part of this tradition. As a time marker, it signifies the last day of the year. Again, this expresses the dual nature of the ending and beginning being present at the same time. Its colour is dark greenish brown, the colour of the tree's leaves, although the tartan ogham correspondence is given as 'royal scarlet' and 'blood red', the colour of the under-bark and resin. The corresponding bird of Ioho is the eaglet.

Ioho is the last vowel of the conventional rubric of the ogham script. It has the phonetic value of 'I'. The last five characters are diphthongs, and in modern usage, they can be ascribed different meanings. Their magical correspondences are less well established than those of the first 20 characters. The first of these last five letters is sometimes known as Koad, with the phonetic value of 'K', but in some other interpretations it is the diphthong 'Ea', whose equivalent is that of the Eadha, the Aspen tree (*Populus tremula*). But, as 'Ea', the first of this unconventional rubric can signify Earth, corresponding with the Anglo-Saxon rune 'Ear', which means 'the grave'. It has the bardic number of 13, the number of Death in the Tarot, and the yew-rune, 'Eoh' is also associated with death.

Colin Murray saw this ogham as Koad, which signifies the unity of all eight festivals of the traditional year. Here it is described as the sacred grove, the location in which all things, hitherto separate, become connected together. At such a point, all things become clear. The associated colours of Koad are all the 'forty shades of green', described in 'tartan ogham' as 'light green and speckled'.

Oi or Oir has the phonetic value of 'Oi'. As Oi, it is the gooseberry bush, (*Ribes uva-crispa*). This plant is a cultivated species, and it is probable that the Gooseberry is not indigenous to the British Isles. The Welsh word for this fruit bush is a name related to Oir, *eirinen fair*, but in the Irish language, it is *spíonán*. During the 1970s, in his teachings to the druidic 'Golden Section Order' however, Colin Murray sometimes called this ogham 'Tharan', with the phonetic value of 'Th', which would relate it to the thorn oghams, Huath and Straif. This is associated with the spindle tree, (*Euonymus europaeus*), the sacred tree of the central point, as with the rune Gar. Traditionally, as Oi, this ogham is associated with childbirth, being used magically to ease the passage of the baby from the womb into the world. Its colour is usually white, although in his tartan ogham correspondences, Frank McGaugh sees it as red, the colour of the spindle tree's fruits.

The 23rd ogham tree is Ui or Uinllean, which has the phonetic value of 'Ui'. According to *The Book of Ballymote*, this ogham is associated with the honeysuckle (*Lonicera*). However, modern ogham users connect it with the beech tree (*Fagus sylvatica*), a chieftain tree. Sometimes this ogham is rendered as 'Phagos', with the phonetic equivalent of 'Ph' or 'F'. The European beech is a large tree which flowers in May, and produces its nuts in October. Thus it marks the period between the festivals of Beltane and Samhain (1 May and 1 November), the markers of the summer half of the year in the Celtic calendar. The name of this tree in modern Irish is *feá*, and the Welsh *ffawyddean*. *Feá* is a version of the name of the 'F' character in runes, 'Feoh'. Whatever it is called, the magical characteristic of this character is hardness and resistance, the solidity of knowledge and tried-and-tested actions. It refers to the solidity of ancient wisdom, the cultural or physical foundation which must be in place before any constructions can be made, either in the physical or the figurative meaning. Its colour is tawny, (the 'light roebuck' of tartan ogham), the colour of the leaves of the copper beech.

Pethbol is the 24th ogham character, with the phonetic value of 'P'. Pethbol is equivalent to the guelder rose or snowball tree, (*Viburnum opulus*), a close relative of the wayfaring tree, which does not grow in Ireland. Like its runic counterpart, it is a character of mystery, about which little is commonly known. Peith has been connected with the rune Peorth, with the meaning of 'a lively tune', meaning the dance of life. Colin Murray saw it as a special step which leads into the labyrinth which is inner knowledge. This links it with the mystic Crane Dance, performed upon labyrinths throughout Europe, and the crane-skin 'medicine bag' which ancient shamans used to hold their sacred power-objects. Its magical number correspondence is given as 3 or 5 in the Irish bardic mysteries, and its colour is that version of red now known as pink, after the pale, transparent red fruits of the tree, which are ripe in September and October.

The 25th ogham is given various names – Péine, Amancholl, Xi and Mór. Clearly this ogham is yet another contentious character. As the phonetic value of 'Ae', Amancholl, it has the ascription of the witch hazel, (*Hamamelis virginiana*). As an ancient ascription, this is problematical because the witch hazel is not indigenous to Europe, having been introduced from New England around the seventeenth century. Thus it is not possible that this tree is the original correspondence. As 'Ae', this ogham is also connected with the sacred grid of the four of eight 'ifins'. The tree of this ogham is the evergreen Scots pine,

(*Pinus sylvestris*, modern Irish *péine*, and the Welsh, *pinwyd-den*). With the yew, the Scots pine is the only other indigenous conifer tree. In esoteric lore, it is a tree which shows the way. In the countryside, it is a marker on the ancient trackways known as 'leys', where prominently visible clumps of Scots pine mark the path ahead. In the darkness, the pine is the tree of illumination, and, as the eight ifins composed of pine, Péine recalls the traditional technique of illumination employed in central Europe until the eighteenth century. This used a *kienspan*, a chip of resinous pinewood, lit at one end. Péine is thus the bringer of illumination, both on an intellectual and on a spiritual level. This connection with the illuminating fire is apparent also in the ceremonial burning of the sacred pine cone, the East Anglian 'Deal Apple' or the Irish *buarcín*. This coniferous fruit signifies the container of wisdom, the matrix which holds together the material world according to the universal laws of existence.

This ogham character has suffered more interpretation than most. As the 25th, it goes beyond the conventional 24-fold division of things customary in the Northern Tradition (as, for example, the 24 hours in the day, the 24 half-months of the year, the 24 characters in the Welsh bardic alphabet and the 24 runes of the Elder Futhark). Because of this, it is considered to be outside the conventions of the other 24 characters. In addition to its ascriptions as witch hazel or pine, this ogham has two further interpretations. They are 'Xi', spirit, and 'Mór', the sea, more general in descriptive terms. As Xi, this character is seen as blue-green (or sea green) in colour, whilst in tartan ogham it is 'black, variegated'.

CRYPTIC OGHAMS AND OTHER VARIANT FORMS

In its treatise on ogham, *The Book of Ballymote* states that there are 150 kinds of the script. Many of these are cryptic and poetic systems of the letters. They include Ogham Coll, in which the 'characters' are composed of symbols that resemble the Roman letter 'C'.

C – one C begins this Ogham fine.
CC – two C's right joined in O, you may combine in human speech set out with taste and show.

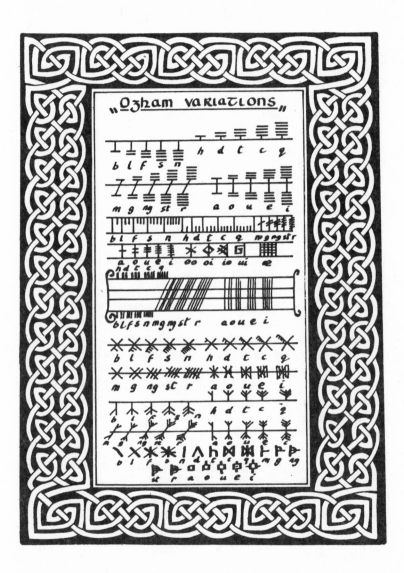

Fig. 35. Variations of the Ogham script.

CCC – three C's well formed give U in equal rows.
CCCC – four C's make fair seen by learning's eye.
CCCCC – five C's produce the ancient vowel I.
CC – two C's thus placed, the Irish Ifin Ogain.
ᑎ ᑎ – two C's in a groove, UA in power retain.
Ɔ – one C thus placed, AO in order takes.
ᑎ– One C turned upside down OI bespeaks.

Thus it lays down in the Book of Ballymote:

A	O	U	E	I	EA	O	UA	OI	AO
c	cc	ccc	cccc	ccccc	c	ɔc	ᑎᑎ	ᑎ	ɔ

The ogham of consonants, a version of consonantal ogham, 'Ogham Consaine', was another cryptic system, based on letter transference. *The Book of Ballymote*; 'Bh constitutes A; Ft rightly form U; Ng bravely make I; Ll of two L's make Ia; Pp in Ogham Io; Dl invariably O; Sc make E; Mm from their backs give Ea; Bb of two B's produce Ua; and Gg as directed'.

One very important esoteric aspect of ogham, mentioned in connection with the characters' descriptions, is the use of certain objects or places as descriptive of the letters. Bird ogham has already been dealt with. In Lin ogham for example, the place-names of pools of water are connected to their initials, for example, Banba (B), Luimneach (L), Febhal (F), Sinaind (S), Nearcnid (N), etc. Din ogham used terms connected with a hill to describe the letters, whilst Dean ogham used parts of the human anatomy. Ceall ogham (Battle ogham) gave each letter to a weapon or other piece of military equipment, for example B corresponded with 'beanchor', a horn. Numerous other objects and descriptions were used in ogham. Sciences, Christian saints, herbs, meats, etc. were used, and the principle is open to modern uses. One could imagine a modern country ogham, where B was represented by Belgium, L by Luxembourg, F by France, S by Spain, N the Netherlands, etc. The possibilities are unlimited. In former times, by such means, initiates could communiate with one another simply by mentioning the animals, birds, weapons, etc. that corresponded with the letters. Unsuspecting listeners could not understand what was being said. The scope in symbolic prose and poetry of this sort of esoteric correspondence is immense. Any piece of literature can contain hidden messages based upon the names of things and places.

Secret visual communication was also possible, if facilitated by Muc ogham (colour ogham), which ascribes a colour correspondence to each letter. In this system, B is expressed by 'ban' (white); N by 'necht' (clear), and Ng by 'ngias' (green), for example One thing that complicates the use of the Muc ogham today is that the colours used are different from those used in modern colour taxonomy. In former times, different cultures have had their own ways of interpreting colour which may not be the same as the modern way of looking at things. But if used properly, Muc ogham can give a richly symbolic possibility to artistic work, abstract patterns, ornament, heraldry, fabrics and clothing – all of which can possess hidden meanings. In recent years, Frank McGaugh has worked on a system of colour ogham which he relates to the tartans of the Scots clans. Because each of the ogham letters has a corresponding colour, he explains that the patterns of Scots tartan have colour sequences that spell out the clan name. The origin of the complex tartans we know today is relatively recent, most dating from the early part of the nineteenth century. It is unlikely, then, that the colour-ogham correspondences of tartan go back to ancient times. But it is quite possible that the nineteenth-century designers of tartans consciously incorporated a colour system into their designs. It may have been based on the old colour oghams, or it could have been a survival within the Gaelic tradition, parallel with the meanings of the Gaelic alphabet (see below).

In former times, there were all sorts of ingenious alterations made to the ogham alphabet in order to make it unintelligible to all but those who held the secret key. Some of these methods paralleled the cryptic runes in their technique. The method known as Sluag ogham increased the number of strokes threefold, making it into the ogham of the Multitudes. There was the Wall-Fern ogham; the Piercing ogham; Fionn's Tooth; Fionn's Window and Fionn's Shield, the last three forms of ogham being named after the legendary Irish giant Fionn MacCumhaill (Finn McCool). Fionn's oghams are based on position within a circular or square framework and, as such, can also be related to certain aspects of traditional cosmology, such as the directions, time of day, or spiritual states of being.

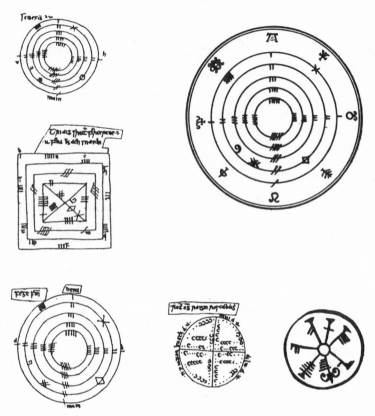

Fig. 36. Versions of Fionn's Wheel and Fionn's Shield.

Another cryptic ogham went by the name of 'the Adder in the Heath', a strange name for snakeless Ireland, indicating that this form of ogham may have originated in Great Britain or even on mainland Europe.

In another form, ogham was employed as a form of semaphore or sign language. This used the fingers to represent the characters. Fingers laid across the central stem of the nose to represent letters was called Sron ogham, whilst Coir ogham used the fingers against the foot or shinbone. Bar ogham was a hand sign language which used the fingers of one hand laid across the other one to make standard or cryptic ogham characters.

The magical application of ogham involved certain formulae whose nature is obscure. Irish ogham inscriptions have yielded several unusual formulae. An inscription of a magical nature is known from a stone at Glenfahan, where the letters LMCBDV are cut. Another inscription was found on an amber bead, described as a magical amulet from Ennis, taken to the British Museum. This inscription was MTBCML. This bead was used formerly as a cure for sore eyes, and to ensure safe births. In 1888, at a place called Biere, near Quedlinburg in Saxony, eastern Germany, a large number of limestone tablets was found by A. Rabe, a schoolmaster. There were 1200 specimens of inscriptions, including several in ogham. The carvings were dated as coming from the Merovingian period (seventh century). They had representations of hammers, axes, shields, swords, javelins, spearheads, arrows and bows, accompanied by inscriptions in unmistakable ogham. There were also other, more cryptic, symbols that might be tent runes and numerical oghams. In his *Studies in Irish Epigraphy*, R. A. S. MacAlister, the expert on oghams, commented that the discovery of these 'Biere stones' seemed to settle, once and for all, the use of ogham as a medium of magic.

A note on Tifinag

There is an alphabet which one may encounter in connection with the Celtic ogham alphabet which really has only been

Fig. 37. The Tifinag script.

associated with it in recent times. This is the alphabet known as Tifinag, which is said to originate in Libya. It has an alphabet composed mainly of dots or depressions with a few other characters which fit in with the mainstream of Phoenician-derived alphabets. However, the connection with the oghams is through the many highly contentious claims that have been made for the origin and meaning of rock carvings in North America. There is a school of thought which attributes many of these rough scribings to the ancient Celts, interpreting them in terms of consonantal ogham, ogham Consaine. Few of these marking, however, resemble the undoubted ogham inscriptions of the British Isles, being irregular and imprecise marks on the rock. Champions of the 'ancient American ogham theory' also interpret other makings, found with or separately from the linear scribings, as 'Tifinag', an obscure script said to be used in Libya in ancient times. The whole of this area is very obscure, and many of the published inscriptions bear little resemblance to either the ogham or Tifinag scripts.

THE BARDIC ALPHABETS

The degrees and roll of wood-knowledge,
The root of sciences, for the weaving of a song of praise.
HARRI AP RHYS GWILYM (1530)

The bardic tradition of Britain, often called druidism today, is of great antiquity and complexity. Within its mysteries are contained several systems of secret and magical writing. Llewellyn Sion of Llangewydd was the principal collector of information on the bardic alphabet known as 'coelbren' which we have today. He was born early in the sixteenth century, and, when old enough, became one of the disciples of Thomas Llewelyn of Rhegoes and of Meurig Davydd of Llanisan. Both of these men were eminent bards of the Glamorgan Chair. Under their tuition, Llewellyn Sion rose to eminence as a composer of elegant verse in the correct ancient Welsh canonical forms. Through his fame as a bard he became a wealthy man, selling transcripts of manuscripts. Fortunately, his work brought him into contact with eminent men who had collections of ancient Welsh manuscripts. It was from these that Llewllyn Sion was able to make copies, and thus to preserve much knowledge which otherwise might have been lost. These texts included ancient and rare books in the castle of Rhaglan, from the collection of Sir William Herbert, which later succumbed to arson during the English Civil War. In 1560, Llewellyn Sion presided in the Bardic Chair of Glamorgan, the seat of his teachers. As a man of great traditional learning, Sion wrote a book, entitled *Atgofion Gwybodau yr Hen Gymry* – a major treatise on ancient Welsh poetry, geneology, memorials, agriculture, law, medicine, handicrafts and chemistry. Unfortunately, the manuscript was sent to London for publication, during which process the author died at the age of 100. Inexplicably, on Sion's death, his great work was destroyed, an appalling loss.

As with the other major sacred and magical alphabets, the letters of coelbren are said to be derived from the basic structure of existence. As with the myth of the discovery of the runes, the origin of bardic letters is ascribed to mystic

Fig. 38. The name 'Brigantia' in the Gaelic alphabet, compared with the same name in Coelbren, Stave-Ogham and standard Ogham.

revelation. The origin of letters is seen as simultaneous with the creation of the universe, stemming from the name of god. The bardic tradition, preserved in the ancient Welsh texts, collected together as *Barddas*, relates:

> *When God pronounced his name, with the word sprang the light and the life, for previously, there was no life but God himself. And the way it was spoken was of God's direction. His name was pronounced, and with the utterance was the springing of light and vitality, and man, and every other living thing; that is to say, each and all sprang together.*

To the bards, the creation of all things was seen as a manifestation of a primal vibration – in Celtic Christian terms, the word of God. From the light, the most perfect manifestation of the divine, came the revelation of the concept of writing:

> *Menw Hen ap y Menwyd (Menw the Aged, son of Menwyd), beheld the springing of the light, and its form and appearance . . . in three columns; and in the rays of light, the vocalization – for one were the hearing and seeing, one in unison with the form and sound of life, and one unitedly with these three was power, which power was God the Father. And by seeing the form, and in it hearing the voice – not otherwise – he knew what form and appearance voice should have . . . And it was on hearing the sound of the voice, which had in it the kind and utterance of three notes, that he obtained the three letters, and knew the sign that was suitable to one and other of them. Thus he made in form and sign the Name of God, after the semblance of rays of light, and perceived that they were the figure and form and sign of life . . . It was from the understanding thus obtained in respect of this voice, that he was able to assimilate mutually every other voice as to kind, quality and reason, and could make a letter suitable to the utterance of every sound and voice. Thus were obtained the Cymraeg, and every other language.*

As in the Jewish tradition, the holy name of God, from which all things were held to emanate, was rarely uttered for respect and fear of the consequences. However:

> *It is considered presumptuous to utter this name in the hearing of any man in the world. Nevertheless, every thing calls him inwardly by this name – the sea and land, earth and air, and all the visibles and invisibles of the world, whether on the earth or in the sky – all the worlds of all the celestials and the terrestrials – every intellectual being and existence . . .*

The Welsh name of God was symbolized by the Awen, a sigil written as three lines radiating from above. This symbol is directly comparable to the Jewish tetragrammaton. Each of the three lines of the Awen have a specific meaning: 'Thus are they made', *Barddas* recounted:

> *the first of the signs is a small cutting or line inclining with the sun at eventide, thus /; the second is another cutting, in the form of a perpendicular, upright post, | ; and the third is a cutting of the same amount of inclination as the first, but in an opposite direction, that is, against the sun, thus\; and the three placed together, thus /|\.*

This symbolizes the threefold or tradic nature of all things. Curiously, this symbol is still used today, but in the guise of the 'broad arrow' that denotes British Government property. In its proper usage, it was the bardic symbol for wisdom, and hence is the sigil of modern Druidism.

The Awen also has an alternative alphabet form OIV, even closer to the concept of the tetragrammaton, but triadic in typical bardic fashion. According to tradition, the sense for O was given in the first column of light, the sense of I to the second or middle light column, and the sense of V to the third, making the word OIV. *Barddas* informs us that:

> *it was by means of this word that God declared his existence, life, knowledge, power, eternity and universality. And in the declaration was his love, that is coinstantaneously with it sprung like lightning all the universe into life and existence, co-vocally and co-jubilantly with the uttered Name of God, in one united song of exultation and joy – than all the worlds to the extremities of Annwn [the underworld].*

This is a concept identical with the 'mother' characters of the Hebrew alphabet, Aleph, Mem and Shin.

But, despite the lofty origin of this notation, three characters were inadequate for the everyday uses of record, literature and magic. A more comprehensive system of writing was required. The invention of writing is attributed to Einigan Gawr (Einigan or Einiged the Giant). After the death of his father, Huon, son of Alser, Einigan invented writing to preserve a memorial of what he did. This appears to have happened amongst the Celts of mainland Europe, as attested by the following from Llewellyn Sion: 'He came to his father's kindred in the Isle of Britain, and exhibited his art, and they adjuged him to be the wisest of the wise and called him Einigen Wyddon (Einigan the Wise)'. Because the first letters were cut on wood (the old word 'pren'), both the letters, and the tablets on which they were inscribed, were known as coelbren, 'the wood of credibility'. This connection of wood-writing with knowledge in the Welsh tradition can be detected today in a number of Welsh words which are primarily concerned with wood, *wydd*. These include *arwydd*, a sign; *cyfarwydd*, skilful; *cyfarwyddyd*, information; *cywydd*, a revelation; *dedwydd*, having received knowledge; *derwydd*, a druid; *egwyddawr*, an alphabet; *gwyddon*, a wise man; and *gwynwyddigion*, men of sacred knowledge.

From their form, and from the information recorded in ancient Welsh writings, these bardic letters appear to have a dual origin. Like the oghams and the runes, they are angular letters primarily intended for cutting on wood or stone. According to *Cyfrinach Y beirdd – Lluniad Llythyrenau (The Bardic Secret – Formation of Lettters)*, the original letters were very basic. It is possible that ogham was the model for the letters cut on wood but, equally, some of the characters show the influence of the Roman alphabet, whilst others are unmistakably runic. This places the bardic letters among the group of alphabets, derived ultimately from the Phoenician, where various characters, although different from one another, nevertheless display the 'family likeness'. According to tradition, it was from three basic forms of the Awen, and them alone, that the first 16 letters were formed. They were constructed from the primary columns, the three principal letters in the form of rays of light. Accordingly the memory of seeing could thus take place simultaneously with the memory

Fig. 39. Versions of Coelbren Y Beirdd: 1–3, after Llewellyn Sion; 4–5, after Meurig Dafydd.

of hearing; and, by means of signs, every sound of voice could be rendered visible to the eye . . . The individual characters of the bardic alphabets were called *llythyrau*, from *lly*, meaning various or manifest; and *tyr* to cut. Another name was *abcedilros*, a parallel with the words alphabet or futhark which intimate the first few letters of an abecedarium.

According to tradition, there were ten characters in the possession of the Cymry (the Celtic Britons, now the Welsh) from the beginning, before they came into the Isle of Britain, which concurs with the story of Einigan Gawr. This continental Celtic alphabet is very obscure, as it appears to have been a secret known only to the bards. Even after the coelbren was devised, these ten characters were kept as a secret by the bards. The 16-letter coelbren was devised during the reign of the British king Dyfnwal Moelmud ap Dyfnvarth ap Prydain ap Aeth Mawr (Dunvallo Molmutius). 430–390 BCE, as recorded in Geoffrey of Monmouth's *Historia Regum Britanniae (The history of the Kings of Britain, c.* 1136). In the reign of Belli Mawr ap Manog (King Beli the Great, son of Manogan), these characters were 'divulged' to non-initiates, and each was given a new form. Then it was stated that there should be no king, judge or teacher in the country who could not read and understand the esoteric meanings of this alphabet. But a 16-letter coelbren was found to be insufficient, and, by the time of Taliesin Ben Beirdd (Taliesin, Chief of the Bards, sixth century CE), it had been increased to 18. It was at this time, with the introduction of the Christian religion, that OIV began to be used for the name of God. Taliesin is supposed to have further enlarged the alphabet to 20 characters. 'The language of twenty letters is in Awen', he wrote. But there is another contender for the creator of the 20-letter coelbren, Ithel felyn (Ithel the Tawny). This development took place at the same time that the runes were formalized in northern Europe. These 20 characters continued in use until the knowledge and use of Latin ceased in Britain.

Ceraint fardd Glâs (Geraint, the Blue Bard, *c.* 900), is credited with enlarging the alphabet further by using 'auxiliary symbols'. This made the coelbren 24 characters in length, the alphabet used for 'black and white' (i.e. in writing) until the late middle ages. This 24-character coelbren was used for secret communication and also for divination in the form of dice. Interestingly, this version has the same number of characters as the Elder Futhark runes and the Old English alphabet before the invention of J and W. The fully developed form of coelbren, such as that described by the bard Ieuan Llawdden, rector of Machynlleth, who flourished around 1440–80, has 38 characters, but this was only used for carving on wood, 24 remaining as the standard.

Throughout recorded history, at least since the time of Taliesin, the Bards of the Island of Britain have used the metaphor of 'wood' to describe words, especially poetry. Taliesin himself, who lived from 520 CE until 570, wrote of himself:

I am the fund of song,
I am a reader,
I love the branches and the tight wattles.

The sprigs and compact wattling are the slivers and assemblages of wood upon which the British bards, like their Irish counterparts, used to write. Extant bardic poetry records that this tradition continued unbroken into the second millennium. For example, Rhys Goch ab Riccert, who lived 1140–70, wrote:

The wooden axe of an unpolished bard,
Has been hewing a song to Gwenllian.

Another famous bard, Iolo Goch (1315–1402), left the following words:

I will bear for Owain
In metrical words, fresh and slow.
Continually, not the hewing of Alder wood,
By the chief carpenter of song.

His contemporary, Dafydd ab Gwilym (1300–68) said, 'This will address them on wood', whilst another contemporary,

Fig. 40. 'Standard' Coelbren Y Beirdd, after Ieuan Llawdden.

Rhys Goch Eryri (1330–1420); 'No longer will be seen the mark of the axe of the flower of the carpenters on a song-loving and wise one'. And almost a century later, Ieuan du'r Bilwg (1460–1500): 'May thy praise go – thou art a soldier – Upon wood, as long as day and water continue'.

Although characters were usually carved onto wood, a system of pyrographic printing using hot iron brands was developed by the bards. Perhaps it is the first example of 'movable type' printing, for it is reputed to date from before the Roman occupation of Britain (44–410 CE).

It was in the time of Llyr Llediaith [Llyr of Defective Speech, father of Bendigaidfran, or Bran the Blessed] that the way of burning the 'cyrvens' with an iron stamp was understood, that is, there was an iron for every letter, heated red hot, with which they burnt on an 'ebill' or a board what was required; and sometimes they formed letters on wood with the small prickings of a hot fork.

But although wood was considered the true medium for bardic poetry, during the Roman occupation writing on other materials was introduced to Britain. Bendigaidfran, father of the famed Celtic king Caradog, or Caractacus, is reputed as having brought to Britain the technique of writing on a scroll. He is said to have learnt the technique during his seven years' captivity in Rome as a hostage on behalf of his son. On his release, he taught the British scribes the manner of dressing the skins of goats to make parchment. But its use was not taken up by the more conservative bards, who kept their wooden tablets. Because of this, their writings became known as the Coelbren y Beirdd (the woodscript of the bards). According to bardic tradition, paper was first made by Moran, a resident of Constantinople, who ground up flax, and spread it out thinly to make sheets of paper. But this flax paper, used by the British bards, was considered inferior to *plagawd*, which it resembled: 'Plagawd was a plant of the lily kind, which was brought over from India; and on it they wrote with black, or some other colour. After that, plagawd of skin was made, being manufactured by art'. According to some bards, it originated in Egypt, not India. Perhaps it was identical with papyrus.

But although the use of these writing materials largely

superseded the use of wood, knowledge of the wooden writing, coelbren, remained part of the education of the bard: 'The three things which a bard ought to make with his own hands are the coelbren, the roll and the plagawd'. However, writing on wood, formerly employed by all literate people, was marginalized. Whilst the bards continued to teach the tradition, in later times only a few of them actually used wood to write upon in the old way. But then, after the defeat of the last Welsh Prince, Owain Glyndŵr (Owen Glendower, 1349–1415), as a punishment for rebellion, the English king forbade the importation of paper or plagawd into Wales, and its manufacture there. This was to prevent learning and written communication between Welsh people, or with foreigners. Bards were forbidden to travel around their circuits, or to make official visits to families, as in former times. But this act of persecution failed to have its desired effect. Instead, it caused a revival of the ancient coelbren of the bards of the Isle of Britain. Perhaps it was this attempt at cultural genocide by the English monarch which actually ensured the survival of the ancient letters. Instead of using the now forbidden plagawd and paper, the bards revived the ancient traditional methods of writing on wood, which, though still remembered, had gone out of use by then.

According to Llewellyn Sion, the wooden frameworks which carried the letters were made as follows:

They gathered rods of Hazel or Mountain Ash in the winter, about a cubit in length, and split each into four parts, that is, the wood was made into four splinters, and kept them, until by the working of time they became quite dry. Then they planed them square, in respect of breadth and thickness, and afterwards, trimmed down the angles to the tenth part of an inch, which was done [in order] that the cuttings of the letters, that is, the symbols, which were cut with the knife on one of the four square surfaces, should not encroach visibly upon the next face; and thus on every one of the four faces. Then they cut the symbols, according to their character, whether they were those of language and speech, or of numbers, or other signs of art, such as the symbols of music, of voice and string. And after cutting ten such bars as were required, they prepared four splinters, two

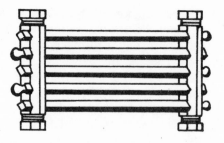

Fig. 41. 'Peithynen' framework, as used by the Welsh bards.

*and two, which were called 'pill', planed them smooth,
placed two of them together side by side across the frame,
and marked the places for ten holes. After that, they cut the
holes, that is, half of each of the ten holes, in one splinter,
and the same in the other; and they did the same with the
other two splinters; and these are called 'pillwydd'. Then
they took the symbolized or lettered bars, and made a neck
at each of the two ends of every bar, all round, the breadth
of a finger, along the bar. Then they placed the lettered
sticks by their necks on the pillwydd at one end, and in like
manner at the other end; and on that the other pillwydd at
each end, hole for hole. And on both ends of the two
pillwydden they made necks, as places for strings to tie them
firmly together at each end of the symbolized sticks. And
when the whole are thus bound tight together, the book that
is constructed in this manner is called 'peithynen' because it
is framed; the pillwydd at each end keeping all together, and
the 'ebillion', or lettered staves, turning freely in the
pillwydd, and thus being easy to read. That is, one face of
the ebill is read first, according to the number of its face,
then it is turned with the sun, and the second face is read,
and it is turned so for every other face, and thus from ebill
to ebill until the reading is finished. A number from one to
ten being on the turning face of each of the ebillion, the
numbered face is the first that is to be read, and then the
others in the order of their course with the sun.*

*There are forty sides to the ebillion in every Peithynen;
after that, another Peithynen is formed, until the conclusion
of the poem or narrative. And where more than ten ebillion*

are required, and less than a score, as many ebillion as are required are placed together in one entire Peithenyn. The reason for assigning ten as the particular number of succession, is, that ten is the division-point of number, and under the number of decades are all numbers arranged, until language cannot give them names.

Nineteenth-century engravings of druids often depict the ancient Celtic priests holding these wooden frameworks. When their use was revived after the defeat of the Owain Glyndwr, the construction of these 'wooden books' was an act of national resistance against the English ruling class:

After recovering the knowledge of the coelbrens, that is, the one of the bards and the one of the monks, nearly every person, male and female, wished to learn and construct them. From thence, they became the trade of sieve-makers and basket-makers, and upon them was cut the record of everything that required the preserved memorial of letter and book. And thus it was until the time of Henry the Seventh, who, being a Welshman, took his countrymen under the protection of his courtesy, and placed them, at his own expense, under the instruction of monks, and furnished them gratuitously with as much paper and parchment as was required; and they were taught whatever they would of the two languages, Welsh or English, and many learned both. On that account the knowledge of letters was more frequent among the common people of Wales than of England.

As with the oghams in Ireland, there were many variant esoteric forms of coelbren, and many ways of using them. When they were used by initiates to communicate with one another, very small ebillion were used 'a finger long, having notches so that they may be used by two persons or more, who are confidants. It is by placing and joining them together . . . that words and phrases are formed . . . they are called The Charms of the Bards, or Bardic Mystery'. These bardic charms could be used for direct communication, by creating words illegible to the common folk, or as a means of divination. The divinatory aspect is even stronger in the 'coelbren of simple letters'. This describes coelbren characters cut onto individual pieces of wood. A version of this used a set of four cubic dice:

Every one of the pieces was four sided, having six surfaces to each, and a letter on each surface, differently coloured, so that what was wanted might be obtained at first sight without much searching. The arrangement of twenty-four was found to be the best for those coelbrens; and for obtaining mutual knowledge by means of the said coelbrens secrets were ascertained, which caused much astonishment as to how it was possible.

Another name for this is the Palm Coelbren:

that where twenty-four are cut on small dice, that is inasmuch as each dice has six sides, and a letter on each side, there will be on the four dice twenty-four letters, besides what may be obtained otherwise, when the dice is reversed, in order to show a different letter . . . by holding some of these in the palm of the hand, and putting them together in the presence of a man of secrecy, dumb conversation can be carried on.

Coelbren is the name for bardic letters cut onto wood. But when they are cut onto stone, they are known as 'coelvain'. 'Secret coelvains' were similar to the charms of the bards, being small stones bearing bardic letters. These were moved around, as necessary, to make words and transmit information. Sometimes, cryptology was used to further confuse the curious.

THE GAELIC ALPHABET

The Gaelic alphabet is another little-known Celtic system that stands in its own right. Like ogham, each letter corresponds with a tree, with the exception of two, which are fire and garden. Gaelic has 17 full characters, with an 18th, the letter 'H', which is considered as an accent and not a character in its own right. As with many other abecedaries, each character corresponds with a number. The letter order is the same as the Graeco-Roman system, unlike ogham. The correspondences of Gaelic have esoteric meanings, as with ogham. But the first letter of the Gaelic alphabet is A, called Fhalm, the elm tree, with the number of one. The second letter is B, Beath, the

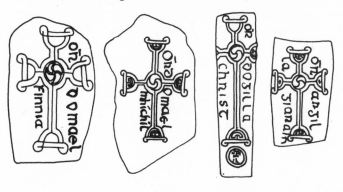

Fig. 42. Eighth-century inscriptions in the Gaelic alphabet on Christian grave-slabs at Clonmacnois, Ireland.

birch tree, with a value of two, equivalent to the first character of the oghams. The third is C, Calltuinn, the hazel tree, value three. Fourth comes Doir, the oak tree, with a value of four, the letter D. Fifth, and number five is Eubh, the aspen tree, the character E. Sixth is number six, the letter F, which is called Fearn, the alder tree. The next, seventh, character is not named after a tree. It is the letter G, Gart, which means a garden or vineyard, equivalent to the number seven. The letter I comes next, being called Iubhar, the yew tree, with the numerical value of eight. Ninth is number nine, the rowan tree, Luis, the letter L. Tenth is Muin, the vine, equivalent to the letter M and with a value of 10. This is followed by N, Nuin, the ash tree, with the number 11. Twelfth is number 12, the letter O, óir, the furze, followed by Beith-bhog, the poplar tree, which stands for the letter P and the number 13. Next comes 14, Ruis, the alder tree and the letter R. Fifteenth is the letter S, Suil, the willow tree, numerically, 15. Number 16 is Teine, which means fire, the letter T, and finally, Uhr, the yew tree, the letter U and the number 17. In the Gaelic alphabet, there are variations from the ogham system. The yew tree is represented twice, by the Iubhar and Uhr, the letters I and U. In ogham, the character equivalent to U, Up, corresponds with the heather. Also, in Gaelic, the elm tree, Fhailm, is the

Fig. 43. Celtic cross at Nevern, west Wales, with cryptic inscription, tenth century.

primary character, not the birch tree, Beath, the equivalent of ogham's Beth. The use of Fhailm as the first letter reflects the Norse tradition that the first woman, Embla, was fashioned from an elm tree. As woman is the fount of all human life, this is most appropriate. It also reflects the matrifocal nature of ancient northern European society. Teine has its more logical ascription of fire, unlike its ogham counterpart, which is assigned to the holly. Overall, the Gaelic alphabet seems more coherent than ogham, for there are no awkward correspondences or herbal ascriptions that disrupt the consistency. Although little used today, the Gaelic alphabet is a very useful symbolic system when used for divination or other esoteric work.

VARIATIONS IN NORTHERN EUROPEAN ALPHABETS

Like all systems of human communication, ogham, coelbren and the runes have many variants. The basic form of oghams is more standardized than the other alphabets, partly because, before its present resurgence, it had a much more limited currency than the others. The Gaelic alphabet is even more standardized, being a version of the Roman. Much has been written about the 'purity' of magical alphabets, most recently, the runes. Protagonists of one or other of the many variants have insisted that their version is the true one, and that all others are 'corrupt' versions of it. But in this context, we should note the viewpoint of Prince L.L. Bonaparte, who in the first half of the nineteenth century wrote:

> *Language is a natural production, living and growing, as much as a tree or flower; and no natural development can be called a corruption. The only corrupters of dialects, that I know of, are the* literary men *who 'improve nature', by writing them, not as they are, but according to their notions of what they ought to be – i.e. in accordance with the 'rules of grammar' derived from modern languages . . . As though grammar were anything but a systematic statement of usage! What would be thought of a botanist who should mutilate his specimens of flowers and plants to improve their symmetry, or make them fit into pre-shaped artificial systems, instead of following nature, and drawing his laws and systems from her!'*

(Quoted by James A.H. Murray in his book *The Dialect of Southern Scotland*).

Fig. 44. Variant characters from Celtic manuscripts.

Bonaparte was correct, of course, there can be no other criterion of correctness than usage. The modern usage of the runes, coelbren or ogham is the way things are *now*. Whether these usages correspond with the usages of antiquity does not matter: the usages of antiquity are the matter for historians. Today, we do not speak Anglo-Saxon, Gothic or Old High German. Our Roman alphabet contains forms and letters that would have been unintelligible to Julius Caesar. And our 'Arabic' numerals are quite different from those which were adopted in Europe in the fifteenth century. Like everything living, magical alphabets evolve, and it is only for very specific reasons that we might choose to use a certain form over another.

5
Magical and Alchemical Alphabets

Just as in earlier times, many secret alphabets were used in the medieval period for magical purposes. Of course, the primary reason for using them, the enlightenment of the individual, was uppermost. However, the emphasis of the period, which comes down to us through magical writings, appears to have been more towards the operative side of magic than solely the aim of spiritual development. But the search for the spark of illumination, the quest of the spiritual seeker through the ages, was still an important driving force. This search was expressed well by the German mystic, Meister Eckhart, who wrote:

Upon this matter a Pagan sage has a fine saying in discourse with another sage: 'I become aware of something in me that flashes upon my reason, I perceive of it that it is something, but what it is I cannot see. It seems to me only, that, if I could conceive it, I would comprehend all truth.

In this period, various fresh means were devised so that this process could be facilitated. New magical alphabets were one method.

The Medieval period has left us a large number of secret alphabets, stemming mainly from the occult and alchemical traditions. Medieval alphabets are characterized by their often chaotic array of characters taken from a number of disparate sources. Clearly, many of them are the invention of individuals, devised for the recording of secrets. Some contain a mixture of characters that are versions of sigils taken from the alchemical and astrological fields. Others are modifications of known

171

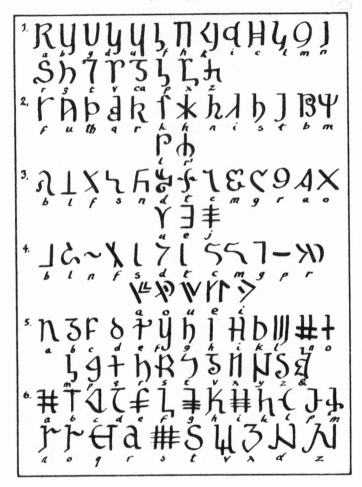

Fig. 45. Late-Celtic magical alphabets: 1–2 and 5–6, from medieval Irish manuscripts; 3, Bobileth; 4, Beth-Luis-Nion.

ancient scripts, such as Hebrew, Greek and Roman. The cryptographic traditions of the Greek, Runic and Celtic alphabets were also continued in the medieval period. These were in use alongside 'standard' Hebrew, Yiddish, 'standard' and cursive Greek forms, various runes and local alphabets, such as Gaelic and Westphalian. The Slavonic alphabets of eastern Europe, especially Cyrillic and Glagolitic, also served as a source for certain letters.

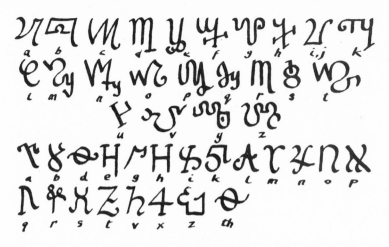

Fig. 46. Alchemical alphabet, 1579 (*top*); Roman version of Canaanean (*bottom*).

Many of these alphabets can be found in ancient alchemical and magical texts, and occasionally on tombs and foundation stones. Perhaps the most public of these is in the ceiling fresco by the Venetian artist Tiepolo in the Residenz of the Bishop of Würzburg, Germany. This 'inscription' was painted on a block of stone standing in a group representing 'Asia'. It contains characters typical of the magical alphabets current in the Renaissance and Baroque eras. Many of these alphabets were employed in the preparation of talismans and magic circles used in the conjuration of spirits. Magical grimoires often illustrate the various pantacles required to conjure and command individual spirits; these have corresponding inscriptions in one or other of the magical alphabets then current. Often, the various names of God in the Hebrew and Greek traditions were written in appropriate occult characters in order to provide the power and protection that the magician needed to accomplish his or her working. These characters often included various astrological sigils considered appropriate to the working, and more personal signs of meaning to the magician. In his *The Tragical History of Doctor Faustus*, the classic play dealing with black magic and its supposed consequences, Christopher Marlowe wrote of the then current beliefs concerning the conjuration of the spirits. This includes the use of alphabet magic:

Faustus, begin thine incantations,
And try if devils will obey thy hest,
Seeing thou hast pray'd and sacrific'd to them.
Within this circle is Jehovah's name,
Forwards and backwards anagrammatiz'd,
Th'abbreviated names of holy saints,
Figures of every adjunct of the heavens,
And characters of signs and erring stars,
By which the spirits are enforc'd to rise:
Then fear not, Faustus, but be resolute,
And try the uttermost magic can perform.

Almost every work of ceremonial magic published since the sixteenth century has contained some use of one or other of the common magical alphabets. Sacred words written in these alphabets were used as essential parts of the rite. Precise words in precise characters written at precise times according to precise prescriptions were held to be essential for success. For example, *The Grimoire of Honorius* tells of the complex techniques that the ritual magicians of this era felt they had to perform in order to accomplish their ends. As with many such operations, before the working text was written, a long period of preparation was required. The parchment upon which the text was to be written had to be prepared from the skin of a lamb nine days old. This was sacrificed according to certain rituals, and specific parts of it were offered up burnt. The skin was then spread on the ground for nine days, and sprinkled four times a day with holy water. On the tenth day, just beore dawn, this skin was covered with the ashes of the burnt offering, and the ashes of a cock sacrificed for the purpose. Then, on the following Thursday, after sunset, the flesh of the lamb was interred in a secret place, and characters from an occult alphabet written on the earth of the grave, using the left thumb.

When this involved procedure had been completed, the lambskin was stretched for a further 19 days, and on the 19th day, the fleece was removed, and buried with a similar ritual involving another inscription. Finally, the skin was dried in the sun for three days, and further characters cut upon it, this time using a new knife. When this was done, Psalm 71 was recited, and more characters cut. Further psalms and characters followed in due order, until the operation was complete. Upon this parchment, then, the appropriate pantacles and sigils could then be written so that the whole ceremony could be accomplished satisfactorily. This involved the usual principles of 'infernal necromancy', involving the conjuration of Lucifer, Astaroth, Frimost and other demonic entities, which were then compelled to do the will of the magician. As with the Hebrew, Islamic and Odinic traditions, Honorius's magic used a series of the names of God. These 72 names are given in Appendix 8. Complex rules such as this were considered essential if the magic was to be effective. Any slight alteration in the inscription, even an omission or addition to the ceremony, was certain to end in failure.

Medieval and Renaissance magic was a synthesis of various traditions. At the time, Jewish qabalistic speculations were developing rapidly; the magical traditions of ancient classical paganism; local pre-Christian traditions, and new developments in philosophy and science were melded together to

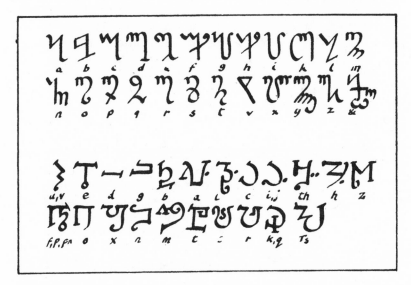

Fig. 47. The Theban alphabet (*top*), and the Alphabet of the Magi (*bottom*).

create new systems. So it is that magical alphabets of the era may be based upon any of the known secular or sacred scripts of Europe, as well as incorporating alchemical, astrological, geomantic and personal sigils. Alphabets such as Theban, which still has a considerable currency in esoteric circles, was first revealed at this time. Whether or not they had ancient antecedents, it was customary to assign their origin to antiquity, preferably to some ancient and notable sage. One such is Apollonian script. This is a medieval alphabet which nevertheless is ascribed to the great Pagan preacher Apollonius of Tyana. It was recorded in 1586 by B. de Vignere in his *Traicté des Chiffres, ou Secrètes Manières d'Escrire*. Apollonian is based upon the Greek alphabet, with a few characters that resemble those in the Gothic alphabet. Along with a few scripts of this era, Apollonian has undergone development in modern times. In his book, *Amulettes, Talismans et Pentacles dans les Traditions, Orientales et Occidentales* (1938), J. Marquès-Rivière gave a version of Apollonian that refers to the Roman alphabet, but with the Greek characters Theta, Psi and Omega as well. Even in the twentieth century, these magical alphabets have continued to develop.

In his *Les Origines de l'Alchimie* (1885), M.P.E. Berthelot gives two other, related, secret alchemical alphabets, which he calls the 'Hellenic' and the 'Greek Astrologic'. They are based upon the Greek alphabet, being personalized cursive forms. The common feature of most of these alphabets lies in the multiple sources of their characters. In different alphabets, the same character can be found serving for different phonetic values. Also, during the late medieval period, the arrival of Arabic numerals in central Europe caused an alteration in secret alphabets, which until then had used several characters which resembled closely the figures, 2, 3, 4, 5, 6 and 9. These characters were dropped from later magical alphabets, and they are almost completely absent in versions used today. The ease of use of these arithmetically superior Arabic digits spelt the death-knell of the older systems of numerical notation. These older numbers survived for some centuries in the wooden stave-calendars of Britain and Scandinavia, and in the secret monogram-like year-notation of occultists.

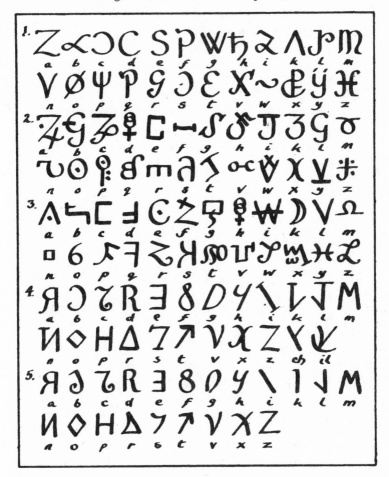

Fig. 48. Renaissance magical alphabets: 1–3 from Sommerhoff; 4, Secret Etruscan; 5, Noachite, according to Rivière.

THE VEHMGERICHT, THE INQUISITION AND THE ALPHABET OF WESTPHALIA

Secret organizations have always needed secret means of protecting their information. Today, the secret police of many countries keep files of suspects in secure buildings, or on computers that they hope are inaccessible to hackers. But, in the past, records were kept on documents written in secret

Fig. 49. Vehmic and Inquisitorial alphabets: 1–3. Vehmic; 4. Inquisitorial.

alphabets and ciphers. In medieval Europe, there were two main organizations which used secret scripts to keep their unsavoury secrets to themselves and they were typical of the groups that have found a need for secret alphabets. They were the Vehmgericht and the Inquisition. The Vehmgericht or Secret tribunal was a confederation of vigilante groups. These bands of secret executioners went about their business in German-speaking parts of the Holy Roman Empire. According to tradition, the organization was founded in the year 772 CE by the Emperor Charles the Great (Charlemagne). Charles, after having subdued the Pagan Saxons in a 33-year long war of attrition, instituted a reign of terror against his subjects.

According to tradition, in order to wipe out resistance, he had 30,000 Saxons deported westwards across the Rhine, and replaced them with an equivalent number of Christian Gauls. This occupied district them became known as West Gaul or West Wales (Westphalia). The heads of the Gaulish families were encouraged to suppress paganism and keep the Saxons in subjection.

Of course, total suppression of the subject Saxons was impossible to achieve. So the system stabilized into one of oppressor and oppressed, with constant attempts by the conquerors to wipe out Pagan survivals. In order to perpetuate this tyranny in a systematic manner, the Vehmgericht organization was founded by five knights. The Vehm thus came into being, inevitably fighting an endless sectarian war in the countryside. Despite its overtly Christian ideals, the Vehm itself contained within it elements of earlier, pagan, tradition. One clue lies in its name. In 1824, James Skene, a Scottish authority on this organization, wrote that he thought that the name Vehmgericht was 'derived from *Baeume Gericht* [Tree Law] as the trees constituted the only ostensible circumstance of its existence, and afforded the first and only indication to the world of its proceedings, by unhappy victims that were found hanged upon them.' Also, the name 'Vehm' has connections with the forest law, such as the rights of lords to put livestock there. There are close connections, too, with the folk traditions of the outlaws and supernatural beings of the forest, such as Robin Hood, the Wild Man and the Wild Hunt, all of which originated in Pagan custom and belief. More specifically, there appears to have been a connection with the tree-letter mysteries of Celtic magic usage. Apart from this, the other rites and ceremonies of the Vehm were certainly within the magical-geomantic practices of the Northern Tradition.

At first the Vehm appears to have been little more than a quasi-legal paramilitary organization but, in the fifteenth century, it was institutionalized by King Robert, who gave it new constitutions. It was then that it was organized into regional chapters and allied to the inquisitors of the Church. One of the titles of the Archbishop of Köln (Cologne) became 'Stadholder of the Holy Secret Tribunal', showing the intimate connexion between Church and Vehm. One of the chief centres of the organization was at Dortmund, known as *Die Krumme*

Grafschaft (The Crooked County). General chapters of the Vehm were held there, sometimes attended by the Emperor himself. Finally, with changes in society, the Vehm gradually lost its meaning, and faded out. The last Freigraf (local chief) of the Vehm, Zacharias Löbbecke, died at the age of 99 in 1826.

Ostensibly, punishment at the hands of Vehmic functionaries was conducted in defence of the Catholic Church and the Holy Roman Empire. In practice, as with the Inquisition, and the witch hunts of Protestant countries, the existence of this organization gave its members almost unlimited powers to torture and murder almost anybody. Members of the Vehm were able to exercise a secret reign of terror in which they could settle personal scores, kill rivals and exercise power over the weak. While it was in existence, the Vehm, allied with the Inquisition, and with general witch-, Jew- and Gypsy-hunters, was an instrument of Church and state terror. In later years, only certain categories of crime were punished by the Vehm. These were connected mainly with the laws of the Church. They were heresy, apostasy, sacrilege, witchcraft, adultery, rebellion, and robberies conducted in league with Jews. Other non-religious crimes punished by the Vehm were theft, rape and murder.

The Vehm was most associated with Westphalia, a land held sacred, like the English county of Rutland, on account of its red earth. Every member of the Vehm had to be initiated on this red earth, *Up Roder Erde Gemaket*. The knowledge of secret alphabets was part of this perverted tradition. In early times, Westphalia had possessed two local alphabets, one of

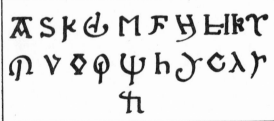

Fig. 50. The traditional Westphalian alphabet.

180

which had letter-names and correspondences in the magical tradition. The Westphalian 'Runenalphabet' (which was not runic, although some letters are related to both runes and Gothic) had the characters Alma, Bina, Calda, Dotta, Emera, Faveta, Ges, Helled, Is, Cana, Lida, Mis, Non, Ota, Ponta, Quinon, Rorot, Sisso, Tonta, Uegon, Yr and Za. Each of these possesses a meaning, as with the runes.

However, the earlier Westphalian alphabets, which might have been known generally, were not used by the secret order. The Vehmic alphabets and that used by the Inquisition are different, being allied more to several medieval magical alphabets used elsewhere. Ironically, considering their attitude towards Jewish people, some of the letters in their secret alphabets are clearly derived from Yiddish letters. By using these alphabets, secret knowledge could be retained and the mysteries of the order transmitted to initiates. The element of fear generated by using something occult must also have played a part in the use of these letters. But, with the passing of Vehmic activity, these characters passed from active use into the realm of antiquarian and scholarly interest. They are never used today.

Fig. 51. Renaissance magical alphabets. 1–2, after Selenus; 3, Templar.

HOUSE, HOLDINGS AND STONEMASONS' MARKS

Housemarks and holdings marks were used in central and northern Europe as a means of indicating the ownership of property. These marks were branded onto cattle, clipped into the coats of horses and cut into the ears of sheep. They were chalked, painted or printed on sacks. They were stamped, carved and painted onto house fronts, on boats and wagons, and ploughed into the surfaces of fields. They were stamped into timber floated down river, so that the owner could identify his wood when it reached its destination. Often, they were carved onto small mark-tags (*merkelapper*) which travelled with goods carried by ship. They were commonplace in medieval trade. Perhaps the largest ever discovery of runic examples was made by Asbjorn Herteig and his archaeological team when, after the disastrous fire of 1955, they excavated Bryggen, the old Norwegian hanseatic wharf district of Bergen. On each of these, the owner's name was written in runes.

Fig. 52. Housemarks (*top two lines*) Norwegian Bumerker; (*line 3*) tradespersons' marks); (i) Kirchentellinsfurt, Germany; (ii) Peter Vischer, (iii) Welser; (iv) Hans Burkmair; (v) Weavers' and Dyers' guild, Bury-St-Edmunds; (*line 4*) heraldic signs (i–iv) Polish, (v) Swedish; (vi–vii) Swiss; (viii–x) English; (*line 5*) merchants' marks (i–iv) Castel Durante, Italy, sixteenth-century; (v–vi) potter's mark, Faenza, 1548; (*line 6*) porcelain marks (i–ii) Strasbourg; (iii) Delft; (iv) Ludwigsburg; (v) Anspach; (vi) Limbach; (vii) Tabary, Sèvres; (viii) Loughton Hall.

Symbolic house marks are still a feature of many old towns in central Europe, where they can be seen carved and painted proudly on house fronts.

These house and holdings marks contained esoteric meanings, being derived from various signs, including Roman, Greek and Runic letters. One recurrent motif is a character that resembles the Arabic numeral 4, which is the ancient sigil of Hermes, the deity of trade. This sigil is common in German-speaking countries, and the medieval weavers' and dyers' guilds of Bury St. Edmunds used it, too. This symbol, along with others, was incorporated into the marks of tradesmen, which are generally very attractive signs in their own right. Even today, many modern German tradespeoples' house marks retain the hermetic '4'. In some places, in the manner of the rules of heraldry, there was a tradition of adding lines or other marks to the original house mark. This was done to denote the son, grandson or other descendant of the founder. By this means, very complex and unwieldy signs were built up. Some continental European heraldry contains a number of sigils of the house-mark type which are probably derived from house marks. In Poland, the arms of the Kosieska, Lis and Pilawa groups of families are notable in this respect, whilst the Swiss Schelter arms are notable for carrying the Hermetic '4' vigil as part of a house mark.

As well as tradespeople, burghers and untitled nobility, members of various crafts also had their own personal marks, smiths' and carpenters' signs being commonplace. Sometimes, these marks were administered by the authorities. For example, in 1398, the magistrates of Aberdeen issued an order that every baker would have to mark each roll and loaf with their personal craftsman's mark. Usually, the Scottish bakers' marks were circles of dots or 'pricks'. This practice is recalled by the nursery rhyme 'Pat-a-Cake, Baker's Man':

Pat-a-cake, Pat-a-cake, Baker's Man,
Make me a cake
As fast as you can,
Pat it and prick it,
And mark it with 'B',
And put it in the oven,
For baby and me.

The Company of Coopers had a system of marks, based on the circle, emblematic of the casks and barrels that they made. In England, carpenters' and joiners' marks went out of use at the end of the sixteenth century, but the principle of trade marks, and hall marks for silver and gold, continued, and is in use today. I have in my possession a nineteenth-century cold chisel formerly belonging to the Great Eastern Railway company. It bears a craftsman's mark. From the medieval period, the stonemasons, who built churches, castles, city walls and bridges, developed a complex and coherent system of marks. Like the smith or carpenter, each stonemason signed his own work with his personal mark. These were derived partly from house and holdings marks, and also from Byzantine mono-grams and sigils. A proportion of stonemasons' marks are runes. For example, in Germany, the Tyr rune can be found in the Frauenkirche at Esslingen, along with Sigel, Ing, Odal and Wolfsangel. Ur exists as a stonemason's mark in Strasbourg cathedral. In England, the rune Ear can be seen in Ely Cathedral, whilst Eoh, Erda and Wolfsangel are carved in King's College Chapel at Cambridge. Ing can also be seen at Beverley Minster. Numerous other examples could be cited from most parts of Europe.

Along with the other medieval crafts, the stonemasons were organized in a guild which had its own rituals, ceremonies and secret means of recognition. In the high medieval period, the craft was organized in lodges which were under the jurisdiction of central authority. Each central lodge of operative masons had its own 'mother diagram', a geometrical pattern from which were derived all of the marks used by its members. Stonemasons in German-speaking countries had to swear an oath that they would not vary their own personal mark, once chosen. These individual marks had to conform to the geometry of the 'mother diagram'. In his book, *Hof- und Hausmarken*, published in 1870, Professor Homeyer wrote that about 50 years earlier, a Dr. Parthey had given him such a 'mother diagram'. This was from the cathedral of Strasbourg, the central lodge for Alsace. This diagram was attributed to an early stonemason, Arnold von Strassburg.

In the year 1828, the mason Kirchner of Nuremberg was in possession of a book that recorded the derivation of all the individual masons' marks from a common source. Professor

Franz Rziha in his 1883 work, published in Vienna, *Studien über Steinmetz-Zeichen (Studies on Stonemasons' Marks)*, demonstrated that a series of 'mother diagrams' were derived from certain fundamental geometrical patterns. All known masons' marks fitted into these 'mother diagrams'. In the 68 plates that illustrated the book, Professor Rziha fitted 1145 stonemasons' marks into their corresponding diagrams, demonstrating the universality of the system. He showed that there are four basic geometrical diagrams upon which all of the stonemasons' signs were based. The first two diagrams were based upon the medieval systems known as *ad quadratum* and *ad triangulum*, the geometry of the square and equilateral triangle respectively. The other two are more complex. Professor Rziha called the other two *Vierpasse* and *Dreipasse*. Vierpasse corresponded to the square geometry with added features, whilst Dreipasse used different combinations of equilateral triangles and circles. All of these diagrams are capable of limitless extension, and so a very elaborate and esoteric geometry is at the base of stonemasons' personal marks.

Professor Rziha discovered the 'mother diagrams' for several major centres of medieval stonemasons, including Nuremberg,

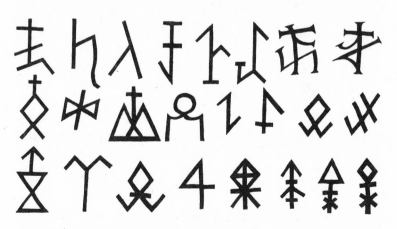

Fig. 53. Stonemasons' marks (*top line, left to right*); (i–iii) Strasbourg cathedral; (iv–vi) Frauenkirche, Esslingen-am-Neckar, Germany; (vii–viii) Strasbourg, Bishop's palace; (*middle line*) King's College Chapel, Cambridge; (*bottom line*) (i) Melrose Abbey; (ii) Bridlington Priory; (iii) Ely Cathedral; (iv) Stonyhurst College; (v–viii) railway masonry, English, nineteenth century.

Dresden, Strasbourg, Cologne, Vienna and Prague. Through the stonemasons' signs, many of which were derived from Greek and runic characters, the geometry of the macrocosm was reproduced at the smallest level. Through this esoteric geometry, the barely noticeable marks carved on individual stones encapsulated the transcendent structure of the universe. The marks used by stonemasons were continued long after the central lodges were closed owing to the changed conditions which called most cathedral building to a halt. Around the second half of the eighteenth century, the central authority system broke down, and after that operative stonemasons were attached to individual places. The system of marks continued, however, and is still in use at places like Ulm. The stonemasons' marks visible on old canal and railway bridges all over northern and central Europe attest to the continuation of the tradition outside church buildings and repair. That was until the advent of reinforced concrete terminated the need for the craft of the stonemason.

The final parts of this geometrical letter story came with the curious 'alphabet' from the dubious *Oera Linda Chronicle*, whose letters were based on a sixfold division of the circle (see Chapter 5). Lastly, in the early part of the twentieth century, the Austrian mystic Guido Von List and his followers took this ancient masonic derivation of personal sigils from a basic diagram as the geometrical basis for the Armanen system of runes (see Chapter 3). Significantly, like the curious Oera Linda letters, this was also based upon the sixfold division of the circle – *ad triangulum*.

MAGIC GRID CIPHERS

There were a number of secret alphabets or ciphers connected with various Masonic and Rosicrucian orders, which appear to have arisen in the seventeenth or eighteenth centuries, perhaps using the principles that underly stonemasons' marks. Whatever their origin, esoteric ciphers of this type were very popular around the Napoleonic period. Most of them are based upon a positional or geometric form that gives the place of a Roman letter within a grid of nine squares, very similar to the Hebrew Aiq Beker, from which it is probably derived. One such grid is as follows:

A	B	C	D	E	F	G	H	I
J	K	L	M	N	O	P	Q	R
S	T	U	V	W	X	Y	Z	&

The characters of this script are created by drawing the appropriate part of the grid. For the first letter, this is all that is done. But for the second letter, the part of the grid is drawn, along with a single dot. The second letter in any part of the grid is marked by two dots within the shape. The letters so produced have an obvious parallel with the marks of the stonemasons in that part of an overall geometric form is taken to make the sign. Clearly, with this cipher, it is possible to vary the orientation of the grid, and also the placement of letters within it. If this is done, it makes decipherment very difficult without the original grid. These alterations may be made at random, or, if a magical content is required, according to a magic square or some other recognized system.

There are other versions of this magical cipher. Of these, that known as the Royal Arch Cipher is the best-known variant. It has a grid of nine squares, each of which contains two letters. The remaining eight letters of the alphabet are placed within the arms of an 'X'-shaped figure. Each of the letter's position is thus denoted by the appropriate part of the grid in which it is contained, the second letter of each being marked, as in the first system, by a dot within the figure. Partially related to these ciphers is the Sovereign Princes' Rose

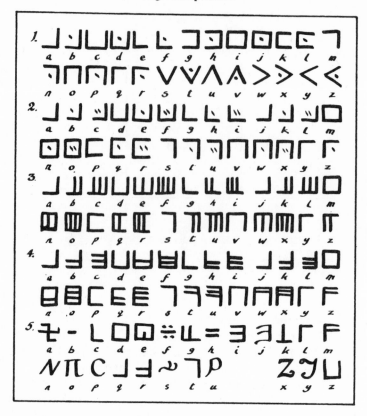

Fig. 54. Versions of the Rose Cross Cipher.

Cross Cipher, described by Helena Blavatsky as a Rosicrucian alphabet. However, although some of the characters in this magical alphabet are related to the letters in 'magic grid' ciphers, the others are not, being typical characters of alphabets like Adamic, the Alphabet of the Magi, the Inquisitorial and Femgenossen (Vehmic) scripts. This type of cryptic script, popular in the nineteenth century, has lost favour in recent years, and is another historic oddity.

MAGICAL USES OF THE ROMAN ALPHABET

Today, with standardized characters in a standardized alphabet, we are not used to variant forms of letters. When we see a capital 'N' written the 'wrong way round' on a medieval inscription, we tend to think of it as the work of a semi-literate, rural person. We view the letter 'Y', the thorn rune 'Th' as an affection when we see it written up on signs such as 'Ye Olde Tea Shoppe'. In general, variant forms of letters are seen today as just plain wrong. But this is an incorrect viewpoint. It is only since the wide dissemination of printed matter that the letters of the alphabet have become standardized completely. If we take a look at historic manuscripts, paintings and inscriptions on buildings, soon we will find variant forms of the familiar characters. And the further back we go, the greater variety we can find. Ultimately, this is the result of conceptions of what constitutes learning. For example, the cosmopolitan scholars who wrote the great illuminated tomes like the *The Book of Kells, The Book of Durrow* and *The Lindisfarne Gospels* were educated to be conversant with several languages and scripts. So it is not surprising that variant letters appear in their texts.

The most scholarly of the ecclesiastical academics in the period of *The Book of Kells* (the eighth century CE) would have been conversant with the Irish, Latin and Greek languages, and perhaps also Welsh, Hebrew, Coptic and Anglo-Saxon. All of these languages had their own alphabets. Bardic Irish was written in ogham, which itself had many variant forms. Latin was written almost exclusively in the Roman alphabet, whilst Greek, Hebrew and Coptic were written in their own scripts. Welsh used the bardic alphabets known as Coelbren and Coelvain, whilst the Anglo-Saxons used runes and the Roman alphabet. Because of this, an educated person in those days would have had access to a wealth of scripts, and would have been able to use them in whatever context seemed appropriate. So it is to be expected that we can find the Greek letter Delta used for 'D' in *The Book of Kells*. Other characters used in these texts are versions of letters found in the bardic, Gothic or Coptic alphabets, the runes, and later magical alphabets. Some of the variant characters are unrecognizable to the modern reader. Fig. 44 shows a selection of these 'alternative letters' from *The Book of Kells, The Book of Durrow* and *The Lindisfarne Gospels*). This interchangeability of characters, obviously done sometimes for decorative effect, is evident within other secret or magical alphabets, such as the Welsh Coelbren and Coelvain, where different bards and scribes used their own favourite forms of the letters, and sometimes added new ones. Ligatures of Roman letters, the equivalent of bind-runes, formerly prevalent, have now gone out of use except in decorative calligraphy and formal inscriptions derived from the calligraphic tradition. In general, however, additional letters were not added to the standard Roman alphabet, although accents, diacritical marks and a few variant letters exist today in specific European languages (such as the German letter 'ß', for double 'S'). Many of the later magical alphabets used by astrologers, alchemists, wizards, witches, warlocks and the Inquisition incorporated various of these letters, arranged in special ways. In times of general illiteracy, it was easy to create means of writing that only those 'in the know' could interpret.

Also, as with other alphabets, there is a magical dimension to the Roman alphabet. The tradition of using the Roman alphabet in an esoteric way is attributed to the Sibylline Oracles of ancient Rome. The name 'Sibyl' was given to any prophetess, the word being derived from the Greek words 'Sio', from 'Zenteo', I consult; and 'boule', the will. Thus a sibyl was a consulted of the will of the gods. Another interpretation of the name is from 'Theou-boule', 'the will of God'. The earliest technique on record is an interesting system of letter divination, supposedly learnt by the Tuscans from Egyptian travellers, and taken over by the Romans when they conquered the Etruscan nation. This is the oracular technique known as the Prenestine Fortune. Although Etruscan, it was through the Roman alphabet that this system was developed. Its name comes from the sanctuary of divination at the town of Preneste, set up by Servius Tullius, sixth king of Rome. This method of divination employed cubes made of Laurel wood on each face of which letters were engraved. A number of these dice were thrown into a silver urn and then taken out at random and arranged in the order in which they were removed. The cubes would produce a series of letters, which were then interpreted.

According to records of his life, the great sage Apollonius of Tyana was an adept at this form of letter-divination. One divination, done before the Emperor Domitian, produced the letters P S F S E L A N T A A S V T I V S V V I V I S. The Prenestine system always interpreted these letters by notarikon, where each letter was taken as the first letter of a word, the whole sequence being an abbreviation of a sentence or two. Domitian's example thus became the Latin *'Praenestinae Sacris Fortunae Sortibus Electum Lente Ascendit Nomen Tuum Ad Alta; Sed, Undique Tandem Insignis, Victor sine Victoria, Urbis Imperium, Unus Imperator, Suscipies.'* Translated, this means: 'Your name, picked by the sacred fates of the Prenestine Fortune, rises slowly towards the height of the future; but finally, everywhere celebrated, a conqueror without victories, you will receive, as sole emperor, the empire of the City'. The veracity of Apollonius's Prenestine divination was demonstrated because the letters drawn out were also the letters of the emperor's father's name: Titus Flavius Vespanianus. Such a remarkable 'coincidence' was seen as certain proof of the veracity of the divination. Although rarely used today, the Prenestine Fortune technique had a long history of use. In the middle ages, it was employed by the bards of Wales, among others. Then it enjoyed a renewed vogue in France in the latter part of the eighteenth century. There, flamboyant practitioners of the art demonstrated this ancient letter magic in public, and a new interest was kindled. This was even more evident after the Revolution, when the suppression of the Church led to a massive increase in interest in all branches of the esoteric sciences.

According to Paul Christian in his *Histoire de la Magie* (1870) (*The History of Magic*), on 10 May 1785, the great magus Count Alessandro Cagliostro (1743–95) demonstrated letter magic to an audience of interested people and sceptics. Cagliostro took a sentence with 203 letters as the text by which the characters within it would be numbered in sequence. Translated from the French, this was: 'Is it possible for the human spirit to look for and discover the secrets of the future in a literal statement of the event which has just happened, or in the definition of a person by the names, titles and acts that constitute his individuality?'. From this seemingly arbitrary basis, he created a circle of letters, from which various words were taken until the whole number had been made into a new sentence by metathesis, transposition of the letters of the original text, by the method better known now as an anagram. Only ten letters remained unused. The new text was: 'The human word is a reflection of the eternal light, illuminating all life here. The initiated Sage can read and recover, in the stated words, a prognostication removed not very far from the destinies that must be accomplished in each individual sphere'. Of the ten remaining letters, T (number 39), C (56), D (70), D (89) N (76), D (123), P (143), N (149) and P (51), he used the Sybilline method of notarikon. Thus, TCDNDDPNP became the Latin: *'Tacentes Casus Denuntiat Nomen; Decreta Dei Per Numeros Proefantur'*, which translates as: 'The Name announces the happenings that remain yet in the silence of the future, and divine decrees are predicted by numbers'. By this demonstration of alphabet magic, Cagliostro proved to his and, apparently, to his audience's satisfaction, that names and numbers lie at the foundation of, and are the keys to, 'the sanctuary of the oracles'.

Sacred alphabet magic

Sacred abbreviations are another dimension of the Roman alphabet. Closely related to the Greek system, they include the names of divinities. The monogram of Christ, IHS, has been discussed already in Chapter 2. But in the Roman catacombs are a number of inscriptions which show the unbroken continuity between the pagan and the Christian traditions. These are the 40 or so inscriptions of the letters D.M. and D.M.S. In pagan terms, these invoke the gods, standing for *Dis Manibus* and *Dis Manibus Sacrum*. But when they were used on Christian monuments, they represent *Deo Maximo* or *Deo Magno* (Great God), and *Deo Maximo Salvatori* (Great God, Saviour). Similar sacred abbreviations in the Roman alphabet play an important part in many esoteric traditions up to the present day.

The Triangular Lodge at Rushton in Northamptonshire is an example of this esoteric tradition. It is a unique Renaissance building which incorporates both sacred geometry and alphabet numerology. It was constructed in 1593 to the design of Sir Thomas Tresham, a Roman Catholic devotee who wished to continue his private worship in a hostile political climate. Tresham was particularly devoted to the Holy Trinity, and consequently, he designed the floor-plan on the basis of an equilateral triangle. Each side of the lodge measures 33 feet 4 inches (one-third of 100 feet, 10.16 metres) in length. There are three Latin inscriptions, each of which has 33 letters. One, however, is the ampersand, which, as a double letter, ingeniously makes up the hundred. The roof is finished with three gables a side, and a triangular-section finial surmounts the roof. The external ornament is highly symbolic. Below the windows of the second storey, on the side of the entrance, are the date, 1593, and the initials of the owner, T.T. Throughout the building, the letter T is used as symbolic of the Trinity. One gable bears the number 3898 in Arabic numerals, beneath which is the seven-branched candlestick of the Jews, the 'Menorah'. On the next gable, there is the Latin inscription *Respicite*, and a sun-dial. The third gable bears the number 3509 and a stone with seven eyes upon it. These numbers represent certain aspects of the Christian doctrine as interpreted by the personal mysticism of Tresham. The Triangular Lodge remains today as a remarkable monument to both a personal vision in particular and Christian qabalistic symbolism in general.

Esoterically, any alphabet is a magical formula in its own right. Early inscriptions of the complete Roman or Gaelic alphabet on stones in Ireland and Britain, known as 'abecedaries', are examples of this usage. A sixth-century example exists at Kilmakedar in County Kerry, Ireland. This is of Byzantine character. The use of the entire Roman alphabet as a sacred formula, representing the entirety of God's creation, can be seen in Christian ritual. In his seminal book, *Christian Worship: Its Origin and Evolution*, Mgr. Duchesne described its place in the Gallican usage for the dedication of churches. This ritual, dating from around the eighth century, contains the precise rite known as the Ceremony of the Alphabet. Firstly, the church pavement is strewn with ashes along its two diagonals. The bishop then proceeds to the eastern corner of the left-hand side, and, passing in a diagonal line across the church, traces on the pavement with the end of his pastoral staff the letters of the alphabet. Then going to the right eastern corner, he repeats the ceremony in another diagonal line across the pavement.'

A later Catholic tradition was to trace the first line in the Greek alphabet, and the second in the Roman one. This ceremony was exclusive to the Western church, being unknown in the Orthodox churches. It appears to have originated in the technical-magical practices of land-taking and laying down boundaries employed by ancient Roman surveyors, the Agrimensores. Their techniques were part of the magical 'Etruscan Discipline', in which the correct place for a house, town, temple or tomb was chosen according to precise rules of geomancy. The transverse cross, upon which the bishop traces the alphabets, recalls the primary lines laid out and measured by the Agrimensores. This large 'X' is, of course, in itself the Greek letter Chi, the first letter of the name 'Christ'. Chi has the gematria value of 600, symbolically equivalent to the Cosmos, the Godhead and the Name (of God). The drawn alphabet itself is closely related to the magic squares and literary labyrinths beloved of the early Church, such as the El-Asnam 'Sancta Eclesia' diagram (see Chapter 6), the laying-on of the appropriate magical power to a piece of ground. Also, the entire alphabet in Greek is the logical expansion of the Christian interpretation of Alpha and Omega. Traced on a cross on the church pavement, it is seen as the impression of a large *signum Christi* on the land, which afterwards is dedicated exclusively to Christian worship. A truncated version of this is still observed in the Anglican Church. But instead of making two complete alphabets, the bishop makes the sign of αXω, Alpha, a Cross (or Chi) and Omega. This is 'in token that he takes possession in the name of Christ of the ground upon which the Church stands'. In the Church of England, the hymn 'Veni Creator Spiritus' is sung during 'the Invocation and the Sign of Alpha and Omega', as the ceremony is known.

Esoteric correspondences and numerology

But despite its use in the Prenestine Fortune, sacred abbreviations and ecclesiastical ritual, the Roman alphabet is still far less developed than Hebrew, Greek, runic, Gothic or ogham. Although the meanings of the letters can be inferred by comparison with the Greek, from which they are ultimately derived, this is rarely done, and there is scarcely any tradition of such work with the Roman alphabet. This is a curious anomaly in magical practice, as it would be relatively easy to build up a powerful and coherent system using the Roman alphabet. But, for whatever reasons, this has not been done. However, there are some notable works that do deal with the Roman alphabet in magical terms. For example, in his *Occult Philosophy*, H. Cornelius Agrippa wrote that the vowels in the Roman alphabet corresponded with the seven planets, these

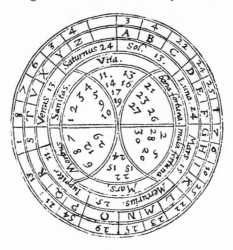

Fig. 55. Alphabetic wheel of H.C. Agrippa, with Roman letter correspondences.

being A, E, I, O U, J and V. Twelve other letters correspond with the twelve signs of the zodiac, these being the consonants B, C, D, F, G, L, M, N, P, R, S and T. The other four letters, K, Q, X and Z, represent the four elements. H, the aspiration, signifies the Spirit of the World. This ascription is the Roman parallel of the Hebrew division of the 22 letters into groups of three, seven and twelve.

In addition to this, like ogham and the runes, the Roman alphabet has a system of colour correspondences. The letters A, I, J, Q and Y are associated with orange, tawny and deep brown; B, C, K and R are ascribed white. G, L and S have scarlet as their colour, whilst D, M and T are mauve and violet. E and N have a blue-grey, slate colour as their own; pale blue is affiliated with the letters U, V, W and X. O and Z are green, with dark blue as the colour of the letters F, H and P.

But despite these correspondences, it is only through numerology that the Roman alphabet has any significant magical connection. The system of numerology, which is much better established, works on a different principle from either Hebrew or Greek. One common version of Roman alphabet numerology appears to have originated with the Hermetic Order of the Golden Dawn, although it has been attributed quite erroneously to Pythagoras! It was taught by Israel

Regardie, among others, and is known as the Pythagorean System. Whatever its origin, it is clear that in magical terms it is a late development, having arisen after the division between I and J and the invention of the letter W. It is based on a system in which each letter is given a value between 1 and 9, as follows:

1	2	3	4	5	6	7	8	9
A	B	C	D	E	F	G	H	I
J	K	L	M	N	O	P	Q	R
S	T	U	V	W	X	Y	Z	

Israel Regardie considered the values of the letters K and V as Master Numbers, which were not to be reduced if at all possible. Regardie stated that in making talismans, it was not particularly important which system of numerology one used, so long as it had internal consistency, and was done with correct magical knowledge. A different system of numbers was devised or transmitted by the palmist and occultist Cheiro. This system appears to have no logical foundation. The correspondences are:

1	2	3	4	5	8	3	5	1
A	B	C	D	E	F	G	H	I

1	2	3	4	5	7	8	1	2
J	K	L	M	N	O	P	Q	R

	3	4	6	6	6	5	1	7
	S	T	U	V	W	X	Y	Z

Interestingly, the fateful sequence 6-6-6 appears in this number system, for the three letters U, V and W. Another, related, numerological system was described by the mystic author O. Hashnu Hara as used by the Qabalists. Clearly, it has no relationship with the Hebrew qabalistic letter-number correspondences, and appears to be yet another arbitrary allocation of number values, which are:

1	2	2	4	5	8	3	8	1
A	B	C	D	E	F	G	H	I

1	2	3	4	5	7	8	1	2
J	K	L	M	N	O	P	Q	R

3	4	6	6	6	6	1	7
S	T	U	V	W	X	Y	Z

Like the other two systems, O. Hashnu Hara's must be post-medieval because of the existence of the letters J and W. Whatever number system one may choose to use, the principles of Roman alphabet numerology remain constant. Unlike the number systems of the Hebrew, Greek and Gaelic alphabets, in which the numbers of the letters are added together, and a total reached, most versions of Roman numerology simply add the numbers together and then reduce them to a single digit. For example, 68 reduces to 5 (6 + 8 = 14; 1 + 4 = 5), or 27 reduces to 9 (2 + 7 = 9). The system is usually applied to a person's name, where all of the numbers corresponding with the letters are added together, and then related to specific qualities. From this, numerologists assert, one's personality, love life, fortune and destiny can be determined.

Another, more recent, system, is known as the Ulian Schemata, developed by D. Jason Cooper. This uses a technique similar to the Greek and Hebrew number ascriptions, where the alphabet is divided into three sections. In the case of the Greek alphabet, these are the three ogdoads, and in the runes, these would be the three aettir. But in the 26-character Roman alphabet, they are two groups of 9 and one of 8:

A	B	C	D	E	F	G	H	I
1	2	3	4	5	6	7	8	9

J	K	L	M	N	O	P	Q	R
10	20	30	40	50	60	70	80	90

S	T	U	V	W	X	Y	Z
100	200	300	400	500	600	700	800

Clearly, as there are at least four systems of letter-number ascriptions, the numerical equivalent of any name depends upon whichever system one chooses to use. As an example of the variations one must encounter, I will take my own name, Nigel Campbell Pennick. In the first system, the correspondences are as follows:

```
N I  G E L    C A M P B E L L    P E N N I  C K
4 9  7 5 3    3 1 4 7 2 5 3 3    7 5 5 5 9 3 2
```

The total of this calculation is 92. Customarily, this is reduced to the digit 2. :The reduction works by adding the figures together until a single digit remains, in this case, 9 + 2 = 11; 1 + 1 = 2). The second system is as follows:

```
N I  G E L    C A M P B E L L    P E N N I  C K
5 1  3 5 3    3 1 4 8 2 5 3 3    8 5 5 5 1 3 2
```

The total of this calculation is 75. Coincidentally, this also reduces to the digit 2.

O. Hashnu Hara's numerology, however, gives a different result:

```
N I  G E L    C A M P B E L L    P E N N I  C K
5 1  3 5 3    2 1 4 8 2 5 3 3    8 5 5 5 1 2 2
```

This adds up to 73, which reduces to 1, (7 + 3 = 10; 1 + 0 = 1). Finally, the Ulian Schemata gives yet another number:

```
 N  I  G E L      C A M P  B E L  L     P E  N  N  I C K
50  9  7 5 30     3 1 40 70 2 5 30 30   70 5 50 50 9 3 20
```

The total of this is 489, which reduces to 21 and then to 3. This numerological technique also takes into account the individual digits of the number, and their relationship, though, like the other Roman systems, it does not approach the matter of gematria. However, the Ulian Schemata does provide the possibility of a Roman gematria. In this system, my name has the same number as the Greek gematria for Theseus (ΘΕΣΕΟΣ), master of the Labyrinth. Clearly, according to this system, I am intimately involved with labyrinthine situations!

Of course, the fundamental problem at the root of this type of numerology lies not only with the system that one chooses, but also with the name that one uses. Some numerologists claim that one can change one's luck by changing one's name from one that carries a less fortunate number correspondence to a more auspicious number. But, as with the number values, there is no generally accepted common view of a person's 'true name'. Some numerologists assert that this is the name which one has borne since babyhood – one's 'given name'. But another school of thought asserts that one's 'true name' is that by which one is known every day, so, for example a nickname or contraction could be one's 'true name'. 'Jenny' would be preferred to Jennifer Ruth Jones, 'Chalky' to John James Archibald White, and so on. Overall, the whole matter of Roman letter numerology is fraught with difficulties and contradictions.

According to Cheiro's system, which is perhaps the most widely used one today, the nine single digits each are related to one of the astrological planets, from which, it is said, comes the character and fortune of the person. As with much Roman alphabet numerology, this system does not follow the traditional principles that one can recognize in Hebrew, Greek and

Fig. 56. Magic pantacle used by John Dee, including Roman letter correspondences.

Gaelic numerology. The planets in this system are not strictly traditional, for they include Uranus and Neptune, which have replaced the traditional ascending and descending nodes of the moon (Caput Draconis and Cauda Draconis, the Dragon's head and tail, respectively). Cheiro's *Book of Numbers* has the following ascriptions: the number one relates to the sun; two to the moon; three to Jupiter and four to Uranus. Five is allocated to Mercury, and six to Venus, whilst Neptune bears the number seven. The final two numbers, eight and nine, are allocated to Saturn and Mars respectively. The astrological attributes of the 'planets' are related to the person through their personal number. According to this sytem, number one, the number of the sun, means that the individual is a positive person who has an active intelligence, expressed in a creative way. The subject is single-minded in his or her ambitions. Their lucky days of the week are Sunday and Monday. They are at their most harmonious with other people who have the number two, four or seven. Their most lucky colours are gold and yellow, and their auspicious gems topaz and amber.

Being of the moon, number two people are supposed to be artistically creative, imaginative, persistent and romantic. Unfortunately, these admirable traits are often tempered by physical weakness. Number twos gets along best with people who have the number one, and to a lesser extent with sevens. The best days for number twos are Sunday, Monday and Friday. Their auspicious colours are green and white, the Royal Colours of Celtic Britain, and their gems are moonstones, pearls and jade.

Three is the number of Jupiter. People with this number are authoritarian, being upholders of order and progress, in a practical and worldly way. The most fortunate days for Jupiter people are Tuesday, Thursday (the day of Jupiter) and Friday. The lucky colours are at the red end of the spectrum: purple, maroon and crimson; their auspicious stone is amethyst. Number three people co-operate best with others who have the number six and nine. Four is the number ascribed by Cheiro and his followers to Uranus. According to the thought of the period when Herschel discovered the planet, Uranus is associated with rebellion and the overthrow of the established order. Because of this, number four people are considered to be strong-willed if lonely rebels, over-sensitive and unlikely to

Fig. 57. Seventeenth-century number-letter-sigil wheel.

be a success in conventional terms. Sometimes they are deeply learned, perhaps in the sciences. The lucky days of number fours are Sunday, Monday and Saturday. Fortunate colours are turquoise blue and grey, whilst the auspicious gemstone is the sapphire. Unlikely to make many friends, nevertheless people of number one are the best possibility here.

Mercury is the ruler of number five. People with this number are said to be bright and rapid in thought, animated, decisive and able. They make good businessmen or successful gamblers, being popular with other people of all numbers. Auspicious days are Wednesday (the day of Mercury), Thursday and Friday. Their fortunate colour is silver or white, and their gemstone is the diamond.

Number six is associated with Venus. This planet brings artistic, aesthetic, qualities. People associated with Venus are resolute, sometimes obstinate in their beliefs. But they are lovers of life, and, with those with whom they can live most harmoniously, people of threes and nines, they are considerate and loving. Auspicious days are Tuesday and Friday (the day of Venus). Number sixes have blue as their lucky colour, and the turquoise as their gemstone.

Seven is the number ascribed to Neptune, a planet discovered in 1846. According to this system, sevens are independent, excitable, people who travel restlessly across the globe. The vocations of writing and the graphic arts are indicated by this number, perhaps accompanied by psychical gifts, but financial success is unlikely. Auspicious colours are green and yellow, with pearls, moonstones and cats'-eyes as the corresponding gemstones. Lucky days are Sunday and Monday, and friendships are most likely with number twos.

The eighth number is allied with Saturn, which brings rugged individuality, and intense beliefs, held together by great personal inner strength. Like people with the number four, eights are considered likely to lead rather solitary lives, being considered rather cold and unemotional. Auspicious days are Sunday, Monday and Saturday, with fortunate colours of black and dark blue. Eights' lucky gemstones are black pearls and dark sapphires.

Nine is the final number, associated with Mars. Martial qualities are indicated: impulsiveness, belligerence and courageousness, tempered by inner strength. Number nines display leadership, but with a tendency to magalomania. Nines make their best friendships with those with three or six as their number. Mars people's lucky colour is fiery red, and their gemstones are garnet, bloodstone and ruby. Their auspicious days are Tuesday (the day of Mars), Thursday and Friday.

The traditions connected with the letters of the Roman alphabet are fragmentary, and few practitioners have worked to forge it into a coherent magical system. Until serious work is undertaken to this end, the Roman alphabet will remain the odd one out among magical alphabets. Because of this present lack, it has not formed the basis for any of the modern schools of magic. As in earlier times, they have based their traditions upon the more sacred alphabets, most notably Hebrew and runic.

6
Magic Squares, Literary Labyrinths and Modern Uses

There are things that are known, and things that are unknown: in between are the doors.

WILLIAM BLAKE

The ultimate spiritual function of every magical alphabet is the transformation of consciousness. As a means of comprehending the inner reality of existence, magical alphabets can act as the trigger that alters awareness. The user of magical alphabets can find her or his thought patterns diverted suddenly from their accustomed channel into new undreamed-of realms. Their transformative nature can provide the user with a completely new viewpoint on life and existence. This transformation is just that described in modern science's Catastrophe Theory, in which a sudden, discontinuous, change is triggered by a slight alteration in conditions. When this happens, it is like the opening of a door, at which a completely new view is revealed suddenly and immediately in its entirety. It is not for nothing that the letters of magic alphabets are known as 'the doors of consciousness'. Through various techniques of meditation and contemplation, this process can be assisted. But whatever the technique, the ultimate intention is the enlightenment of the individual.

THE MAGIC SQUARE AND THE WORD LABYRINTH

In Chapter 1, I dealt with Hebrew magic squares. But, although highly developed there, their mysteries are not exclusively within the realm of Jewish esotericism. They exist also in the Latin tradition, where they are related directly to another form known as the literary labyrinth. As letter squares and grids, they are laid out by a technique in which a certain arrangement of letters can be read in a number of ways. The best-known example of this is the so-called Sator square. This form is known from a number of ancient Roman sites, including Cirencester and Pompeii, and occurs today in magical illustrations. Its form can be either of the following:

```
S  A  T  O  R        R  O  T  A  S
A  R  E  P  O        O  P  E  R  A
T  E  N  E  T        T  E  N  E  T
O  P  E  R  A        A  R  E  P  O
R  O  T  A  S        S  A  T  O  R
```

Whichever way round it is written, this is translated usually as 'Sator, the sower, holds the wheels by his work'. The exact meaning of this is disputed, but it has connotations of fertility and control. It has also a Christian interpretation, for it can be rearranged as a cross that reads 'Pater Noster' (Our Father), with A and O (Alpha and Omega) twice:

```
                A

                P
                A
                T
                E
                R
A  P A T E R N O S T E R  O
                O
                S
                T
                E
                R

                O
```

Other magic squares comparable with the Sator one were used in ceremonial magic. Several are given in the medieval text,

The Sacred Magic of Abramelin the Mage. For example, that intended to transform the magician so that he or she could fly in the air in the form of a crow, is:

```
R   O   L   O   R
O   B   U   F   O
L   U   A   U   L
O   F   U   B   O
R   O   L   O   R
```

Unlike the Sator square, this, and most others, are composed of 'words' with no apparent meaning, though clearly every one has its own coherent interpretation. It is clear that from the earliest times that various combinations of letters were held to have a magical significance. The use of whole alphabets in consecration is an example of this. Formulae exist in all of the magical traditions, but it was in the late Graeco-Roman tradition that the specific form known as the 'letter labyrinth' came into being. These labyrinths are arrangements of letters, derived from a word or a phrase, which are arranged in such a form that they can be read in many ways, and so that other, unexpected, combinations of letters and words exist within the pattern. Overall, they comprise magical formulae which encapsulate not only the original meaning of the word or phrase, but also many other associated meanings, explicit and implicit. There are two basic types of these labyrinthine forms. The first is an arrangement which has a certain shape with a well-defined centre. Overall, they may be circular, square, or can have a spiral progression of letters. Almost invariably, the first letter of these texts is at the centre of the pattern. The other main type, called the 'progressive labyrinth' by the word-labyrinth researcher Piotr Rypson, is rectangular. Here, the first line is the proper text, and the successive lines are formed in transposition of letters to the left or right. This is a system used in crytography since ancient times, closely related to the Sator square and some runic systems.

The tradition of letter labyrinths is known to go back to the Pagan period of Imperial Rome. There was always a recognized connection between the literary labyrinth and the physical labyrinth of the type known from Roman mosaic pavements. A good example can be seen in the Trojan Tablets.

These are six carved stone tablets, known collectively as 'Tabulae Iliacae' (Trojan Tablets). They were found around Rome, and date from around the beginning of the Imperial period (*c.* 50 BCE–*c.* 50 CE). They bear Greek letter labyrinths on one side, and have themes from the Trojan Cycle carved on the opposite side. Among the carvings are illustrations of the walls of Troy, and Achilles carrying his magic shield, made by the divine smith Hephaestus. Both are symbols of physical and magical protection.

The European warrior tradition, of which the Greek is a prime example, customarily used protective symbols on the shield. These had a wide range, both over time and space. They include the Gorgon's head of the Greeks, and the lightning bolts of Jupiter on Roman legionaries' shields. In northern Europe, King Arthur's shield is said to have borne an image of the Virgin Mary whilst Saxon and Viking warriors relied on totemic beasts and runic letters. Finally, there is the complex heraldry of the age of chivalry, which in its central and eastern European forms include runes, house marks and Roman letters. The letter connection with Achilles's impenetrable shield parallels the ogham tradition of Fionn MacCumhaill's letter-bearing magic shield. It is also related to the magical enemy-dazzling 'liuthrindi' shield-patterns of the Northern Tradition martial arts.

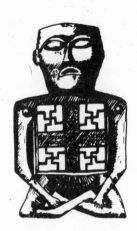

Fig. 58. Norse 'luaithrindi' pattern. Figure-mounting from a bucket in the ship-burial at Oseberg, Norway.

According to the Greek legend, at the centre of Achilles's circular shield, Hephaestus depicted the entire cosmos: the Earth, the sea and the sky; the sun, the moon and the stars. Around the centre of this shield were four rings, in which were shown aspects of life on Earth. Finally, the ocean around the Earth surrounded all. The two Trojan Tablets showing Achilles's shield have the labyrinth-words 'Theodorus made Achilles's Shield', and 'Achilles's Shield by Theodorus according to Homer'. In his *Historiae Naturalis (Natural History)*, Pliny states that Theodorus was 'creator, of the labyrinth on the Isle of Samos'.

In the Christian tradition, letter labyrinths were used by Publius Optatianus Porphyrius, who flourished during the reign of Emperor Constantine the Great, around the year 325 CE. The 'Pater Noster' interpretation of the Sator square may be seen as the origin of this tradition. The Constantinian period saw the incorporation of the letter labyrinth into Christian symbolism. A remarkable instance of this was to be found in the church of St. Reparatus at El-Asnam, Algeria, (formerly the Roman town of Castellum Tingitanum, founded around 328 CE). This sacred building contained two early letter labyrinths in mosaic. One, in the chancel, included the words 'Marinus Sacerdos', commemorating a priest's name. The other was at the centre of a square pavement labyrinth measuring about 2.4 metres (8 feet) in diameter, laid out on the axis of the north door to the basilica. At the centre of this pavement labyrinth, laid out in the typical Roman design, was a literary labyrinth. This was an arrangement of 169 letters in a square, composed of the words 'Sancta Eclesia' (Holy Church). These words can be read in any direction, except diagonally. Thus at El-Asnam there was a labyrinth-within-a-labyrinth. In some ways, this is a direct parallel with the tradition of Achilles's shield, being a representation of the cosmos contained within another. According to Christian exegesis, this labyrinth-within-a-labyrinth can be seen as representing the interrelation between the church (*Civitas Dei*, the City of God), and the outer world (*Civitas Mundi*, the City of the World). It is thus a representation of the ideas in St. Augustine's work, *De Civitate Dei (On the City of God)*. The Furthermore, the 169 letters composing the 'Sancta Eclesia' square are an example of Greek gematria, for the number 169

A	I	S	E	L	C	E	C	L	E	S	I	A
I	S	E	L	C	E	Ā	E	C	L	E	S	I
S	E	L	C	E	A	T	A	E	C	L	E	S
E	L	C	E	A	T	C	T	A	E	C	L	E
L	C	E	A	T	C	N	C	T	A	E	C	L
C	E	A	T	C	N	A	N	C	T	A	E	C
E	A	T	C	N	A	S	A	N	C	T	A	E
C	E	A	T	C	N	A	N	C	T	A	E	C
L	C	E	A	T	C	N	C	T	A	E	C	L
E	L	C	E	A	T	C	T	A	E	C	L	E
S	E	L	C	E	A	T	A	E	C	L	E	S
I	S	E	L	C	E	A	E	C	L	E	S	I
A	I	S	E	L	C	E	C	L	E	S	I	A

Fig. 59. 'Santa Eclesia' labyrinth from El Asnam, Algeria.

```
                    SVLASASALVS
                     LASATASAL
                      SATRTAS
                       TRERT
                       RECER
                       ECICE
                       CIHIC
          M            IHIHI            M
          VI           HIMIH           CV
          IGV          IMXMI           MEC
          GVFERIHIMXVXMDOMINIME
          VFERIHIMXVRVXDOMINIM
          FERIHIMXVRCRVXDOMINI
          VFERIHIMXVRVXDOMINIM
          GVFERIHIEXVXEDOMINIME
          IGV          SEXES           MEC
          VI           TSRST           CV
          M            QTSTQ            M
                       VQTQV
                       AVQVA
                       HAVAH
                       SMAMS
                       ESMSE
                       MESEM
                       PMEMP
                       EPMPE
                      AREPERA
                     ODARERADO
                    ORODARADORO
```

Fig. 60. 'Crux' letter labyrinth of Venantius Fortunatus (540–601 CE).

is equivalent to the Greek words for 'the Amen' ('O AMHN). Thus within something seemingly as simple as a word-square within a labyrinth, a wealth of symbolism is encoded.

The creation of permanent letter labyrinths was the concrete manifestation of the many more ephemeral versions that circulated as devotional texts and talismans. There are several important examples of these, which have been reproduced and used over a long period. One of the best loved was composed of Venantius Fortunatus (*c.* 540–601). His letter labyrinth is a famous version now known as St. Thomas's Cross. This is a cruciform poem which has the word 'Crux' (Cross) at the Centre. The letters from the centre can be read into the four arms as *Crux Domini Mecum* (The Lord's cross with me), *Crux est quam semper adoro* (I adore the cross always); *Crux mihi refugium* (The Cross my refuge); and *Crux mihi certa salus* (Cross my certain salvation). The ingenuity of this aid to meditation is remarkable. The arrangement of the letters assists the reader in arriving at new meanings; adoration is the support from 'ground level' to the centre, whilst salvation is on the higher level, above the centre.

It was in Spain that this form seems to have become especially loved. A letter labyrinth was carved upon the tombstone of Prince Silo of Asturias at the basilica of Pravia in Spain. In the eighth century, he was the founder of the church of San Salvador at Oviedo. This formula is based upon the words *Silo princeps fecit* (Prince Silo made it). Later, Vigilán, a Spanish monk from San Martin de Albeda in Rioja (974 CE), wrote a literary labyrinth in honour of St. Martin, the patron of the monastery. This Spanish tradition of multiple letter correspondences materialized later into a new form in the works of the mystic Ramón Llull (see below). Like some later saint invoking labyrinthine works, Vigillán's labyrinth was based on words which related to St. Martin. By expanding the name, it appears, the protective qualities of this and other saints could be called upon.

A popular version of the letter labyrinth is known as *versus intexti*. In this form, the number of lines in each verse was fixed, and some letters were obligatory. Generally, the page was divided into a grid measuring 35 by 35 squares, making 1225 in all. This number is equivalent by the rules of gematria with the Greek phrase 'The Lord God' ('O KYPIOΣ 'O ΘEOΣ),

'God's Creation' (ΚΤΥΣΙΣ ΘΕΟΥ), and 'The Plantation' ('Η ΦΥΤΕΙΑ), all with the number 1224. The latter word, 'The Plantation' is related also to the Eight Ifins of the ogham alphabet, and the Gaelic letter Gart. It is a metaphor for the sacred grid, that hidden matrix which underlies the material world. Once the *versus intexti* grid had been drawn, a pattern was made of words, and around this main pattern, the verses were written in smaller characters. The whole page was filled up in this way, with additional letters added in the gaps in such a way that they added meaning to the whole composition. Devotional talismans were often built up from a central text. Key words or phrases such as *Helig* (Holy), *De Dios soy amado* (God loves me), *Sanctis Gloria Christus* (Christ's Holy Glory), and *Gott ist mein Trost* (God is my comfort) are repeated in all directions in a qabalistic acrostic. They are arranged so that several layers of meaning may be perceived in reading these groupings of words. They are certainly not arbitrary, for they display a remarkable ability for synthesis and lateral thinking in their creators.

A coherent description of the relationship between the labyrinth pattern and the letter labyrinth was given by the Moravian philosopher known as Commenius, Jan Amos Komensky (1592–1670). This account of the symbolism of both the labyrinth pattern and the letter labyrinth was given in his book *Labirant Svetla a Ray Srdce (The Labyrinth of the World and the Paradise of the Heart)*. Here, the labyrinth is seen as an image of the pilgrim's progress along the correct pathway through a world dismissed as a false spectre of demonic chaos. The labyrinth of the world is envisioned as a city composed of badly matched words and meaningless correspondences. When, after many turns of the labyrinth, the pilgrim reaches the centre, expecting heaven, he finds there that it is the place of the most concentrated evil. This is a Christian version of the Cretan labyrinth mythos in which the hideous evil of the Minotaur lurks, horned like the Christian Devil. Then, having experienced the ultimate evil, Komensky's pilgrim finds a door which leads him to the 'real world' of Christian revelation. At the centre of evil, the word of Christ is experienced, and the pilgrim is transfigured. He then returns to the world, converted.

This central European vision shows the material world as a

labyrinth consisting of a mass of experiences that remain unintelligible to the pilgrim until the centre has been reached. It is clear that this is the same message that was conveyed by the El Asnam church labyrinth so many centuries earlier. If we examine surviving ancient literary labyrinths, it is clear that this type of magical arrangement is read from the centre outwards. Only from the centre are things intelligible. So it was that the Christian road to salvation was described by the Abbot of the Paulite monastery of Czestochowa in Poland, Andrzej Goldonowski (1596–1660). He devised a letter labyrinth which featured the phrase *'A Paulo Pluto decedit victis arena'* features. Here, the power of the saint is invoked as overcoming the power of the underworld as personified not by the Christian Devil, but by Pluto. Whether the Minotaur, Pluto or the Devil, it is from this centre that literary labyrinth originates. This is the mystery of the labyrinth, whether in its physical or its literary form.

During the Baroque period, these word labyrinths became poetic devices which evolved into new forms. Here, the words are written inside graphic shapes, such as grids. The order of reading them being the 'game' or esoteric secret that could unlock the meaning of the labyrinth. Many Baroque literary

Fig. 61. Hebrew poem for the Sephiroth as a wheel of light. Naphthali Bacharach, seventeenth century.

labyrinths are sacred in intention, but others were devised to honour an individual, or just for pleasure. Yet others hover on the borderline between orthodox devotion and invocational magic. One such letter labyrinth is a talisman collected in Hungary around 1700 by István Lepsényi for his *Poesis Ludens Seu Artificia Poetica*. This is in the form of a Latin prayer to the archangel Michael, calling for the possessor to be granted a long life. In some ways, these magical tracts resemble the Icelandic runic *Kotruvers* that were used to ensure success in chess and backgammon games. These forms all attempt to access the inner power of the word through alphabetic formulae which enable the meditator to gain multiple interpretations.

According to the Jesuit commentator Juan Eusebio Nuremberg, whatever form they might take, the orthodox devotional texts are an attempt to penetrate the puzzling 'labyrinth of the world', by means of 'a thousand of labyrinthine ways born in Divine Harmony'. But in modern times, the spiritual and magical quality of literary labyrinths has become overshadowed by their secular successor. Significantly known as 'concrete poetry', these letter assemblages usually represent little more than the typical post-modernist accumulation of chaotic, random, and hence meaningless, symbols. The barrenness of the post-modern wasteland is a far cry from the esoterically rich traditions of the literary labyrinth.

RAMÓN LLULL, MAGIC SQUARES AND THE TALISMANIC ART

In his *Ars Generalis sive Magna*, the Spanish mystic Ramón Llull (otherwise Raymond Lully) published a series of esoteric diagrams. These were a continuation and development of earlier medieval diagrams, Jewish, Islamic and Christian, that attempted to embrace the whole compass of human knowledge and experience. It is the same belief of the encapsulation of all things in the alphabet that underlies the whole-alphabet magic. Llull's intention was to use these wheels as intellectual proofs of his belief in the truth of Christianity. By this means, adherents to the Jewish and Islamic faiths would be converted to Christianity. This process was to be accomplished by means of meditation on the multifarous possibilities brought up by his wheels. Each wheel consisted of a series of moveable concen-

Fig. 62. Diagrams by Ramón Llull.

tric circles upon which were engraved or printed various letters and words which represented specific aspects of human knowledge or divine qualities. After the student had meditated on one setting, one wheel would be moved, and a new combination arrived at. Having finished with that one, another move would produce another new set of relationships, and so on until all of the combinations had been examined. Further wheels and diagrams were produced by Renaissance followers of Llull.

In its concept, Llull's system followed closely the complexities of early clockmakers like the Italian genius Giovanni de Dondi (1318–89), whose brilliant technological ability produced instruments that had dials which showed accurately the position of almost every known astronomical motion. The sophisticated complex gearing and dials of such clocks, developed from earlier Greek and Byzantine mechanical calendars, provided a model for the Llullian vision of the universe. Technically, Llull's system uses a combinatorial analysis of sets of terms. All permutations are possible in his system, and it was through the use of every possible permutation that Llull believed enlightenment could be gained. Just as with the letter systems of Hebrew, Greek, runic and ogham, Llull's method divides every branch of knowledge into a finite set of basic principles which can then be recombined at will. Lull's wheels, then, are a direct parallel with other alphabet systems, though arranged in a then novel and different way suitable for an age of mechanical experimentation. To the German philosopher Wilhelm Gottfried Leibniz (1646–1716), the inventor of calculus, Llull's technique was a vision of a universal system of knowledge, an image of the creation. In some ways, Llull's qabalistic combinatorial 'engines' were the forerunner of the mechanical computers of Charles Babbage (1792–1871), and hence can be considered the occult origin of modern computers.

Because the Hebrew alphabet was held to encapsulate the entire order of creation within its 22 letters, it was believed that any physical or spiritual quality could be represented graphically through these letters. When the letters are laid out on a magic square or kamea, then by joining up the letters by straight lines, a geometrical sigil can be produced that encapsulates the quality described. Topographically, this is almost a reciprocal version of the Llullian technique. Although these sigils can refer to literally anything, this technique is used mainly to describe and invoke certain spirits used in talismanic magic. This type of magic was developed and refined by adepts who, in the Renaissance period, allied themselves to the Rosicrucian view of the world. This Rosicrucian tradition is based upon the legend of the adept Christian Rosenkreuz (Christian Rosycross), who was said to have died in 1484. On the opening of his tomb 120 years later, certain secrets were said to have been revealed. This legend and its implications for human consciousness were revealed in a series of German pamphlets published in the years 1615 and 1615. These were disseminated widely, and rapidly translated and published in other languages. The concepts of Rosicrucianism were extremely important in Renaissance magical thought, and continue to influence the Western Mystery Tradition today. At present, the most influential element of this Rosicrucian current derives from the nineteenth-century magical organization known as the Order of the Golden Dawn. This order's magical system, brilliantly synthesized by some of the best magical minds of their generation, has proved to be the foundation for almost all later magical practice in the Western Tradition.

The symbol of the Order of the Golden Dawn was a rosycross. This badge, emblematical of the Christian Qabalah, incorporated the Christian cross into a scheme which had the 22-petalled flower of the Hebrew alphabet. Towards the centre of this 'inner rose' is a ring of three petals on which the three 'mother' letters were written. This was surrounded by a seven-petalled circuit bearing the seven 'simple' letters. Outside, as the third ring, was a 12-petalled ring which bore the 12 'double' letters of the Hebrew alphabet. Incorporated into this ancient symbolism was the system of colour correspondence propagated by S.L. MacGregor Mathers. Each letter had its own corresponding colour. This inner 'rose', served as a basic 'grid' for the creation of talismans. As with the magic squares and planetary kameas, the 22-petalled rose serves as a positional grid. In this way, a geometrical sigil similar in character to those formed from square grids can be produced. The interpretation of such sigils then depends upon a knowledge or recognition of the 'mother diagram' upon which it is based. This brilliant inventiveness is characteristic of the creative possibilities inherent in the best magical systems. Clearly, by analogy, it is possible to create new magical sigils based upon other arrangements of letters, and other alphabets. This provides further possibilities for expanding our understanding of runic, Coelbren y Beirdd, the Greek and Roman alphabets. The only limitations to this are those that lie within the imaginative capabilities of the practitioner.

ESOTERIC ALPHABETS IN THE MODERN AND POST-MODERN ERA

Some of the most esoteric alphabets or sign systems are those once used widely by tramps, gypsies and other itinerant people. These chalked sigils, intended to be unobtrusive to all but those who needed to read them, signified certain information vital to those living on their wits. Certain signs told the next traveller whether or not he or she could expect hospitality or hostility from the householder upon whose property the sign was marked. There were symbols representing, for example, dangerous dogs, the gullibility of the householder, and the level of zeal of the local police. By using these signs, the traveller could act in a manner appropriate to the conditions. They were an example of mutual aid between strangers with a common cause – survival in hostile conditions.

Any time is right for the creation of new magical alphabets, and so when conditions demand it, they continue to arise. Sometimes, they have been created in order to provide a secret means of communication between members of a sect or magical order. But, occasionally, they have masqueraded as ancient systems, rediscovered or handed down among a close-knit hereditary order. Even divine revelation, or its post-modern counterpart, shamanic insight, may be claimed as the true origin of such scripts. Of course, such claims are impossible to substantiate, even if true, unless there is uncontestable documentary evidence in existence. This type of system was most prevalent in the nineteenth century, when, among others, the writing of the fraudulent 'Princess Caraboo', the enigmatic tablets that gave rise to the Mormon religion and the curious Frisian work known as the *Oera Linda Chronicle* were launched upon the world.

In 1817, the 'tall story' of the self-styled Princess Caraboo was the sensation of the time. According to *Felix Farley's*

Bristol Journal, and a subsequent book, *Caraboo: a narrative of a singular imposition*, also published at Bristol, a woman from that city engineered a hoax in which she masqueraded as the princess of 'Javasu', and was fêted as a celebrity. According to her sensational and completely fictional story, she was a princess from the East Indies who had been kidnapped by pirates and somehow come to Bristol. Attempting to return 'home' by ship, by some means she managed to be introduced to the exiled Napoleon then imprisoned on St. Helena. Then, she was brought back again to Bristol, where she continued the masquerade. During this time, in order to continue her public lionization, she invented an alphabet that purported to be the written language of the equally fraudulent Javasu. But after some time of keeping up this pretence, and living well by it, she was exposed. It transpired that her real name was Mary Baker, an Englishwoman. She had once been married to a Dutch-Malay man, from whom she had picked up elements of the Malay language which she used to hoax her unsuspecting dupes. In Mary Baker's case, her knowledge of an exotic language and some inventiveness in writing enabled her to live well for some time at the expense of her admirers. Doubtless her Javasu alphabet gave many epigraphic scholars a great deal of interest and trouble before it was exposed as fraudulent.

Another curious alphabet features in the foundation of a new religion – the Church of Jesus Christ of Latter-Day Saints, better known as the Mormons. The founder of this religion was Joseph Smith, born in 1805 in Vermont, USA. He claimed to have been visited by a non-material entity that he called the Angel Moroni. This being, he asserted, was a supernatural messenger from a lost tribe of Israel that had emigrated to America in antiquity. This supposed tribe had built the ancient earth mounds that Smith and his colleagues were digging up in their search for buried treasure. Moroni told Smith of some inscribed golden plates buried in one of these mounds, which he dug and found. Inspired in some way to be able to read the script on these plates, which was unintelligible to all others, Smith produced the text known as *The Book of Mormon*. This, added to the standard Bible, became the religious text upon which the present-day Church of Jesus Christ of Latter-Day Saints is based. Unfortunately, these mystic plates of gold disappeared mysteriously after the text was produced, giving

Fig. 63. Anomalous inscriptions from North America: (*top left*) Braxon County, Virginia; (*bottom left*) Cripple Creek, Colorado; (*right*) brass plate, Kinderhook, Illinois.

impartial researchers no chance of finding out the origin of the script or language that they were reputed to bear.

Before, during and subsequent to Smith's 'personal revelation', many inscriptions were discovered or appeared on American rocks and found on artefacts. Among these are the curious plates supposedly discovered during April 1843 in a mound at Kinderhook, Illinois. Like Smith's original Mormon plates, these were dismissed by archaeologists as being the subject of a hoaxer. They were, claimed the sceptics, made by a blacksmith who etched the plates with obscure letters, including some Chinese characters copied from a tea chest. The Inscription Rock, located in an *arroyo* west of Albuquerque, New Mexico, is another such alphabetic artefact dismissed as a fraud. The letters on this rock are said to have been made by a Mormon in an attempt to deceive critics of Joseph Smith's claims. Many other strange inscriptions, ascribed to Atlantean, Lemurian, Chinese, Punic, Israelite, Ibero-Celtic, Irish, Scottish, Welsh and Norse visitors, as well as European esoteric sects of later times, abound in North America. Needless to say, almost every one has been dismissed as fraudulent by sceptical researchers, and has generated equally fervent support as to its authenticity on the other side. It seems that the only people overlooked as the origin of these letters are the Native

Americans themselves, dismissed by generations of racist assumptions. But an impartial observer must reserve judgement, for history abounds with sudden changes of expert opinion, and today's orthodoxy becomes tomorrow's error.

A complete 'ancient alphabet' from northern Europe can be found in publications concerning the *Oera Linda Chronicle*, a work purporting to be a thirteenth-century Frisian work. An edition of this work, which is widely believed to be a hoax, was published at Leeuwarden in the Netherlands in 1876. It

Fig. 64. Alphabet from the Oera Linda Chronicle.

contained a supposed ancient alphabet. Like the later Armanen system of runes, these letters were based upon the sixfold division of the circle. The idea of letters being parts of a fixed geometric form is derived ultimately from medieval stonemasons' marks and from Masonic and Rosicrucian secret alphabets. Some of the letters of this alphabet resemble characters of runic and coelbren, but ultimately it is a version of the Roman alphabet, modified to fit within a circle. There is no traditional or archaeological evidence for this alphabet having existed before the nineteenth century.

In former times, esoteric groups often created their own alphabets, and the twentieth century is no exception. The so-called Pecti-Wita runes are an example of this, created for the Scottish wiccan group of the same name, headed by Aidan Breac, and published by Raymond Buckland. They are not runes, for they bear no resemblance to any system, ancient or modern. Superficially, some characters bear a resemblance to the corresponding coelbren letters. Others are clearly derived from the Roman alphabet. They have no connexion either with the Gaelic letters. This system is complicated by being written phonetically, and it appears particuarly non user-friendly when applied to the Gaelic tongue. It does not appear to have any magical correspondences. Another, even less plausible, alphabet is the so-called Pictish, which has also been used by

Fig. 65. Pecti-Wita 'runes' (after Buckland).

Raymond Buckland, among others. But this script is not ancient, nor Pictish. It is just a decorative version of the Roman alphabet It has no connexion with the ancient Picts, who used ogham and an early version of the Gaelic alphabet on their monuments.

The value of these new alphabets is questionable, for they do not stand within the sacred or magical tradition of, say, the runes or the true Celtic alphabets. They are mainly secret scripts which serve as a means for keeping magical records that cannot be read by prying eyes. In that, at least, they resemble the secret alphabets of old. In some ways, they parallel the secret alphabets created by the master fantasist J.R.R. Tolkien in his seminal 'Swords and Sorcery' fantasy novels concerning the mythical ancient world of Middle Earth. In *The Return of the King*, the final volume of his magnificent trilogy *The Lord of the Rings*, Tolkien described various systems of writing used by the people his world. As befitting an Oxford professor, Tolkien was thorough, providing a consistent and believable linguistic description of these letters. He created the Fëanorian letters, the *Tengwar*, as having 24 main characters and 12 supplementary ones. In this numerical way, the 'alphabet' followed the old European traditions of Greek, the Elder Futhark and Coelbren. Following the Greek-Runic-Gothic tradition, Tolkien gave these characters the names that described certain meanings. By this means, he built up a believable (and magically usable) system.

His other system was based upon the runic forms, although none of them correspond with any known historic runic values. These *Angerthas* comprise 60 characters, many of which take the familiar forms of authentic runes. However, it seems that Tolkien wished to dissociate this fantasy alphabet from genuine meaningful runes, and hence adopted a quite different system. Tolkien's letters have been used since in decorative fantasy art, and also, whether or not he foresaw this use, in magical workings by devotees of his Middle Earth mythos. Tolkien's success with *The Lord of the Rings* was the beginning of the present interest in fantasy worlds and their creative possibilities. His alphabets can be considered the well-thought-out prototypes for many more recent 'secret alphabet' inscriptions invented by some fantasy illustrators. One can see such writing in the illustrations of many modern fantasy role-playing game

Fig. 66. Modern-genre fantasy illustration, using 'Victory' glyphs and words in Gothic, Runic and Coelbren scripts, with appropriate esoteric sigils.

books and magazines. A typical example is illustrated in Fig. 66.

Finally, a new flowering of personal secret alphabets has come since the 1970s with the availability of the paint spray-can. This is in the form of graffiti, a plague of which has swept the cities of the world. New, personal, symbols and characters have been developed by graffiti practitioners, who leave their personal mark or 'tag' wherever they can. Beginning in New York, where the trains of the Subway were literally covered in painted graffiti, the use of the 'tag' has spread to all places where youths can afford to buy paint spray-cans. Like the house and holdings marks of old, these tags serve to tell fellow graffiti merchants that their owner has been there. They are not spiritually transformative. These tags are usually an encoded rendering of the sprayer's initials or nickname, house number, or date of birth. But, occasionally, one may encounter more genuinely 'occult' tags, which are related in some ways to the older marks used by the tramps and gypsies of former times.

POSTSCRIPT

The inner nature of things, expressed in magical alphabets, is rooted in the collective psyche of all human beings. These eternal truths of existence have been recognized throughout history, though in some eras, they have been disregarded. In periods when they *were* respected, they served to guide human actions, and thus have enriched people's lives immeasurably. Even today, these eternal truths of ancient wisdom are not lost, though they may have been marginalized by the demands of modern technological society. But whether in ancient or in modern times, all workable societies have needed, of necessity, to be based on our common human realities. Clearly, our era is in desperate need of a reassertion of this ancient wisdom. Today, through the appropriate use of magical alphabets and their associated lore, we can rediscover the hidden possibilities of consciousness beyond the level of the material and the exclusively human. It is clear from the teachings of all spiritual traditions that throughout the universe are diffused the fundamental elements of existence that we experience as consciousness and spirit. Of course, it has always been possible for any human being to have a direct experience of this quality which we call 'the divine'. Sometimes, it arises spontaneously, but more usually it is attained through the application of certain esoteric techniques, which include meditation and shamanry. Such experiences are possible only because there is no definite boundary between the self and the non-self. Naturally, this holistic nature of the universe includes the links between the individual and the 'rest of' existence. It includes that which we term 'the divine'.

Those who study the esoteric arts do so primarily because they seek a more harmonious and creative means of existing within the circumstances in which we find ourselves – the human condition. Whether we accept it or not, human existence is part of the natural order of things. Without Nature, we can have no being, physical or spiritual. Nature is neither a mechanical device nor a monstrous dumb organism, put there by some divine intelligence just to be tinkered with for human use and pleasure. Such mechanical and organismic interpretations of Nature are fragmental and reductionist, describing it in solely terms of the material that can be seen by dismantling it. On the contrary, from both many ancient traditions, and the experience of modern esotericism, it is apparent that spirituality is inherent in Nature. It has not gone away. It is still there to anyone who seeks it. Equally, it is clear that we can only experience oneness with existence if we work in harmony with Nature. The study and use of sacred alphabets are one means of achieving this, for they are manifestation of the spirituality that is inherent in Nature.

Physically, psychically and spiritually, human beings are part of the Earth, and our life is lived out within the framework of time. This is the absolute reality within which we exist. In our lifetime, there can be no repeats, no 'replays'. Once something has passed, it is gone forever. Each action that we take, each experience in time has but a single chance to be; however it is conducted, that will be its nature for all time. It cannot be corrected or obliterated. Also, nothing that has come into being or passed through our physical, psychic or spiritual constitution can ever be erased. Its existence, in the past or the present, becomes part of our, and the Universe's *Orlög*, that combination of things, events and processes that make up that which composes the 'now'. Although the flow of time and events is a continuous, seamless stream, nevertheless we perceive it as being composed of discrete events. These can be units of time, actions or individual objects, beings and people. This perception, which originates in our consciousness, is the basis of our understanding of the universe. It is the origin of language and notation.

It is certain that any system of notation can only be a fragmentary means of describing reality, which must, of necessity, be removed at least one step from the present actuality of that which is being described. Although most human perception is of a fragmented nature, existence is a holistic continuum. But within these notational systems, whether numerical or alphabetic, for those who can find it, a deeper reality is encoded. Basically, at the simplest level, magical alphabets are the encapsulation of esoteric information. Like computer programs, which are written and operate according to their own internal logic systems, each ancient notation is a form of deep language which contains within it the essence of the modes of thought of its inventors and users. But, ultimately, each magical alphabet can transcend the specific cultural tradition in which it has originated. Each of them are but a particular expression of a kind of magical structure which acts at all levels in the material as well as the non-material worlds. The fleeting nature of all existence is ungraspable, but nevertheless the esoteric techniques that exist within all human cultures can provide us with a means of coming to a creative understanding of it. Of the many methods of describing and, hopefully, making some sense of our existence, the inner magical secrets of the alphabets can provide us with a degree of illumination. In our lives, we are all writers on the unfolding blank pages of existence. Because of this, we should bear in mind the words of Omar Khayyám's *Rubáiyát*:

> *The moving finger writes; and having writ,*
> *Moves on: nor all thy piety nor wit*
> *Shall lure it back to cancel half a line,*
> *Nor all thy tears wash out a word of it.*

Appendices

Appendix I: The Meaning of Hebrew Letters

Letter	phonetic equivalent	everyday meaning	esoteric meaning	numerical value	Tarot trump
Aleph	A	cattle	father	1	Fool
Beth	B	house	mother	2	Magician
Gimel	G	camel	nature	3	High Priestess
Daleth	D	door	authority	4	Empress
He	H	window	religion	5	Emperor
Vau	V	nail	liberty	6	Hierophant
Zain	Z	sword	ownership	7	Lovers
Cheth	Ch	fence	distribution	8	Chariot
Teth	T	serpent	prudence	9	Strength
Vod	I	hand	order	10	Hermit
Kaph	K	palm of hand	force	20	Wheel of Fortune
Lamed	L	ox-goad	sacrifice	30	Justice
Mem	M	water	death	40	Hanged Man
Nun	N	fish	reversibility	50	Death
Samekh	S	prop	universality	60	Temperance
Ayin	O	eye	balance	70	Devil
Pe	P	mouth	immortality	80	Tower
Tzaddi	Tz	fish-hook	shadow/reflection	90	Star
Qoph	Q	back of head	light	100	Moon
Resh	R	head	recognition	200	Sun
Shin	Sh	tooth	sacred fire	300	Judgment
Tau	T	cross	synthesis	400	World

The Ten Commandments are based on a numerical progression similar to the ten Sefiroth. They are associated with the first ten letters of the Hebrew alphabet:

1. Aleph, the Crown: God is first, above and before all.
2. Beth, Wisdom: worship of God only is permitted.
3. Gimel, Intelligence: Peace, harmony with God.
4. Daleth, Love: sanctity of God's household.
5. He, Justice: domestic order.
6. Vau, Beauty: forbids a person to cut short another person's days.
7. Zayin, Firmness: forbids a person to destroy another person's peace.
8. Cheth, Splendour: forbids a person to steal another person's living.
9. Teth, Foundation: forbids a person to destroy the social harmony.
10. Yod, Authority: concerns ethical relations.

Appendix II: Greek Letter Meanings

Letter	phonetic equivalent	meaning	numerical value	corresponding human organ
Alpha	A	cattle	1	head
Beta	B	demon	2	neck
Gamma	C	divinity	3	shoulders
Delta	D	fourfold	4	breast
Epsilon	E	ether	5	diaphragm
Zeta	Z	sacrifice	7	belly
Eta	E	joy/love	8	genitals
Theta	Th	crystal sphere	9	thighs
Iota	I	destiny	10	knees
Kappa	K	illness	20	shins
Lambda	L	growth	30	ankles
Mu	M	trees	40	feet
Nu	N	hag	50	feet
Xi	X	fifteen stars	60	ankles
Omicron	O	sun	70	shins
Pi	P	solar halo	80	knees
Rho	R	fruitfulness	100	thighs
Sigma	S	psychopomp	200	genitals
Tau	T	human being	300	belly
Ypsilon	U	flow	400	diaphragm
Phi	F	phallus	500	breast
Chi	Ch	property	600	shoulders
Psi	Ps	heavenly light	700	neck
Omega	O	riches/abundance	800	head

Appendix III: The Runic Correspondences

Rune name	tree(s)	herb	colour	polarity	element	deity	symbolic meaning
Feoh	elder	nettle	red	female	fire/earth	Frey/Freyja	the primal cow, Audhumla
Ur	birch	Iceland moss	green	male	earth	Thor/Urd	horns of the ox
Thorn	oak/thorn	houseleek	red	male	fire	Thor	the thorn, hammer of Thor
As	ash	fly agaric	dark blue	male	air	Odin/Eostre	the ash Yggdrasil
Rad	oak	mugwort	red	male	air	Ing/Nerthus	wheel under cart
Ken	pine	cowslip	fire red	female	fire	Heimdall	fire of the torch
Gyfu	ash/elm	pansy	royal blue	m/f	air	Gefn	sacred mark
Wyn	ash	flax	yellow	male	earth	Odin/Frigg	wind vane
Hagal	ash/yew	bryony	blue	female	ice	Urd/Heimdall	structural beams, hailstone.
Nyd	beech/rowan	snakeroot	black	female	fire	Skuld	fire-bow and block
Is	alder	henbane	black	female	ice	Verdandi	icicle
Jera	oak	rosemary	blue	m/f	earth	Frey/Freyja	sacred marriage of heaven/earth
Eoh	yew/poplar	bryony	dark blue	male	all	Ullr	vertical column of the yew tree
Peorth	beech/aspen	aconite	black	female	water	Frigg	the womb, a dice cup
Elhaz	yew/service	sedge	gold	m/f	air	Heimdall	the elk, the flying swan, open hand
Sigel	juniper/bay	mistletoe	white	male	air	Balder	the holy solar wheel
Tyr	oak	purple sage	fire red	male	air	Tyr	the vault of the heavens above the cosmic pillar
Beorc	birch	lady's mantle	green	female	earth	Nerthus/Holda	breasts of the Earth Mother Goddess
Ehwaz	oak/ash	ragwort	white	m/f	earth	Frey/Freyja	two poles bound
Man	holly	madder	tiver red	m/f	air	Heimdall/Odin/Frigg	human being
Lagu	osier	leek	green	female	water	Njord/Nerthus	sea wave, waterfall.
Ing	apple	selfheal	yellow	m/f	water/earth	Ing (Frey)	the genitals

Appendix III: The Runic Correspondences – cont'd

Rune name	tree(s)	herb	colour	polarity	element	deity	symbolic meaning
Odal	hawthorn	clover	ochre	male	earth	Odin	land, property
Dag	spruce	sage	blue	male	fire/air	Heimdall	balance, (night, day)
Ac	oak	heap	green	male	fire	Thor	mark tree
Os	ash	'magic mushroom'	dark blue	male	air	Odin	mouth, speech
Yr	yew	bryony/mandrake	gold	m/f	all	Odin/Frigg	yew tree, bow
Ior	linden/ivy	kelp	black	female	water	Njord	Jörmungand, the world serpent
Ear	yew	hemlock	brown	female	earth	Hela	earth-grave
Cweorth	bay/beech	rue	tawny	female	fire	Loge	funeral pyre
Calc	maple/rowan	yarrow	white	female	earth	Norns	grail-cup
Stan	witch hazel/blackthorn	Iceland moss	grey	male	earth	Nerthus	sacred stone
Gar	ash/spindle	garlic	dark blue	male	all	Odin	spear of Odin
Wolfsangel	yew	wolfsbane	blood red	female	earth	Vidar	wolf-hook
Ziu	oak	aconite	orange-red	male	air/fire	Tyr	lightning-bolt
Erda	elder/birch	mint	brown	female	earth	Erda	Mother Earth
Ul	buckthorn	thistle	orange	male	air	Waldh	turning-point
Sol	juniper	sunflower	sunlight	female	fire	Sól	the sun's disc

Appendix IV: Runes and Tarot Major Arcana

Below are three different versions of correspondences between the runes and the Tarot trumps, according to the modern authorities Sigurd Agrell, Edred Thorsson and Hermann Haindl:

Rune name	Agrell's version	Thorsson's version	Haindl's version
Feoh	World	Tower	Magician
Ur	Fool	High Priestess	High Priestess
Thorn	Magician	Emperor	Empress
As	High Priestess	Death	Emperor
Rad	Empress	Hierophant	Hierophant
Cen	Emperor	Chariot	Lovers
Gyfu	Hierophant	Lovers	Sun
Wyn	Lovers	Strength	Fool
Hagal	Chariot	World	Chariot
Nyd	Justice	Devil	Justice
Is	Hermit	Hermit	Hermit
Jera	Wheel of Fortune	Fool	Wheel of Fortune
Eoh	Strength	Hanged Man	Star
Peorth	Hanged Man	Wheel of Fortune	Aeon
Elhaz	Death	Moon	Devil
Sigel	Temperance	Sun	Strength
Tyr	Devil	Justice	Hanged Man
Beorc	Tower	Empress	Death
Ehwaz	Star	Lovers	—
Man	Moon	Magician	—
Lagu	Sun	Star	Alchemy
Ing	Judgement	Judgement	—
Odal	World	Moon	Moon
Dag	World	Temperance	—
Yr	—	—	Tower
Gebo	—	—	Universe

Appendix V: Ogham Correspondences

letter	name	tree	colour	bird equivalent
B	Beth	birch	white	pheasant
L	Luis	rowan	grey/red	duck
F	Fearn	alder	crimson	seagull
S	Saille	willow	fine	hawk
N	Nuin	ash	clear	snipe
H	Huath	hawthorn	purple	crow
D	Duir	oak	black	wren
T	Tinne	holly	dark grey	starling
C	Coll	hazel	brown	crane/heron
Q	Quert	apple	green	hen
M	Muin	vine	variegated	titmouse
G	Gort	ivy	blue	mute swan
Ng	Ngetal	reed	green	goose
St/Z	Straif	blackthorn	bright	thrush
R	Ruis	elder	blood-red	rook
A	Ailm	elm	blue/piebald	lapwing
O	On	gorse	yellow	cormorant
U	Ur	heather	purple	skylark
E	Eadha	aspen	red	swan
I	Ioh	yew	dark green	eaglet
Ea	Ea/Koad	aspen	green	—
Oi	Oi	gooseberry, spindle	white	—
Ui	Ui	beech, honeysuckle	tawny	—
Ia	Io/Pe	guelder rose	white	crane
Ae	Ao/Xi	pine, witch hazel	multicoloured	starling

Appendix VI: Gaelic Alphabet Correspondences

letter	name	meaning	numerical equivalent
A	Fhalm	Elm tree	1
B	Beath	Birch tree	2
C	Calltuinn	Hazel tree	3
D	Doir	Oak tree	4
E	Eubh	Aspen tree	5
F	Fearn	Alder tree	6
G	Gart	Garden, vineyard	7
I	Iubhar	Yew tree	8
L	Luis	Rowan tree	9
M	Muin	Vine	10
N	Nuin	Ash tree	11
O	óir	Furze	12
P	Beith-bhog	Poplar	13
R	Ruis	Alder tree	14
S	Suil	Willow tree	15
T	Teine	Fire	16
U	Uhr	Yew tree	17

Appendix VII: Magic Square Correspondences

number	magic square	day	deity (classical)	deity (northern)	tree	character
1	36	Sunday	Apollo	Sól	Birch	Good
5	81	Monday	Selene/Luna	Mani	Willow	Bad
2	25	Tuesday	Mars	Tiw/Tyr	Holly	Good
6	64	Wednesday	Mercury	Woden	Ash	Good
3	16	Thursday	Jupiter	Thor	Oak	Bad
7	49	Friday	Venus	Frigg	Apple	Bad
4	9	Saturday	Saturn	Loki	Alder	Neutral

Appendix VIII: The 72 Names of God (from the *Grimoire of Honorius*)

Trinitas, Sother, Messias, Emmanuel, Sabahot, Adonay, Athanatos, Jesu, Pentagna, Agragon, Ischiros, Eleyson, Otheos, Tetragrammaton, Ely, Saday, Aquila, Magnus Homo, Visio, Flos, Origo, Salvator, Alpha and Omega, Primus, Novissimus, Principium et Finis, Primogenitus, Sapientia, Virtus, Paraclitus, Veritas, Via, Mediator, Medicus, Salus, Agnus, Ovis, Vitulus, Spes, Aries, Leo, Lux, Imago, Panis, Janua, Petra, Sponsa, Pastor, Propheta, Sacerdos, Immortalitas, Jesus, Christus, Pater, Filius Hominis, Sanctus, Pater Omnipotens, Deus, Agios, Resurrectio, Mischiros, Charitas, Aeternas, Creator, Redemptor, Unitas, Summun Bonum, Infinitas.

Glossary

E-A: East Anglian
G: German
Gk: Greek
H: Hebrew
I: Irish
N: Norse
W: Welsh

aett	group of eight letters in a rune-row (N).
aiq beker	arrangement of 27 characters in a grid of nine squares, 3 in each (H).
alphabet	a sequence of sigils or characters, each of which represents a spoken sound.
Awen	bardic sigil for the name of God (W).
Bifröst	the rainbow bridge linking Earth to the heavens (N).
coelbren	bardic alphabet written on wood (W).
coelvain	bardic alphabet written on stone (W).
colel	the numerical value of 1, the discrepancy allowable in the number-computations of gematria (q.v) (H).
ebillion	lettered staves in the Bardic tradition (W).
futhark	name for a runic-row, based upon the first six letters; F, U, Th, A, R K.
Gaelic	the native language of Scotland, with its 17-character alphabet.
gematria	the technique of giving words number equivalents, based on word-number correspondences (Gk).
hoslur	sacred enclosure used for judicial combat, literally, 'the Hazelled Field' (N).

kienspanhalter	traditional form of lighting, using a stand to hold a wege of pine wood, which is lit. The origin of the rune Ken (G).
mezuzah	scripture-holder used for household protection. Attached to the door-post (H).
Northern Tradition	the mystery tradition of Europe north of the Alps, including Celtic, Germanic, Scandinavian and Baltic elements.
notarikon	the technique of creating new words from the first or last letters of a name or phrase, as with modern acronyms (Gk).
ogdoad	one of the three 8-letter divisions of the Greek alphabet (Gk), cf, aett.
ogham	the Celtic tree alphabet (I).
peithynen	framework holding ebillion (q.v.) (W).
plagawd	an early form of paper used in ancient Wales (W).
qabalah	the Jewish mystery-tradition, based on the 'tree of life' and the Hebrew alphabet (H).
Rosicrucianism	the European mystery tradition, based on the supposed teachings of Christian Rosenkreuz, Christian Qabalah-oriented.
rune	a character from one of the Germanic-Norse families of futharks (q.v.) or alphabets.
temurah	encryption of sacred names or phrases by letter substitution (H).
tiver	red ochre used for marking sacred objects (E-A), from Old Norse *taufr*, magic colour.
transvolution	the process of 'becoming'; the underlying mechanism and outcome of 'the way things happen'.
Vehmgericht	the Secret Tribunal of medieval Germany (G).

Bibliography

Abrahams, Israel, *Jewish Life in the Middle Ages*, Philadelphia, 1896

Angrell, Sigurd, *Senantik mysterierreligion orch nordisk runmagi*, Stockholm, 1931

— — *Lapptrumor och Runmagi*, Lund, 1934

Agrippa, H.C., *De Occulta Philosophia*, with notes by Karl Anton Nowotny, London, 1967

Anon, *The Book of Ballymote*, manuscript in the library of the Royal Irish Academy, Dublin

Arntz, Helmut, *Das Ogom, Beiträge zue Geschichte des deutsche Sprache und Literatur*, Vol. 59 (1935) p. 321–413

Aswynn, Freya, *Leaves of Yggdrasil*, London, 1988

Bahn, Paul G. & Vertut, Jean, *Images of the Ice Age*, Leicester, 1988

Box, G.H. & Charles, R.H. *The Apocalypse of Abraham and Ascension of Isaiah*, New York, 1918

Brandon, Jim, *The Rebirth of Pan*, Dunlap, 1983

Brix, H. *Studier in nordisk Runmagic*, København, 1928

Bromwich, R. *Trioedd Ynys Prydein*, Caerdydd, 19.79

Buckland, Raymond, *Buckland's Complete Book of Witchcraft*, St Paul, 1986

Buick, Reverend George R. *The Recent Discovery of Ogams in the County of Antrim, Proceedings of the Royal Society of Antiquaries of Ireland*, 1898, p. 392–95

Bullhorn, F., *Grammatography: Alphabets of the World*, London, 1961

Casanowicz, I.M., *Jewish Amulets in the United States National Museum, Journal of the American Oriental Society*, Vol. XXXVI (1917), p. 154–67.

Cockayne, O., *Leechdoms, Wortcunning and Starcraft*, London, 1864

Cooper, D. Jason, *Understanding Numerology*, Wellingborough, 1990

Cotterall, Arthur, ed., *The Encyclopedia of Ancient Civilizations*, London, 1980

Cross, T.P. and Slover, C.H., *Ancient Irish Tales*, Dublin, 1969

Davis, W., *The origins of image making, Current Anthropology* 27 (1986), pp. 193–215, 371, 515–16.

Dent, A., *Lost Beasts of Britain*, London, 1964

Dickens, B., *Runic and Heroic Poems*, Cambridge, 1915

Dinneen, Patrick S. *Focloir Gaedhlige agus Bearla*, Baile Átha Cliath, 1927

Diringer, David, *A History of the Alphabet*, Old Woking, 1977

Duchesne, Mgr. L., *Christian Worship: Its Origin and Evolution* (trans. M.L. McClure), London, 1904

Duwel, Klaus, *Runenkunde*, Stuttgart, 1968

Elliott, R.W.V., *Runes: An Introduction*, Manchester, 1959

Evans-Wentz, W.Y., *The Fairy Faith in Celtic Countries*, Oxford, 1911

Fell, Barry, *Windmill Hill Amulets*, Epigraphic Society Occasional Publications, Vol. 15 (1986) p. 36.

Flowers, Stephen E., *Runes and Magic: Magic Formulaic Elements in the Older Runic Tradition*, American University Studies, Series I, No. 53, New York, 1986

Franke, Adolphe, *The Kabbalah*. New York, 1967

Fuller, Major-General J.F.C., *The Secret Wisdom of the Qabalah*, London, n.d, c. 1936

Gettings, Fred, *Dictionary of Occult, Hermetic and Alchemical Sigils*, London, 1981

Ginsburg, Christian D., *The Kabbalah: Its Doctrines, Development and Literature*, London, 1970

Ginzburg, Louis, *The Legends of the Jews*, 7 vols, New York, 1909–38

Gorsleben, Rudolf J., *Die Hoch-Zeit der Menschheit*, Leipzig, 1930

Graf, Erkhard, *Mythos Tarot – historische Fakten*, Ahlerstedt, 1989

Graf, Heinz-Joachim, *Die Runennamen als sprachliche Belege zur Ausdeutung germanischer Sinnbilder, Germanien*, Vol. 9 (1941), p. 254–59

Graves, Robert, *The White Goddess*, London, 1961

Hara, O. Hashnu, *Number, Name and Colour*, London, n.d.

Harding, Mary E., *Women's Mysteries, Ancient and Modern*, London, 1935

Hatt, J.J., *The Ancient Civilization of the Celts and Gallo-Romans*, London, 1970

Henderson, G., *Survivals in Belief among the Celts*, Glasgow, 1911

Hickes G., *Linguarum Vett. Septentrionalium Thesaurus, 1703–05*, London, 1970

Hogan, Eileen, *Ogham: Each letter of the Alphabet is Presented with a Colour and a Bird*, London, 1978

Jensen, K. Frank, *The Prophetic Cards – a catalog of cards for fortune-telling*, Roskilde, 1985

Jones, David, *Epoch and Artist*, London, 1959

Keiller, Alexander, *Windmill Hill and Avebury Excavations, 1925–39*, Oxford, 1965

Koch, R., *The Book of Signs*, London, 1930

Kohler, Kaufmann, *The Tetragrammaton and Its Uses, Journal of Jewish Lore and Philosophy*, Vol. I (1909), p. 10–32

Laing, L., *Celtic Britain*, London, 1979

Lehmann, W., *Meister Eckhart*, Göttingen, 1917

Lévi, Eliphas, *The Mysteries of the Qabalah*, Wellingborough, 1981

– – *The Book of Splendours*, Wellingborough, 1981

Lewis, Frank, *Gwerin Ffristial A Thawlbwrdd, Transactions of the Honourable Society of Cymmrodorion*, 1941, p. 185–205

Lewis, M.J.T., *Temples in Roman Britain*, Cambridge, 1966

List, Guido von, *Das Geheimnis der Runen*, Wien, 1912

Lloyd, H. Alan, *Old Clocks*, 4th edition, London, 1970

Luzzato, Rabbi Moses, *General Principles of the Kabbalah*, New York, 1970

Mabillon, J., *De Re Diplomatica*, Paris, 1781

Macalister, R.A. Stewart *Studies in Irish Epigraphy*, 3 vols, London 1897, 1902, 1907

– – *The Secret Languages of Ireland*, Cambridge, 1937

– – *Corpus Inscriptionum Insularum Celticarum*, Dublin, 1945

MacCana, Proinsias, *Celtic Mythology*, London, 1970

MacCulloch, J.A., *The Religion of the Ancient Celts*, Edinburgh, 1911
MacNeill, M., *The Festival of Lughnasa*, Oxford, 1962
McGaugh, Frank, *Tartan Ogam, Stonehenge Viewpoint*, No. 71, 1986
— — *On the Dating of Tartan Ogham* in *Exploring Rock Art*, ed. Donald L. Cyr, Santa Barbara, 1990, p. 73–77
Mann, Ludovic MacLellan, *Archaic Sculpturings*, Glasgow, 1915
Matthews, Caitlín, *Mabon and the Mysteries of Britain*, London, 1987
Michell, John, *The View Over Atlantis*, London, 1969
— — *City of Revelation*, London, 1972
Moltke, Erik, *Runes and Their Origin: Denmark and Elsewhere*, Copenhagen, 1984
Murray, Colin & Liz, *The Celtic Tree Oracle*, London, 1988
Nowotny, Karl Anton, *Runen und Sinnbilder, Germanien*, Vol. 7 (1939), p. 218–25
Osborne, Marijane, & Langland, Stella, *Rune Games*, London, 1982
— — — — —: *Old English Ing and his Wain, Neuphilologische Mitteilungen*, Vol. 81 (1980), p. 388–89
O'Hehir, Brendan, *The Origin, Development and History of the Ogham Script: Facts and Conjecture* in *Exploring Rock Art*, ed. Donald L. Cyr, Santa-Barbara, 1990, p. 11–12
O'Rahilly, T.F., *Early Irish History and Mythology*, Dublin, 1946
Pennick, Nigel, *The Mysteries of King's College Chapel*, Cambridge, 1974
— — *Ogham and Runic Magical Writing of Old Britain and Northern Europe*, Bar Hill, 1978
— — *The Ancient Science of Geomancy*, London, 1979
— — *The Subterranean Kingdom*, Wellingborough, 1981
— — *Hitler's Secret Sciences*, Sudbury, 1982
— — *Runestaves and Oghams*, Bar Hill, 1986
— — *Earth Harmony*, London, 1987
— — *Games of the Gods*, London, 1988
— — *Practical Magic in the Northern Tradition*, Wellingborough, 1989
— — *Das Runen Orakel*, München, 1990
— — *Runic Astrology*, Wellingborough, 1990
Poncé, Charles, *Kabbalah: An Introduction and Illumination for the World Today*, London, 1974
Powell, T.G.E., *The Celts*, London, 1980
Rees, Alwyn, & Rees, Brinley, *Celtic Heritage*, London, 1967
Rhys, Prof., *The Ogam Inscribed Stones of the Royal Irish Academy and of Trinity College, Dublin. Proceedings of the Royal Society of Antiquaries of Ireland*, Volume XXXII, 1902
Ross, Anne, *Pagan Celtic Britain*, London, 1967
— — *Druids, Gods and Heroes of Celtic Mythology*, London, 1986
— — *The Pagan Celts*, London, 1986
— — & Robins, Don, *The Life and Death of a Druid Prince*, London, 1989
Sadler, Rev. M.F., *The Revelation of St John the Divine, with notes critical and practical*, London, 1905
Scholem, Gershom, *Jewish Gnosticism, Merkabah Mysticism and Talmudic Tradition*, New York, 1965
Spence, Lewis, *The Mysteries of Britain*, London, 1928
Spiesberger, Karl, *Runenmagic*, Berlin, 1955

— — *Runenexerziten für Jedermann*, Freiburg, 1976

Taylor, I., *Greeks and Goths: A Study on the Runes*, London, 1879

Thorsson, Edred, *Futhark: A Handbook of Rune Magic*, York Beach, 1984

— — *Runelore: A Handbook of Esoteric Runology*, York Beach, 1987

— — *At the Well of Wyrd: A Handbook of Runic Divination*, York Beach, 1988

— — *A Book of Troth*, St Paul, 1989

Turville-Petre, E.O.G., & Ross, A.S.C., *Agrell's 'Magico-numerical' theory of the runes, Folk-Lore*, Vol. XLVII (1936), p. 203–13

Wardle, Thorolf *Runelore*, Braunschweig, 1983

— — *The Runenames*, Braunschweig, 1984

Waite, A.E., *The Holy Kabbalah*, New York, 1965

Weber, Martha, *Kaiser- und Königsmonogramme des Mittelalters, Germanien*, Vol. 8 (1940), p. 334–42

Westergaard, Kai-Erik *Skrifttegen og Symboler*, Oslo, 1981

Wirth, Hermann, *Die Heilige Urschrift der Menschheit*, Leipzig, 1934

Wright, Dudley, *Druidism, The Ancient Faith of Britain*, London, 1924

Zeller, Otto, *Der ursprung der Buchstabenschrift und das Runenalphabet*, Osnabrück, 1977